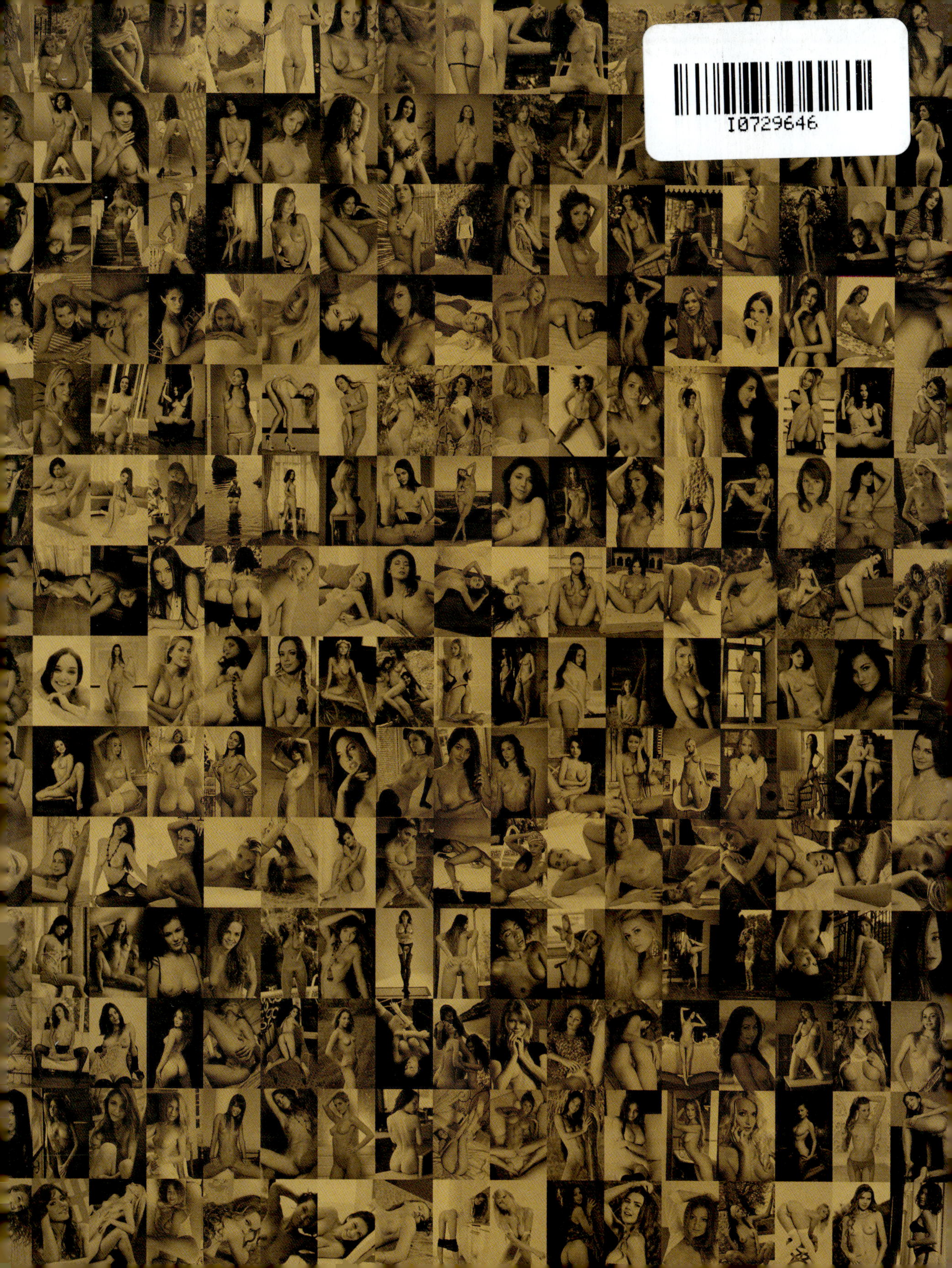

I0729646

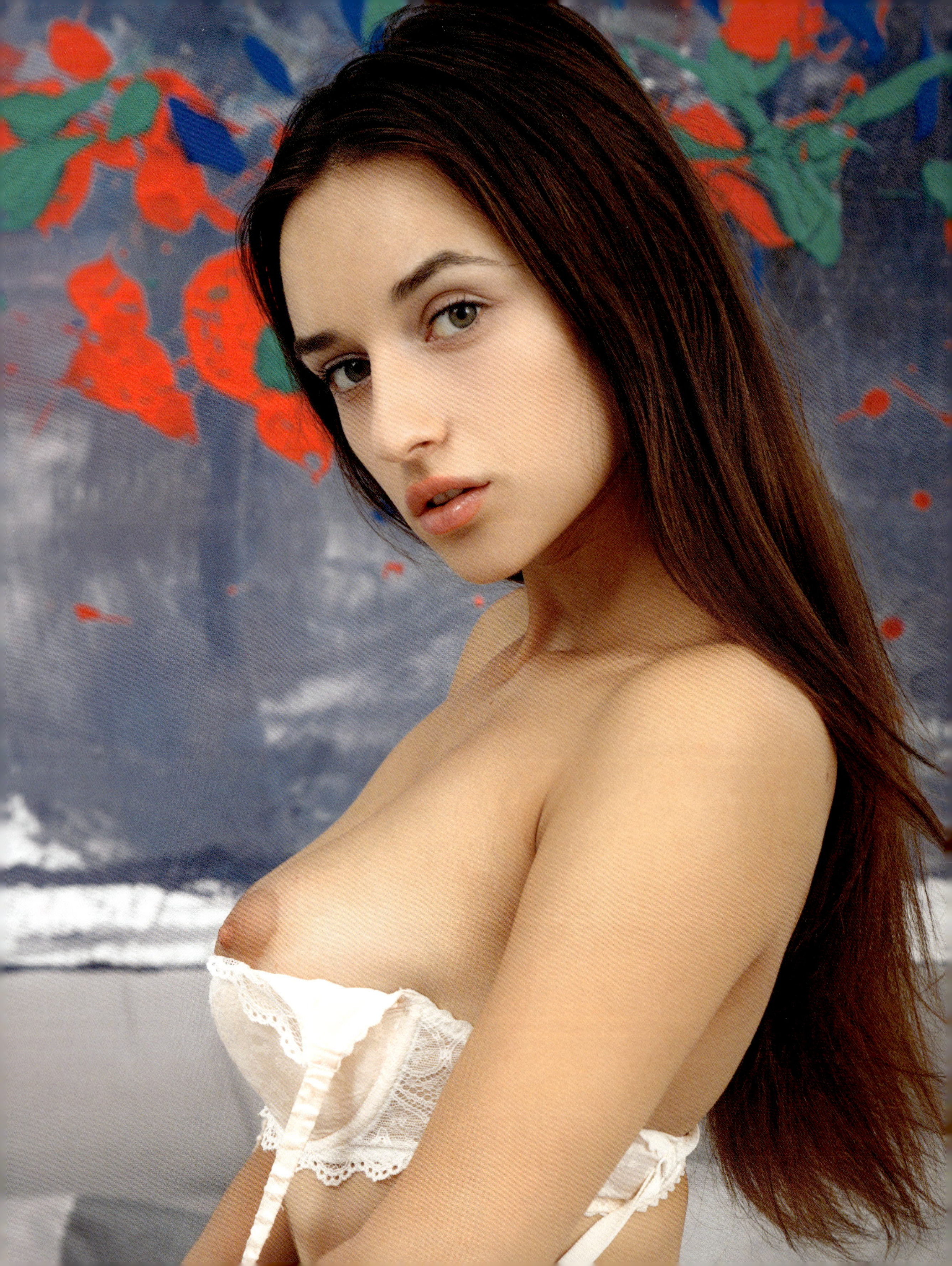

TOP MODELS OF

MetArt.com

WHERE FLAWLESS BEAUTY MEETS ART

GLORIA SOL

COLLECTED AND EDITED BY ISABELLA CATALINA

EDITION Skylight

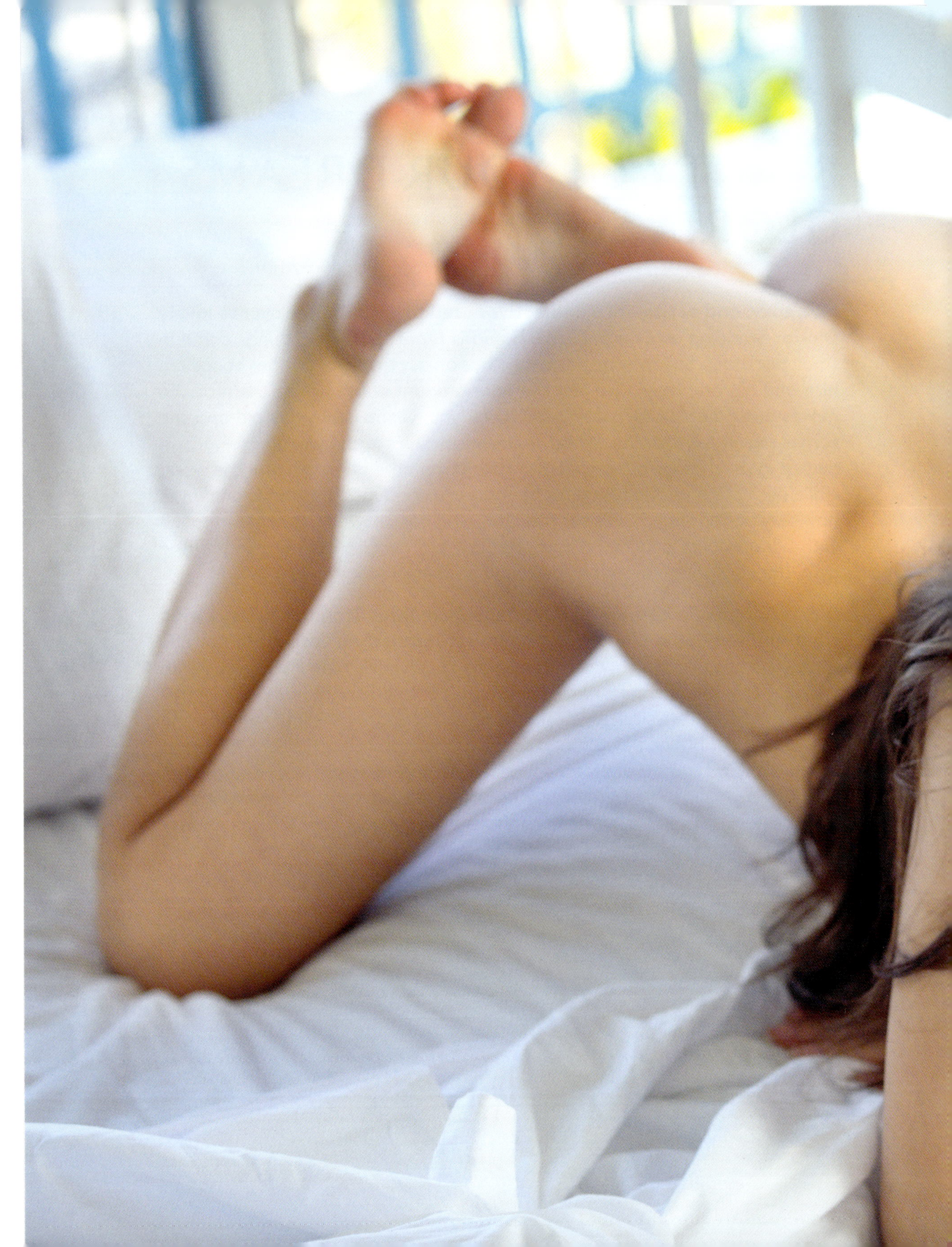

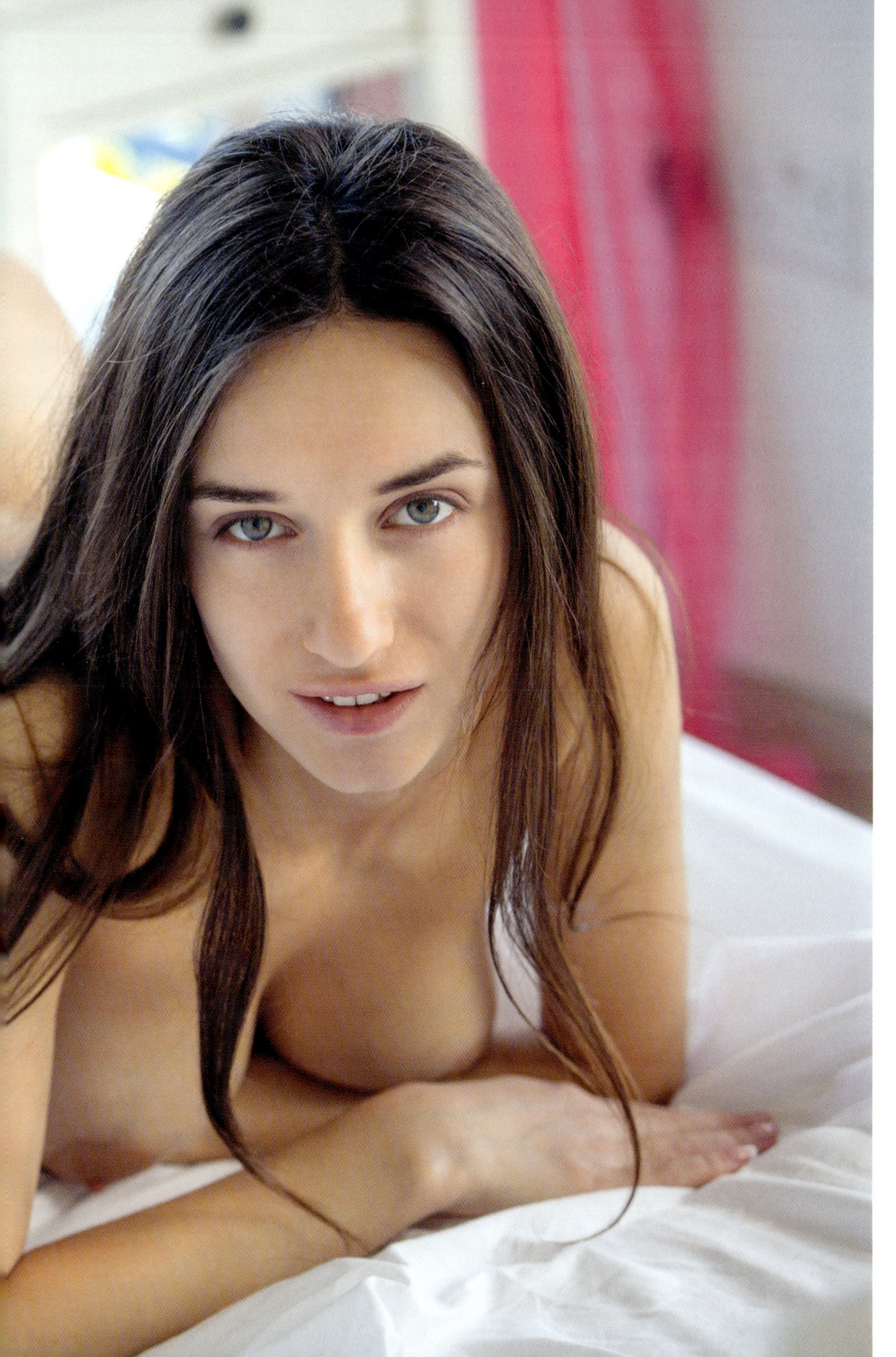

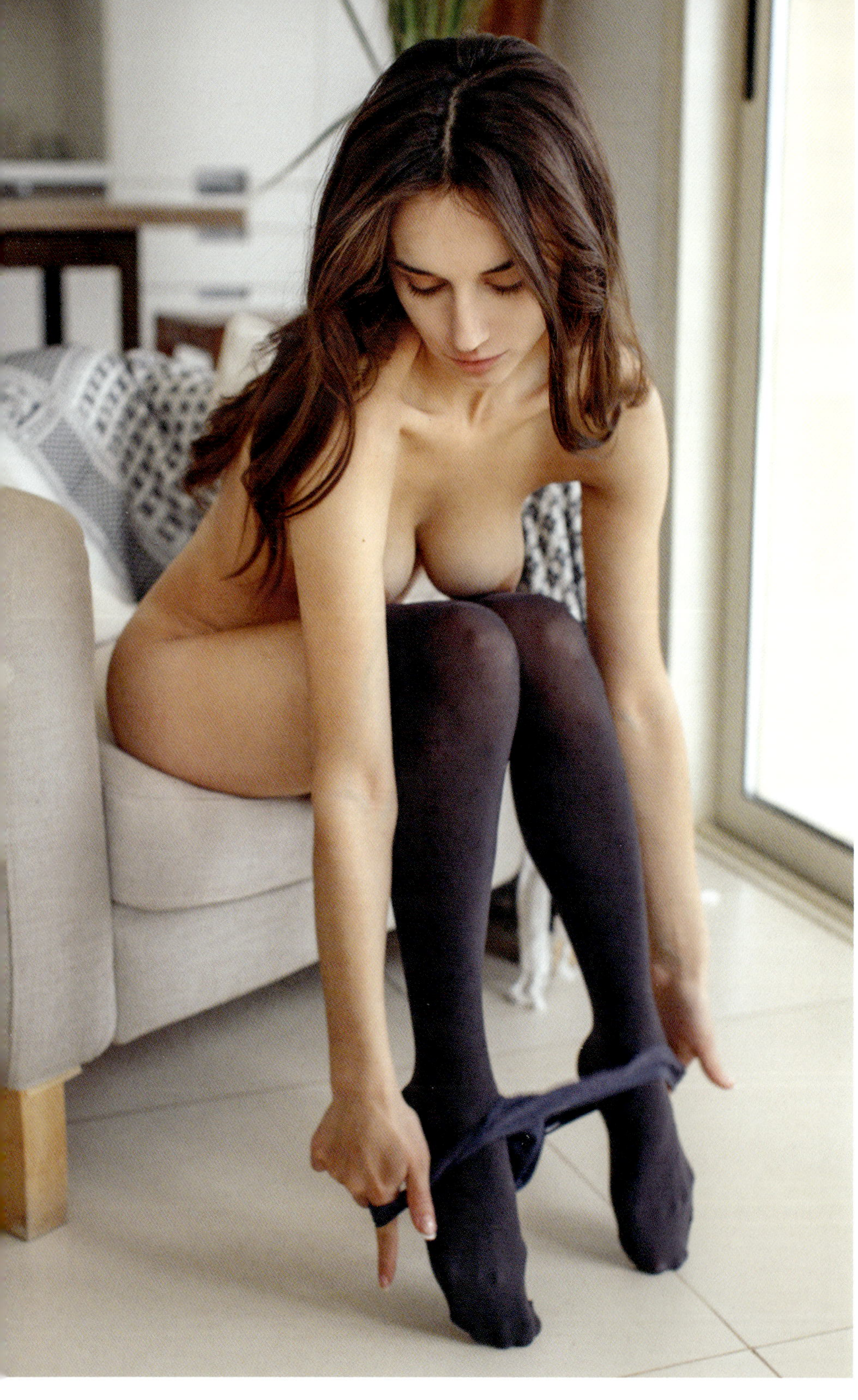

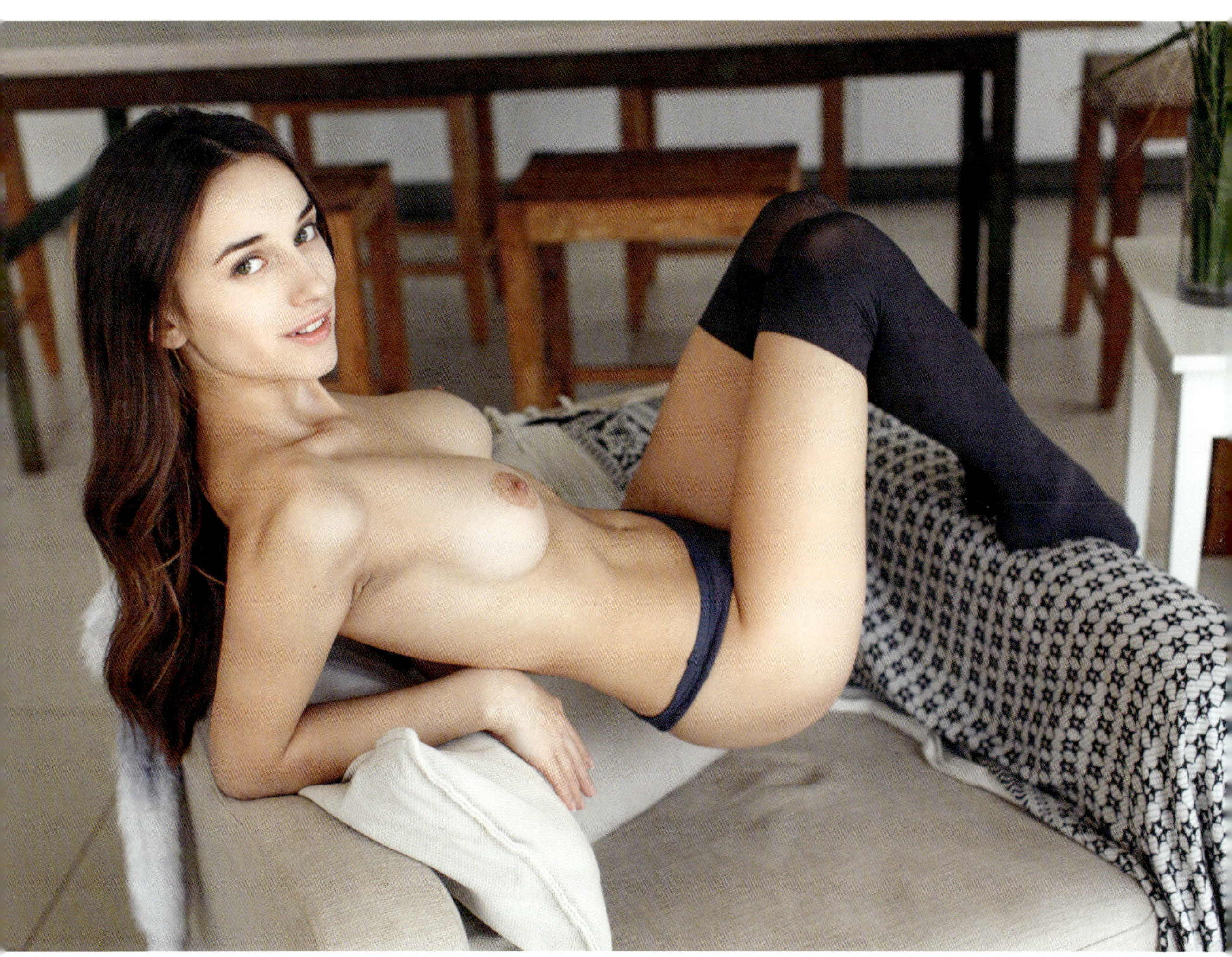

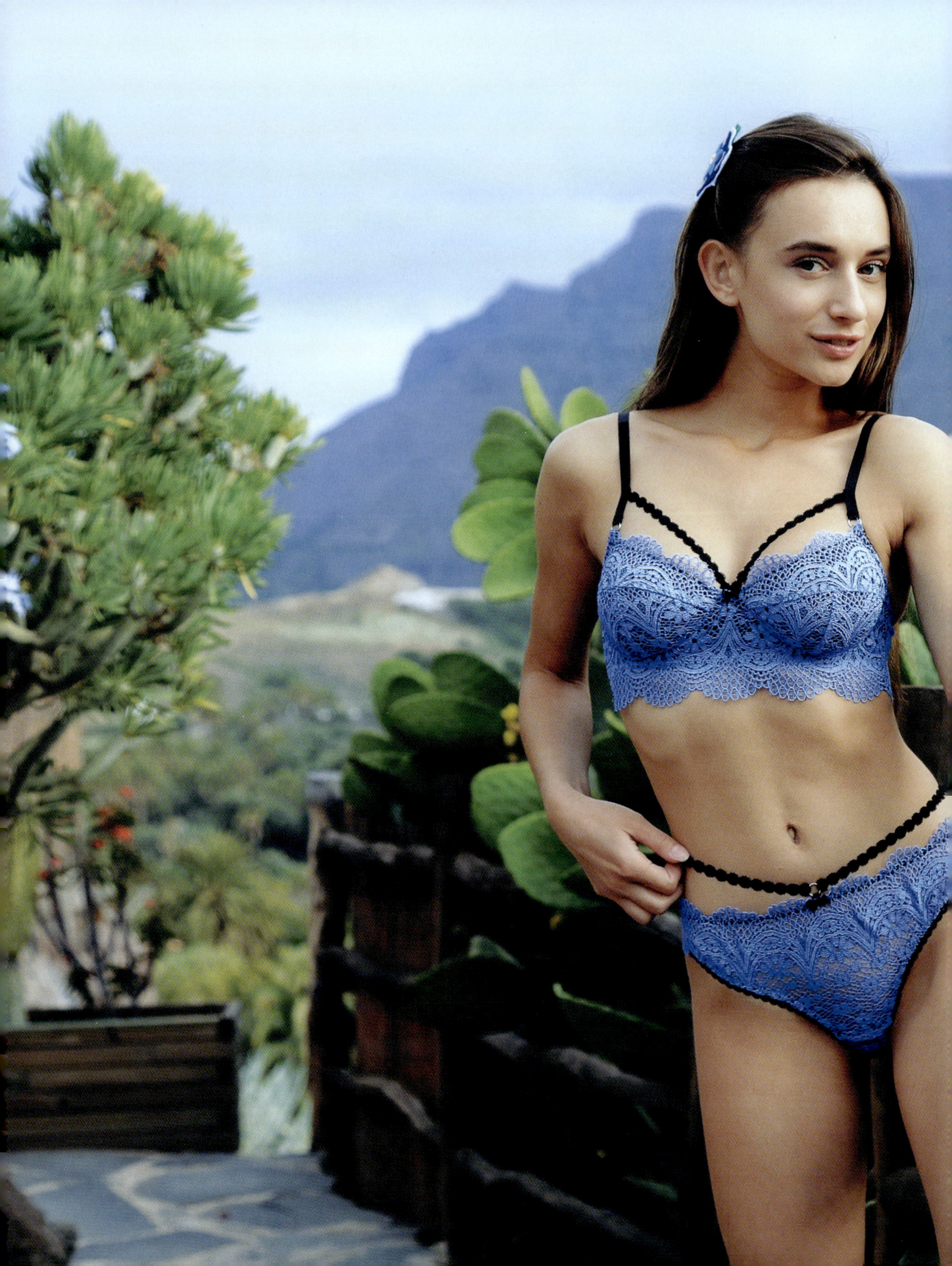

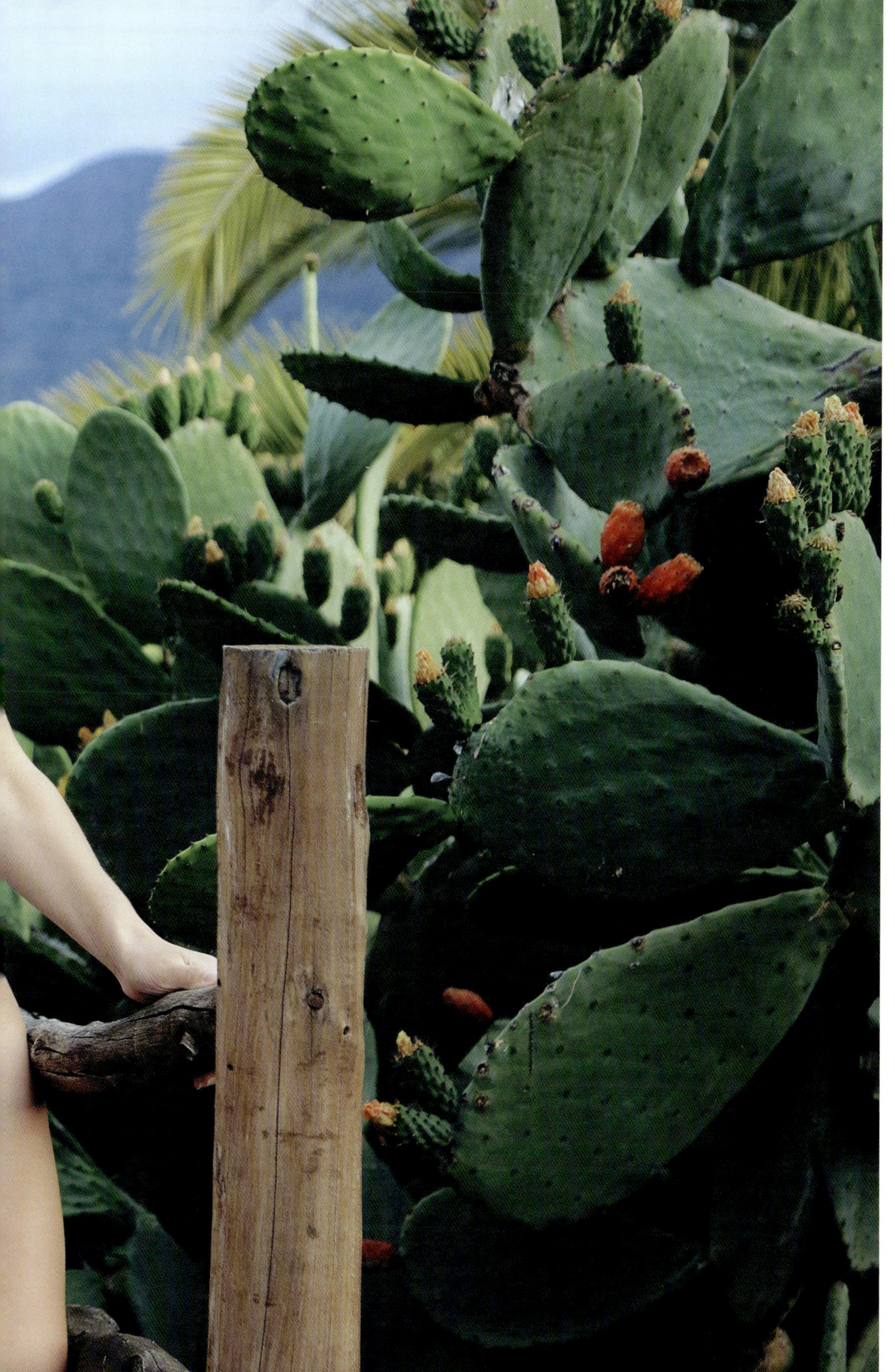

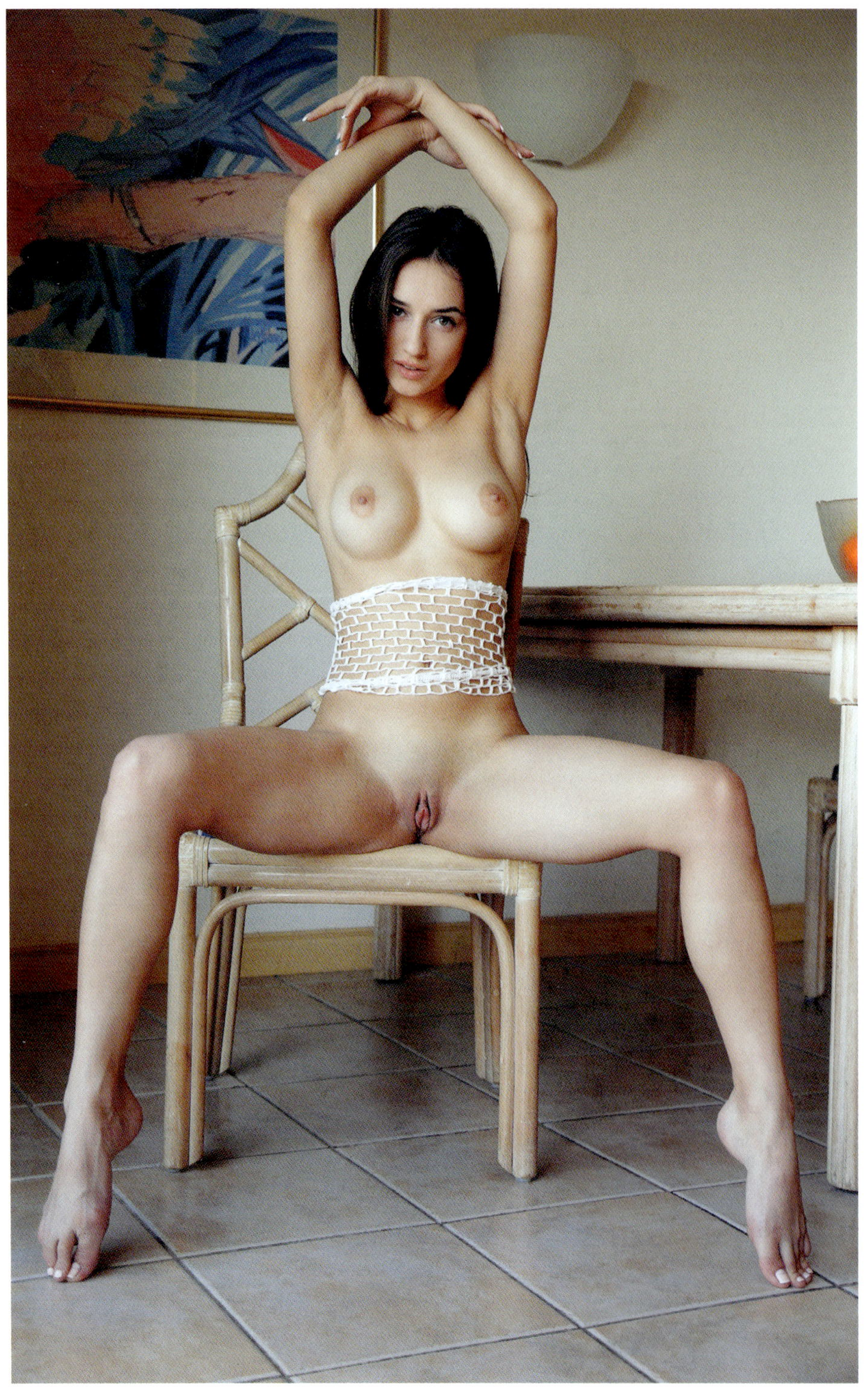

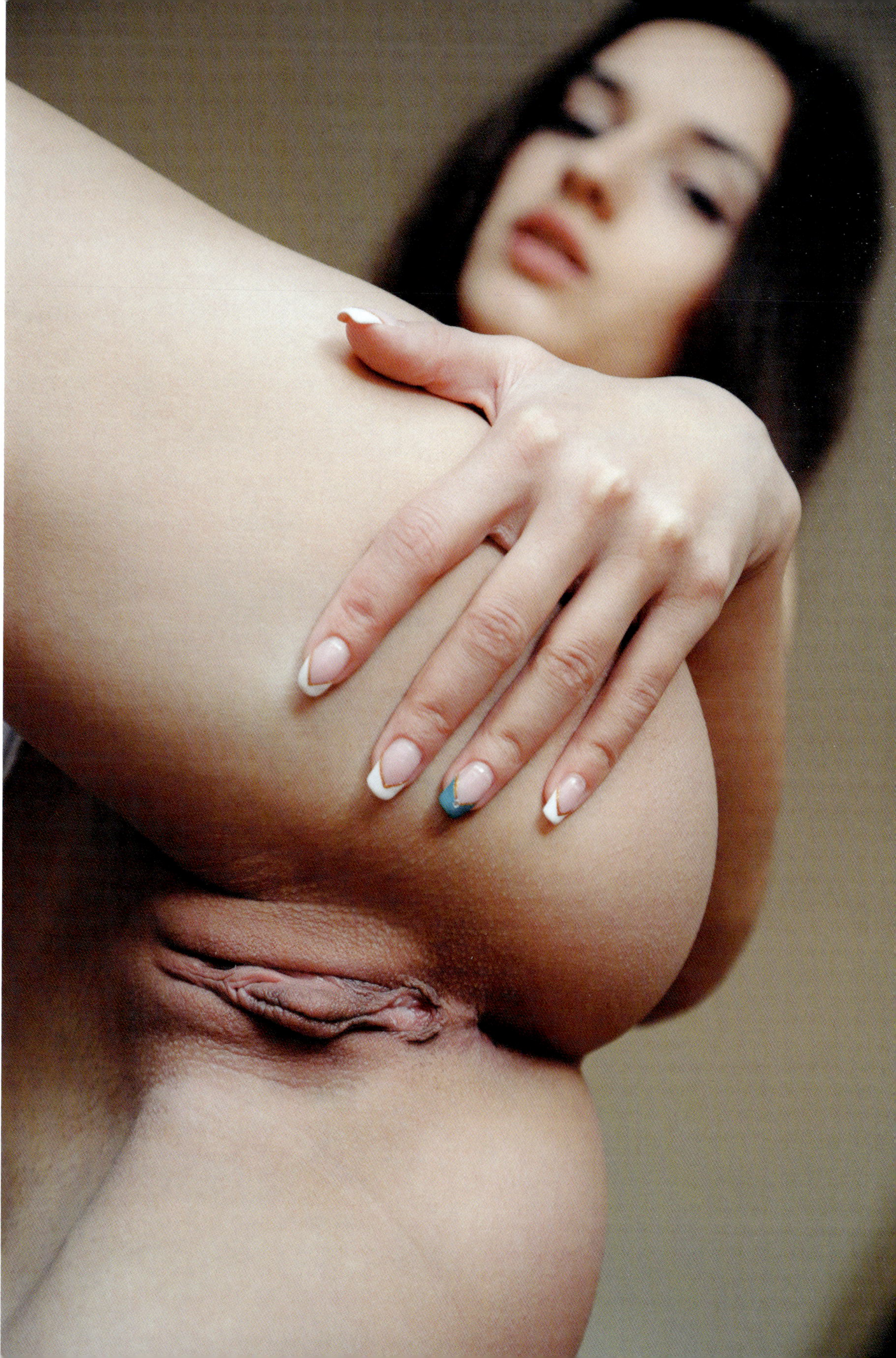

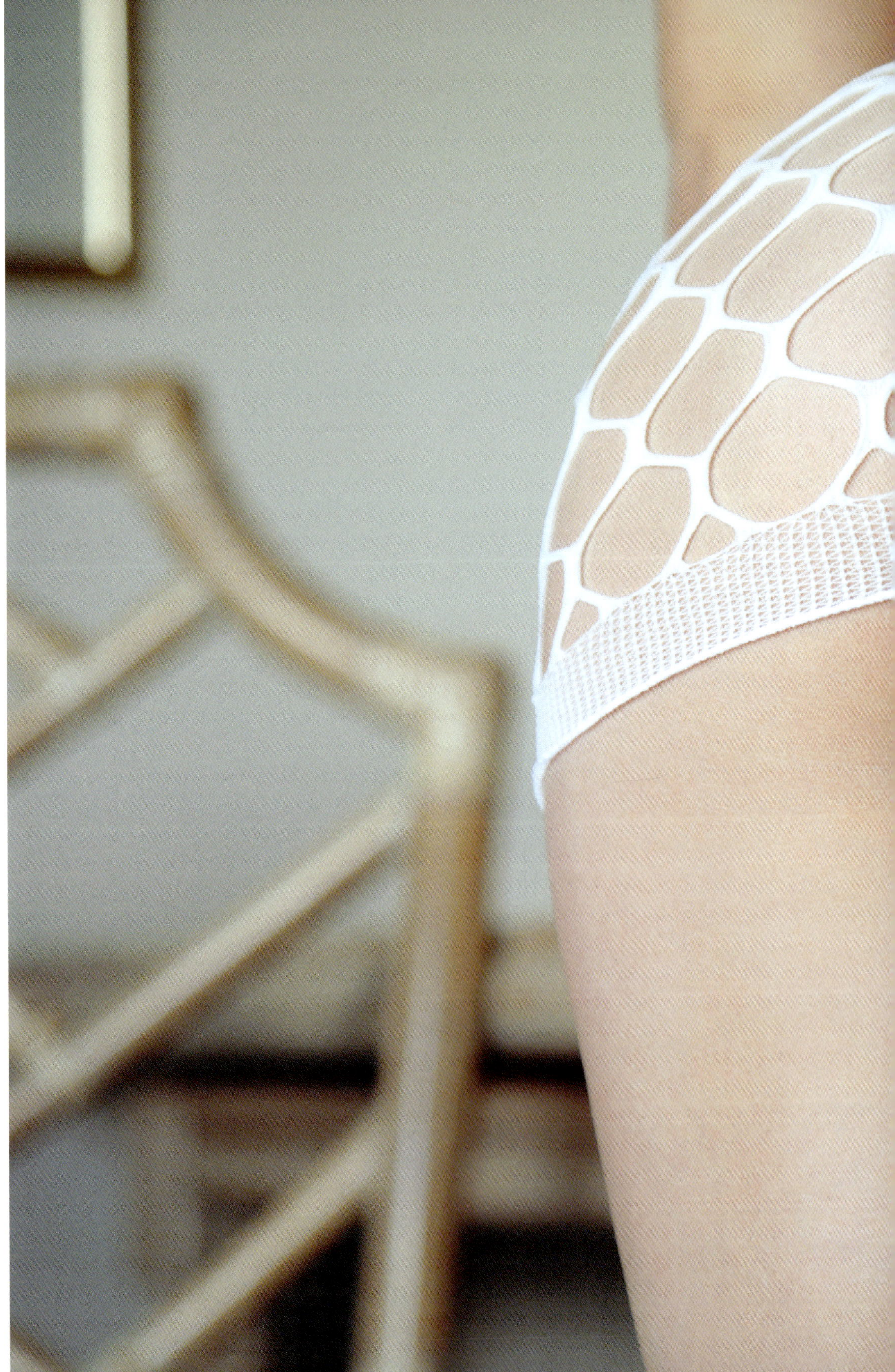

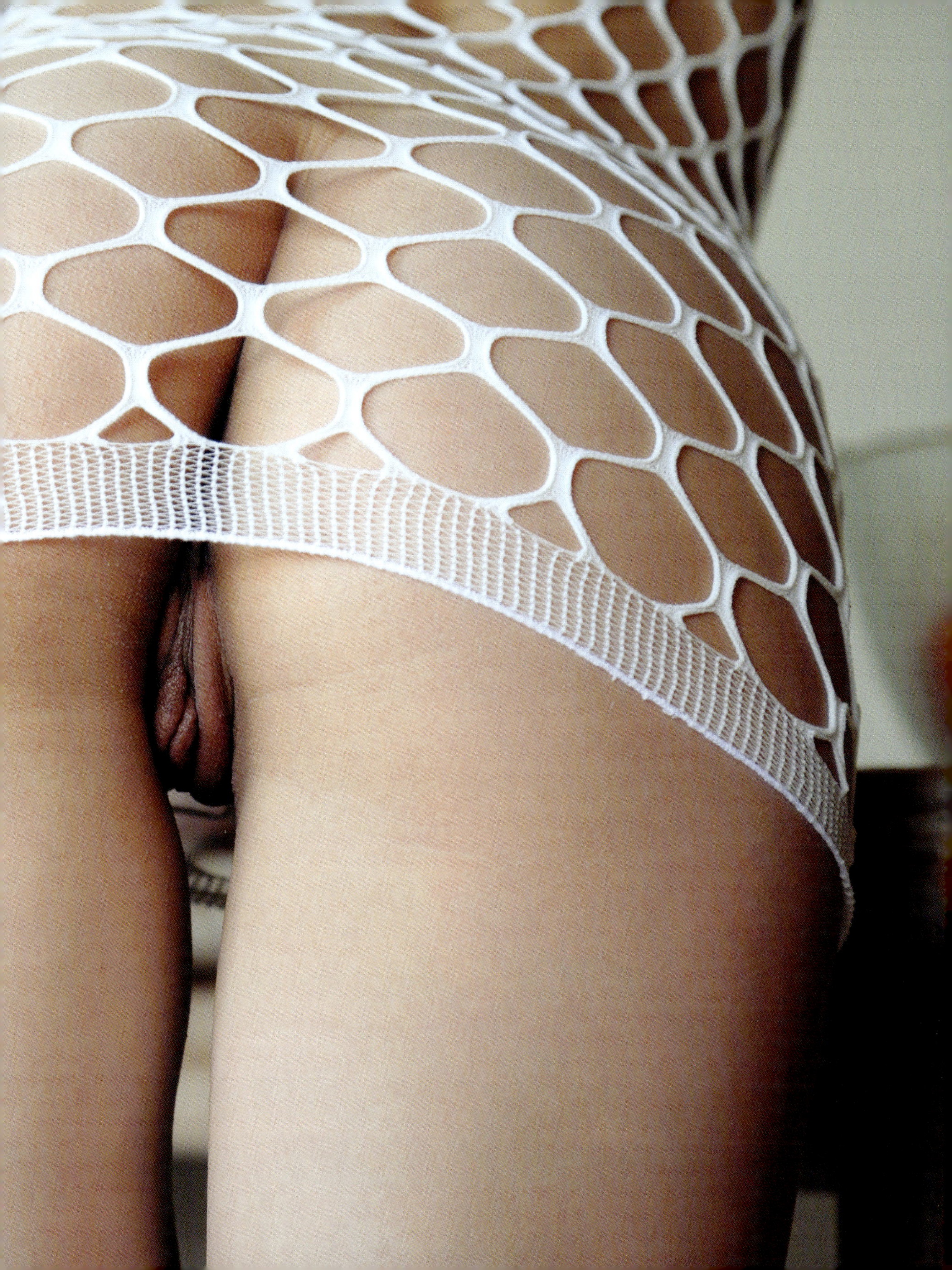

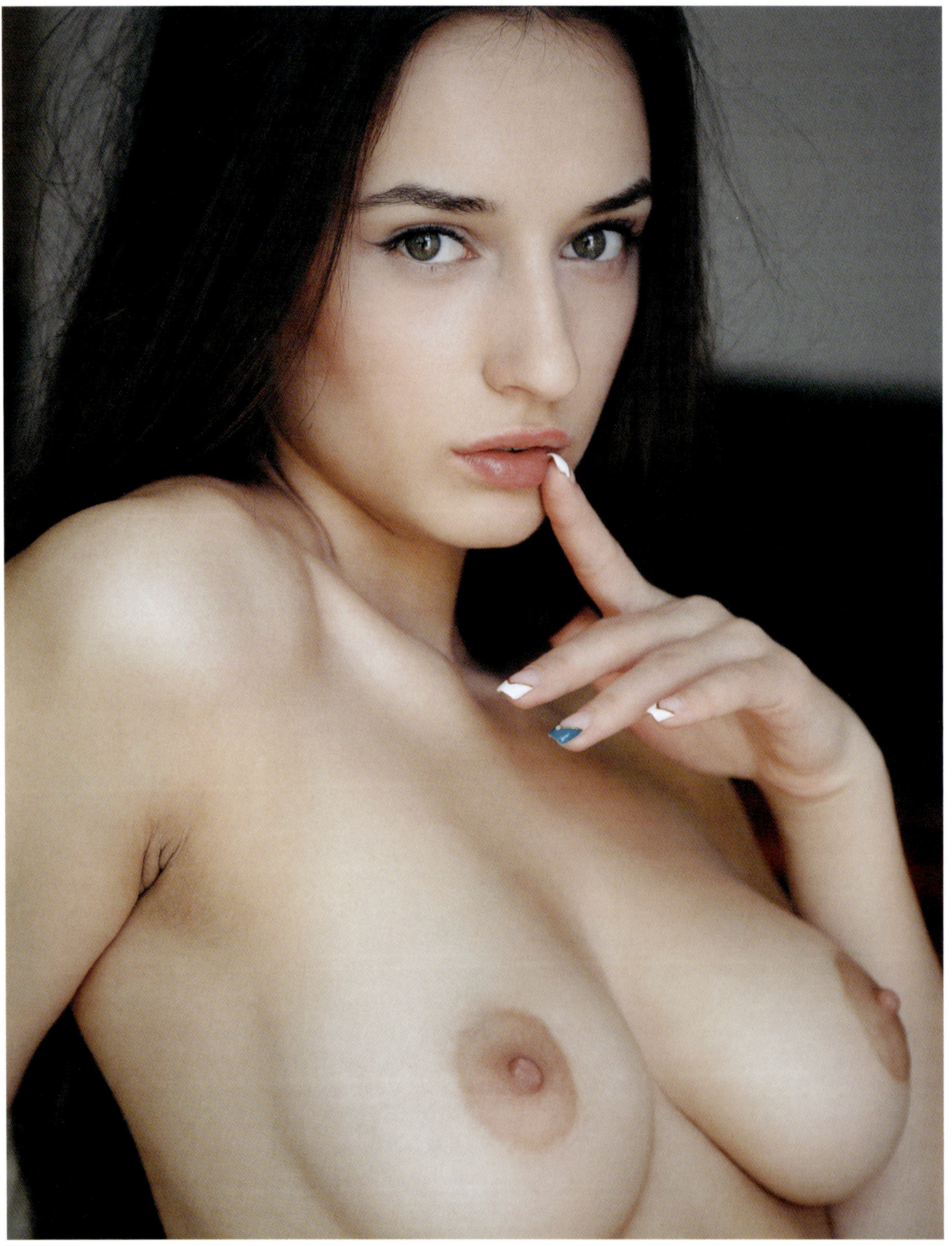

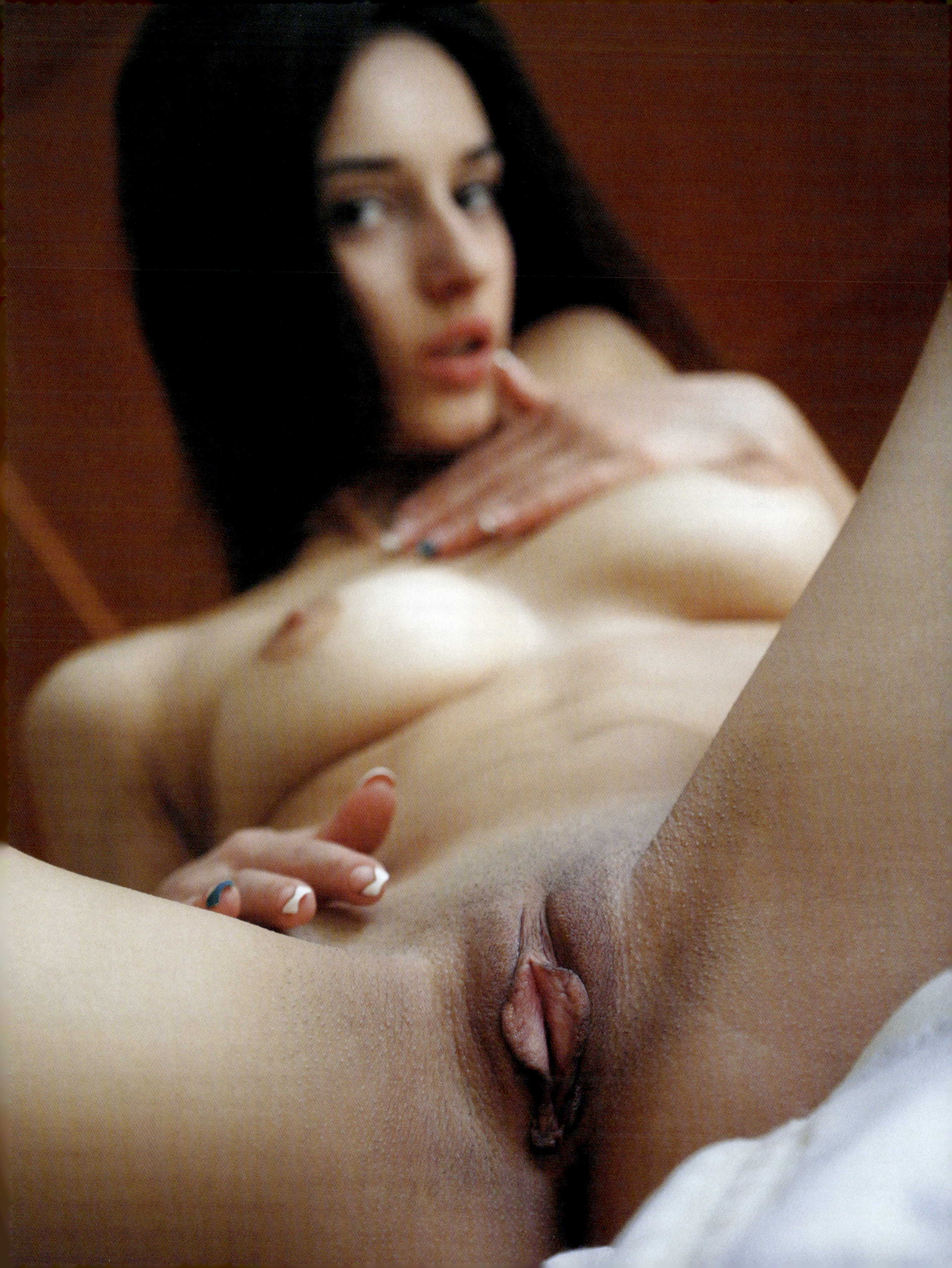

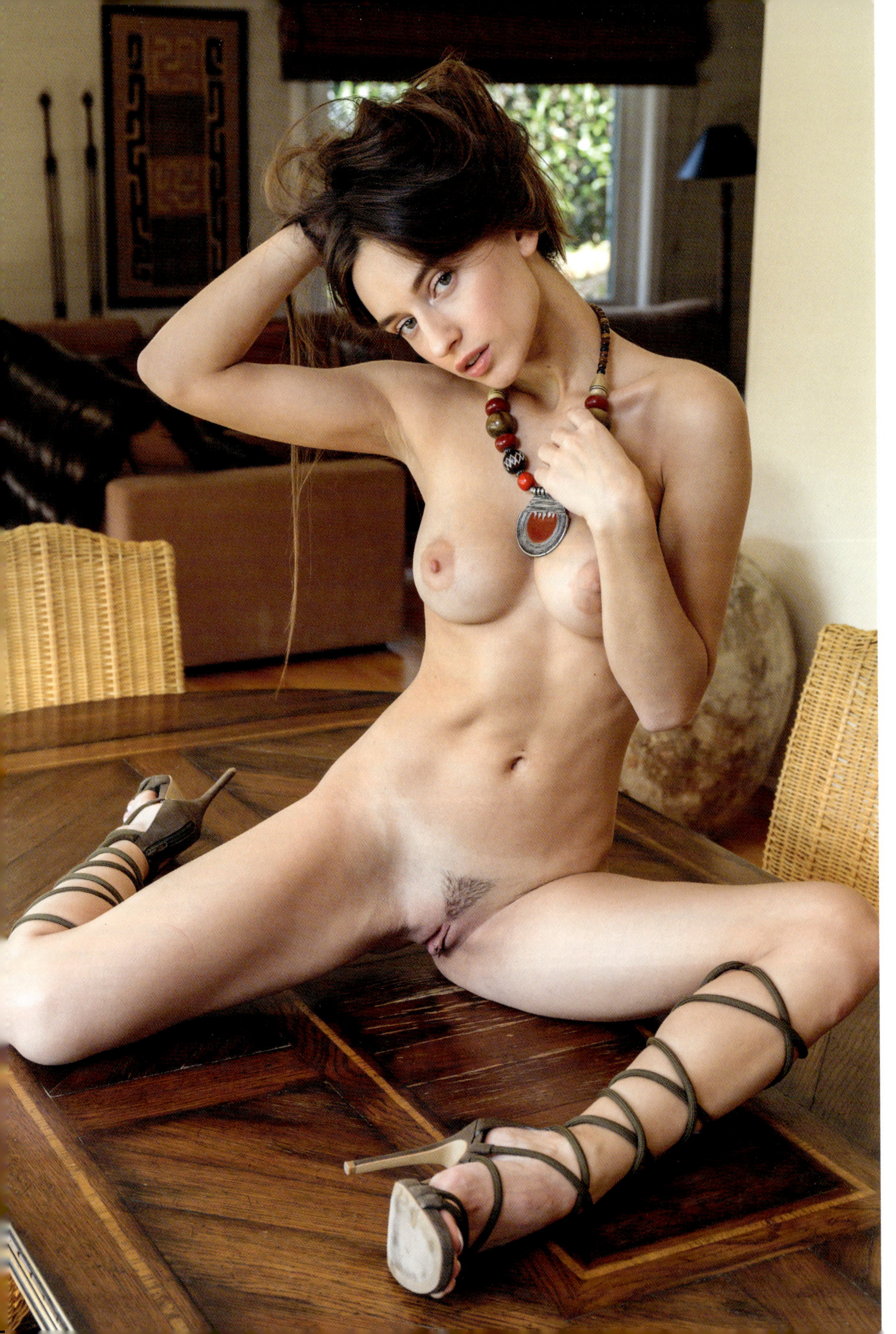

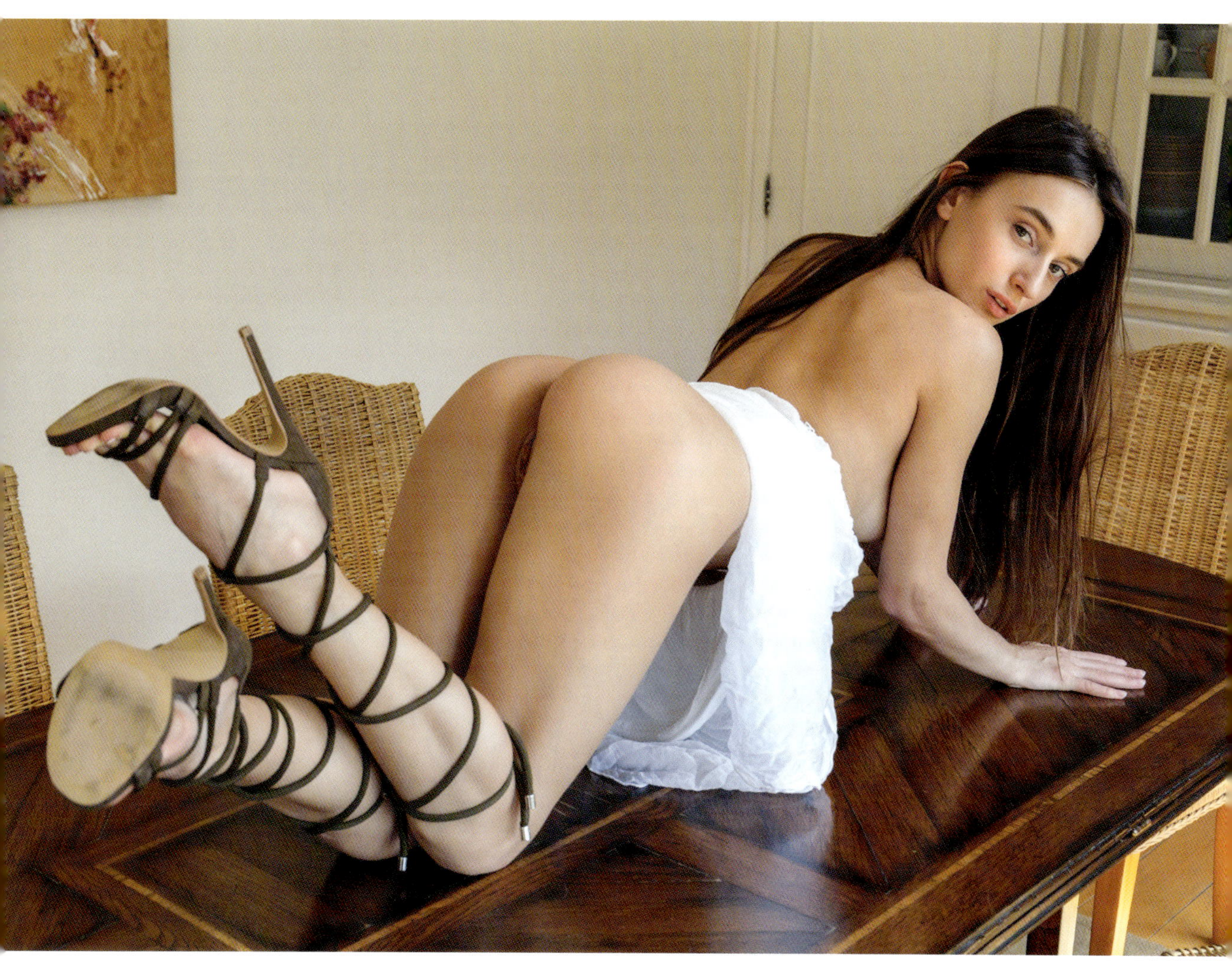

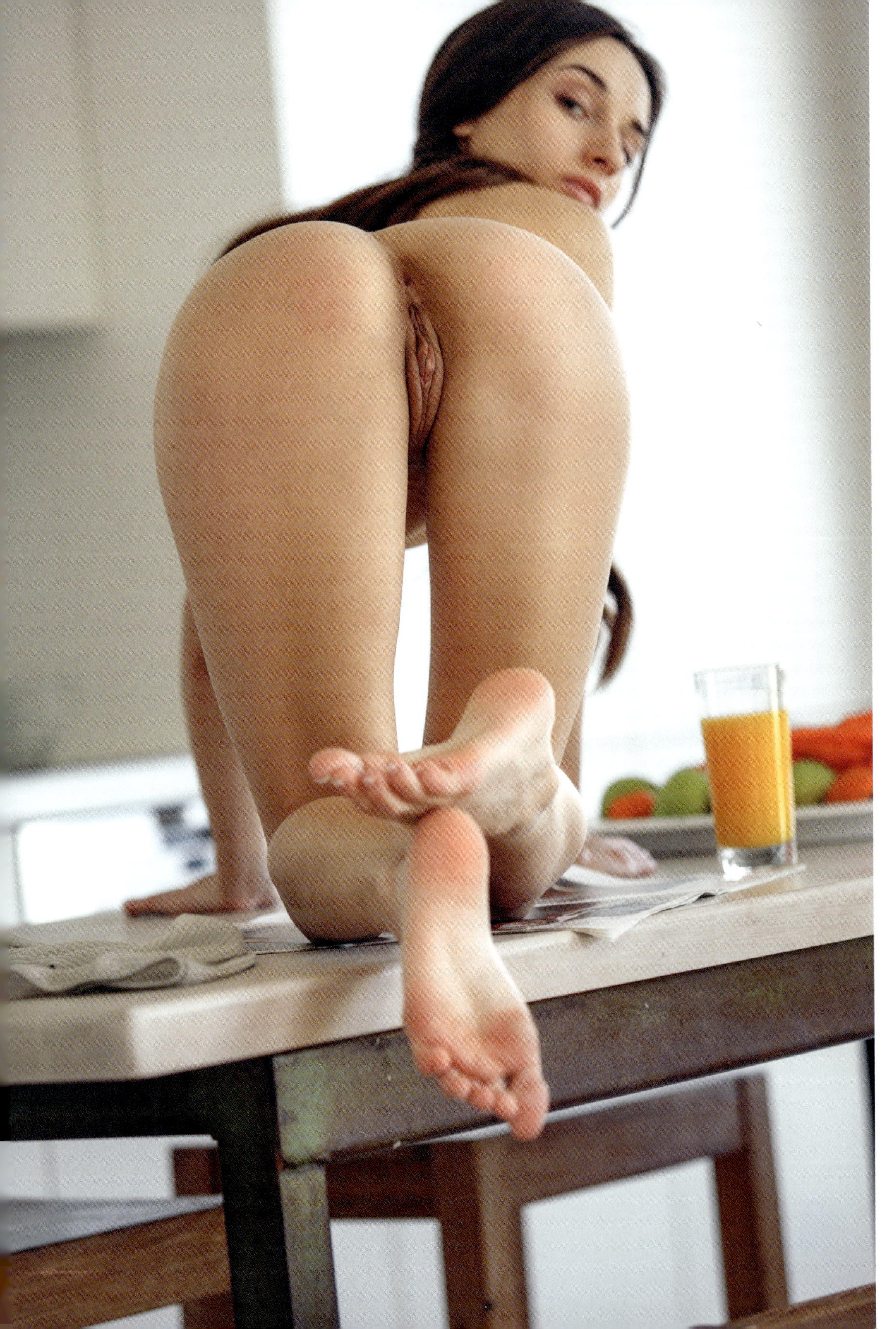

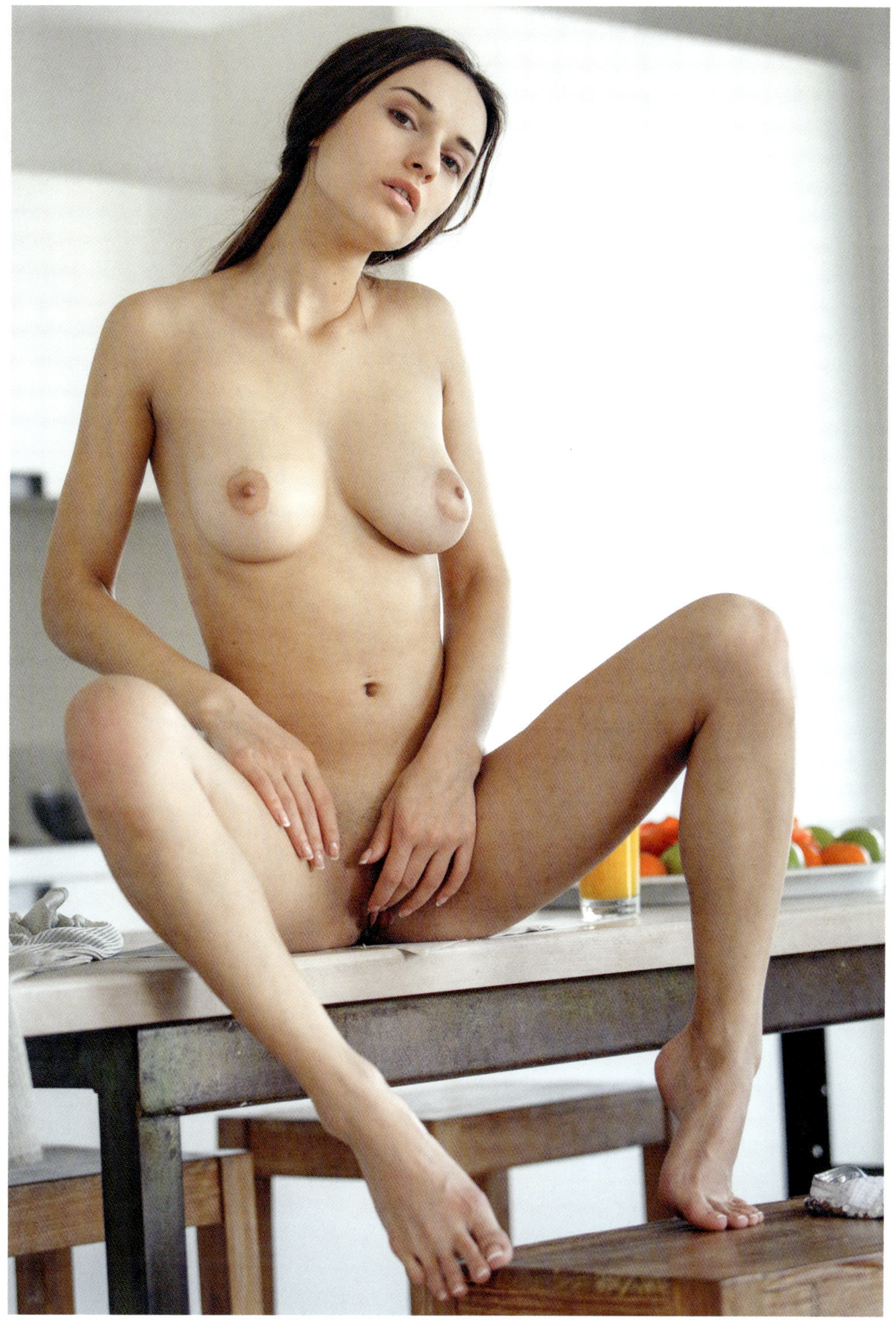

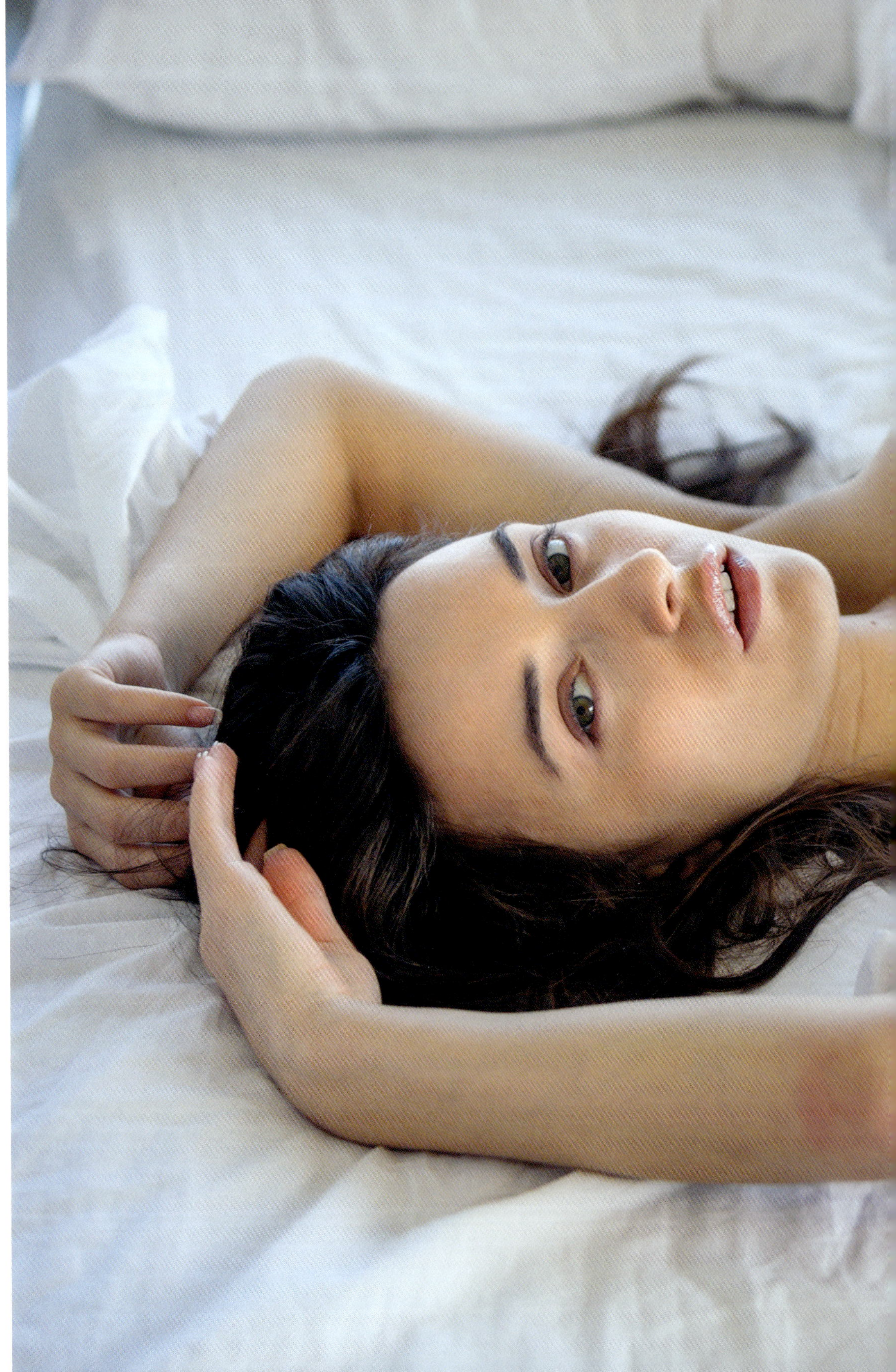

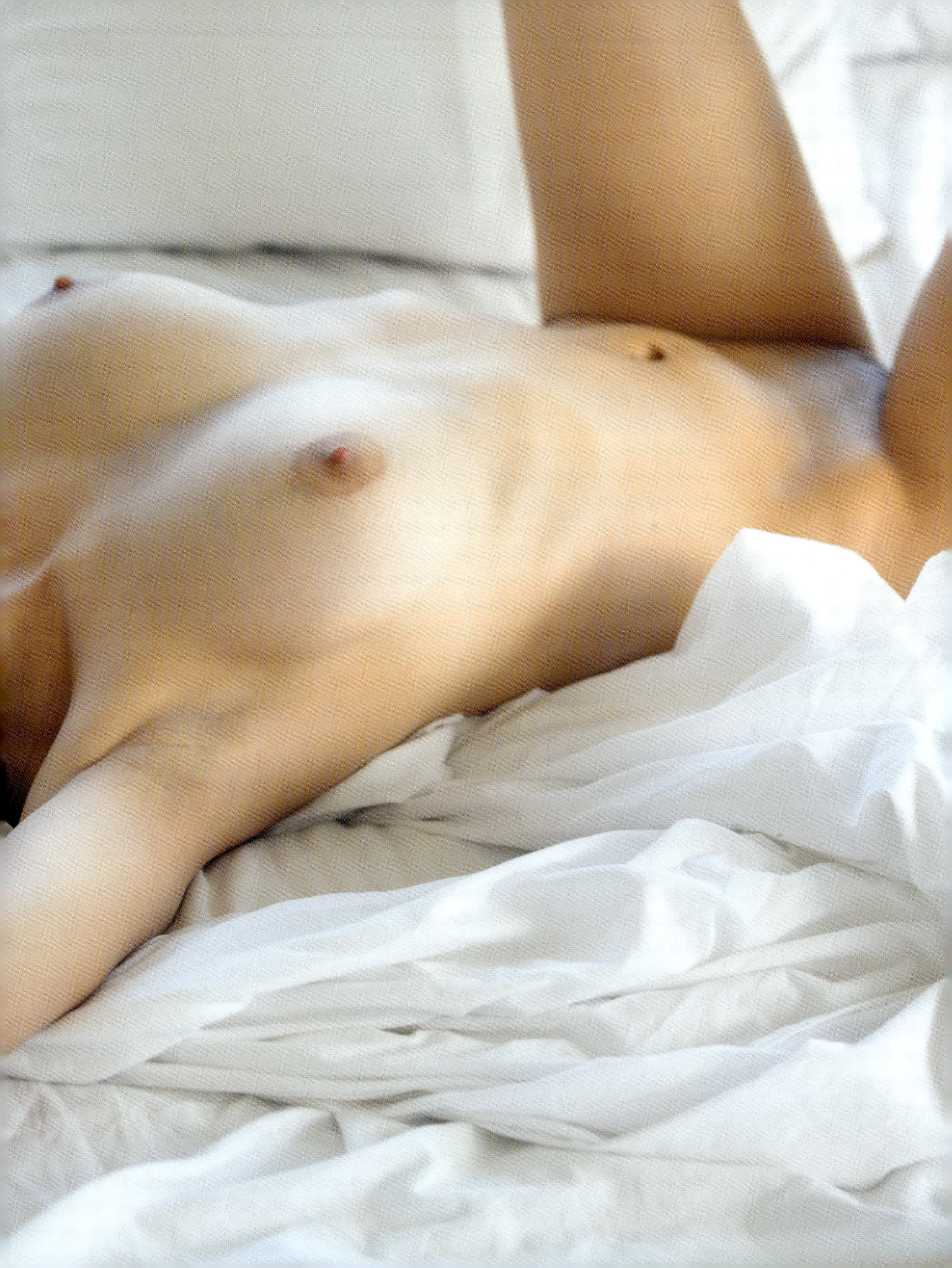

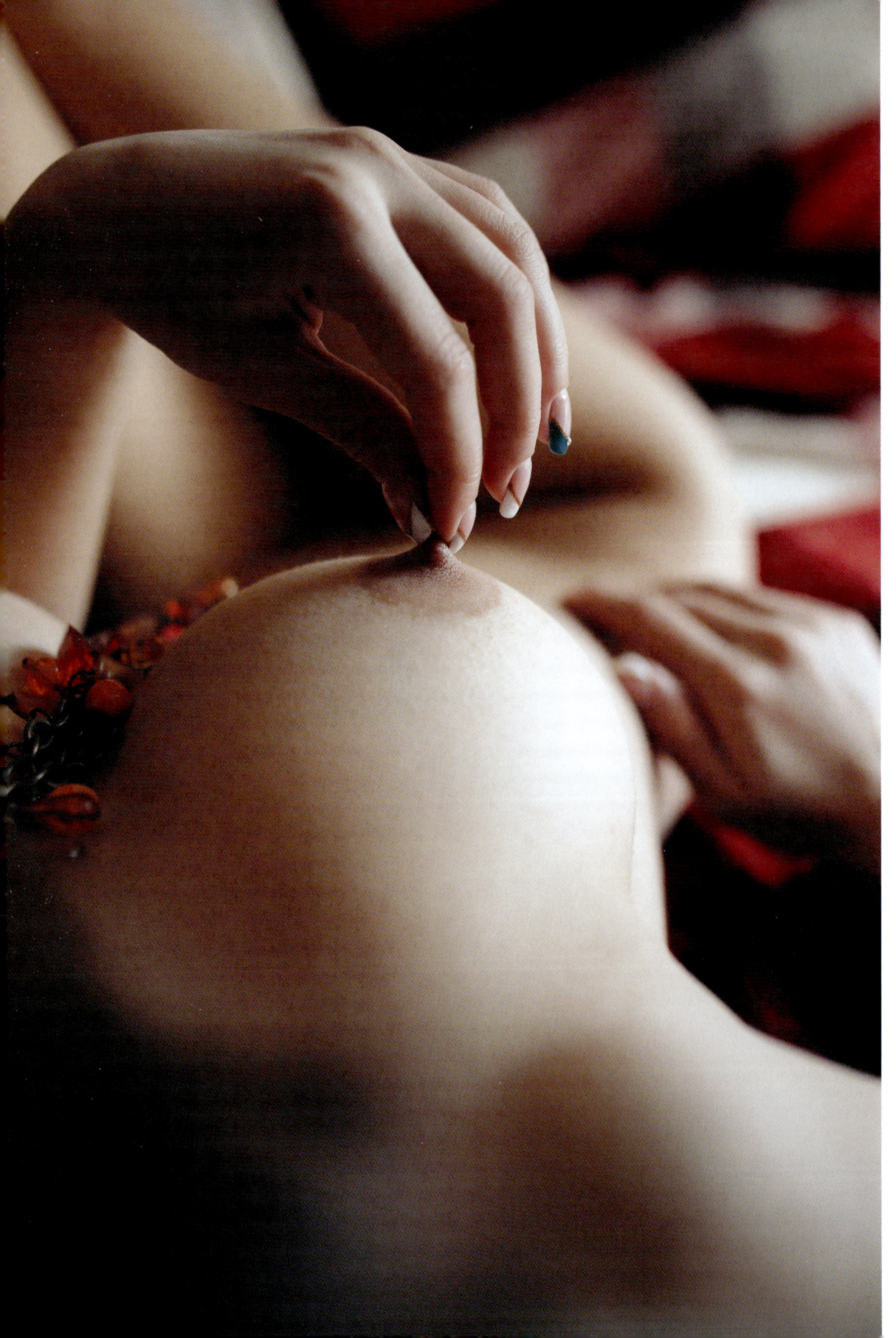

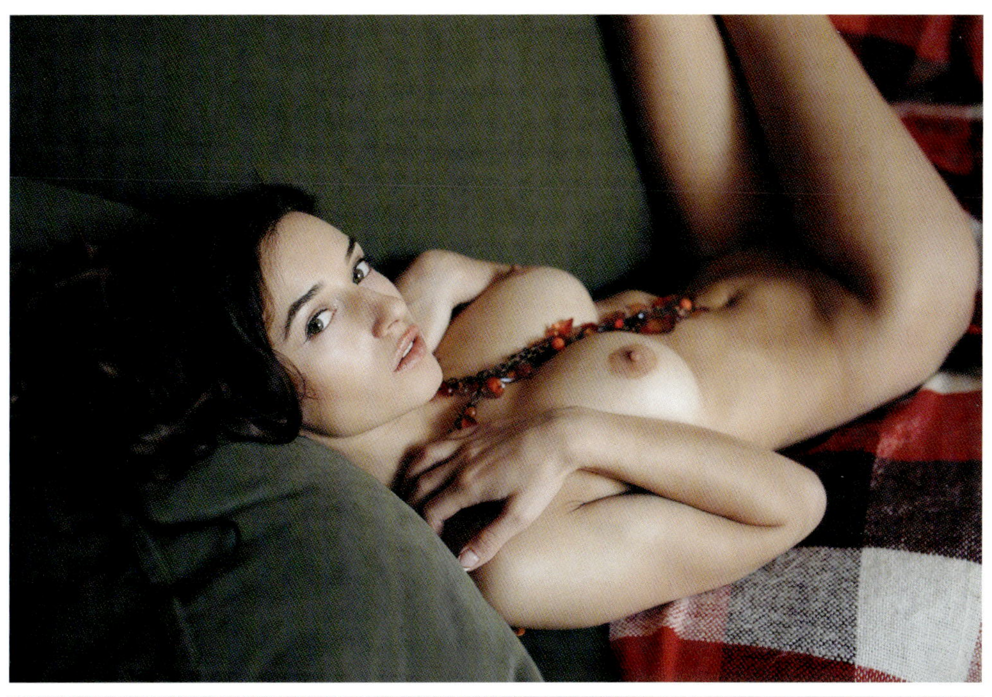

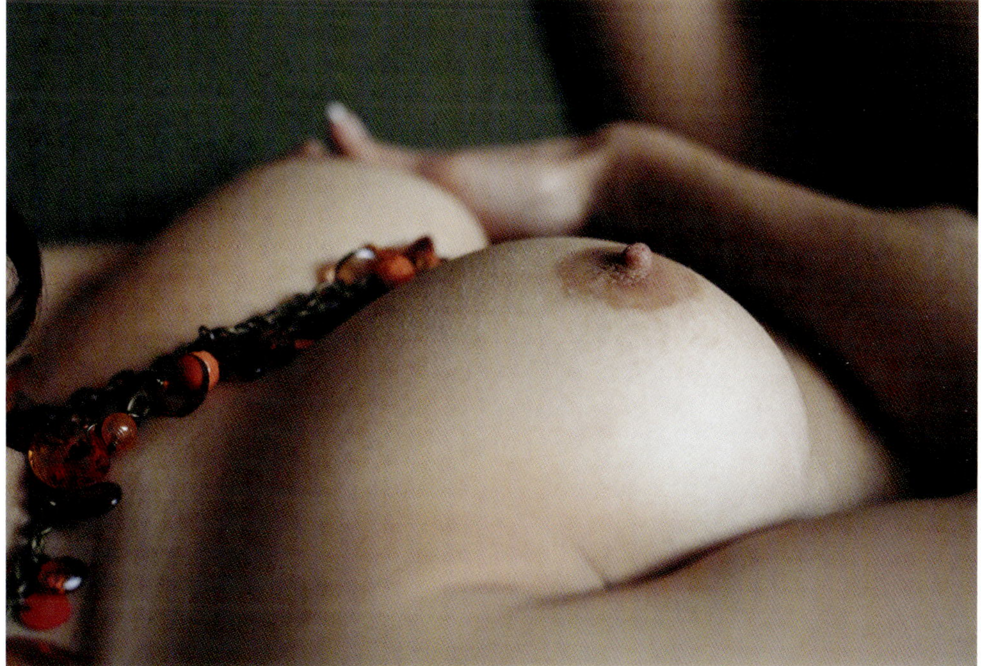

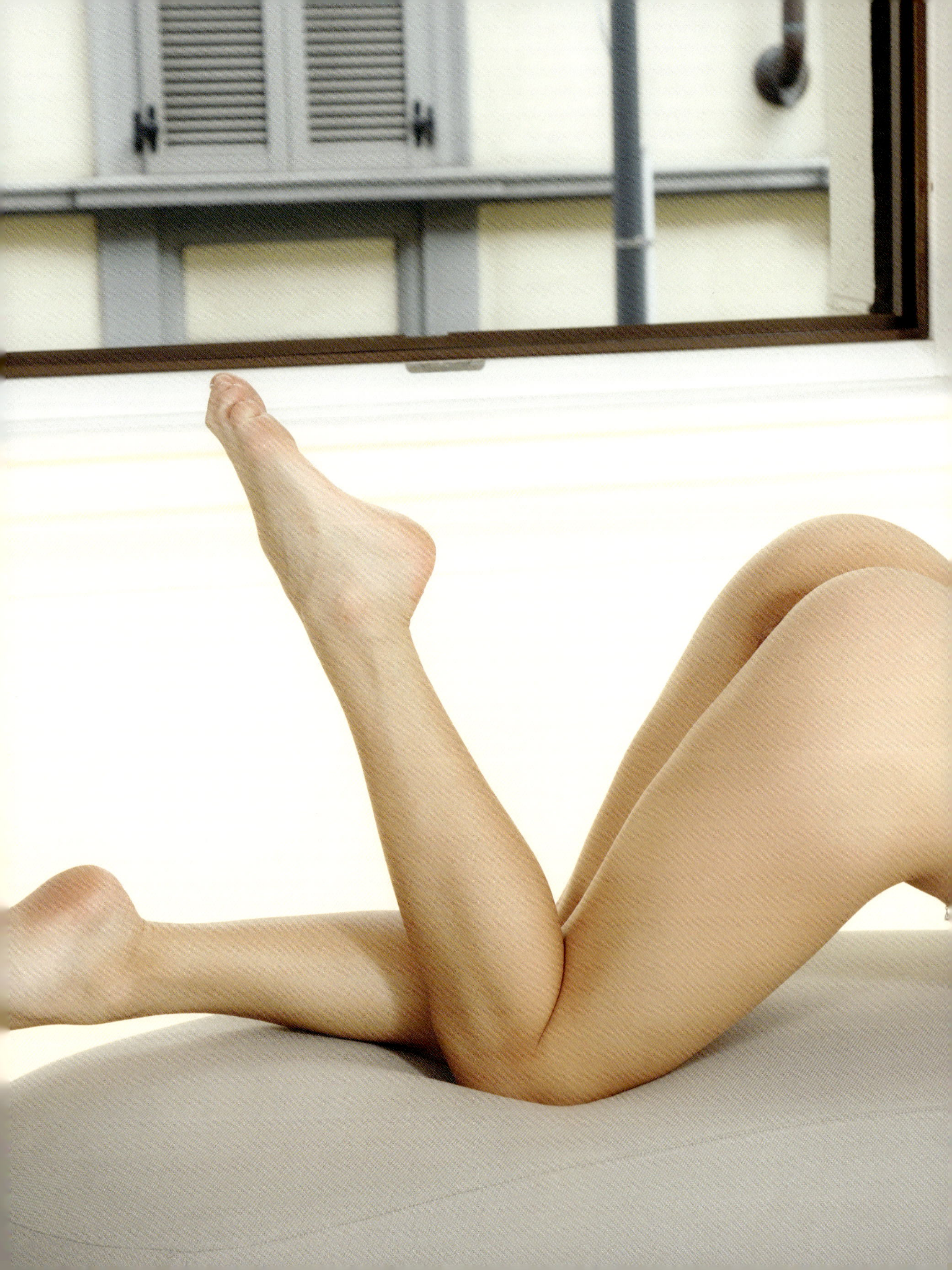

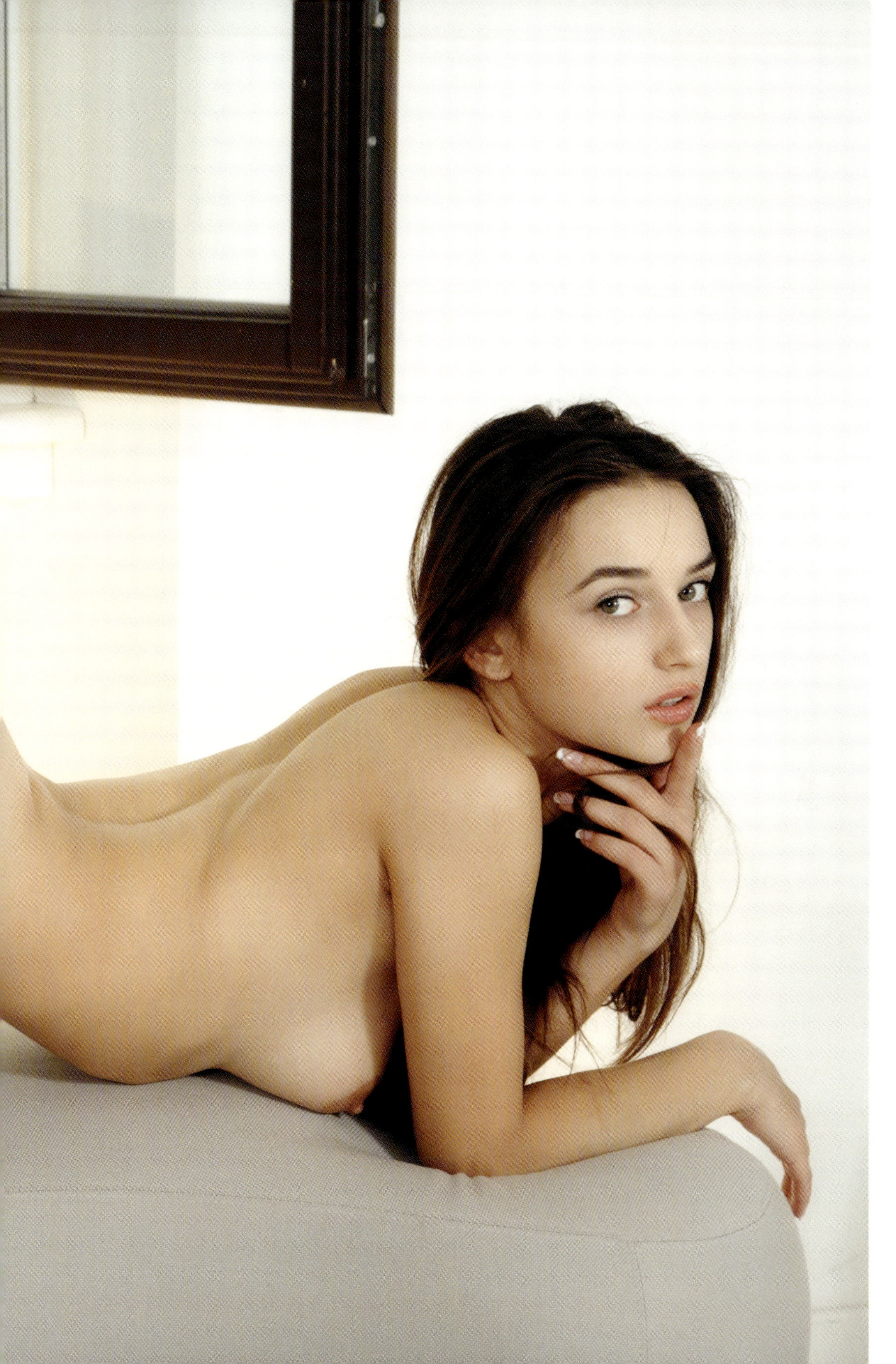

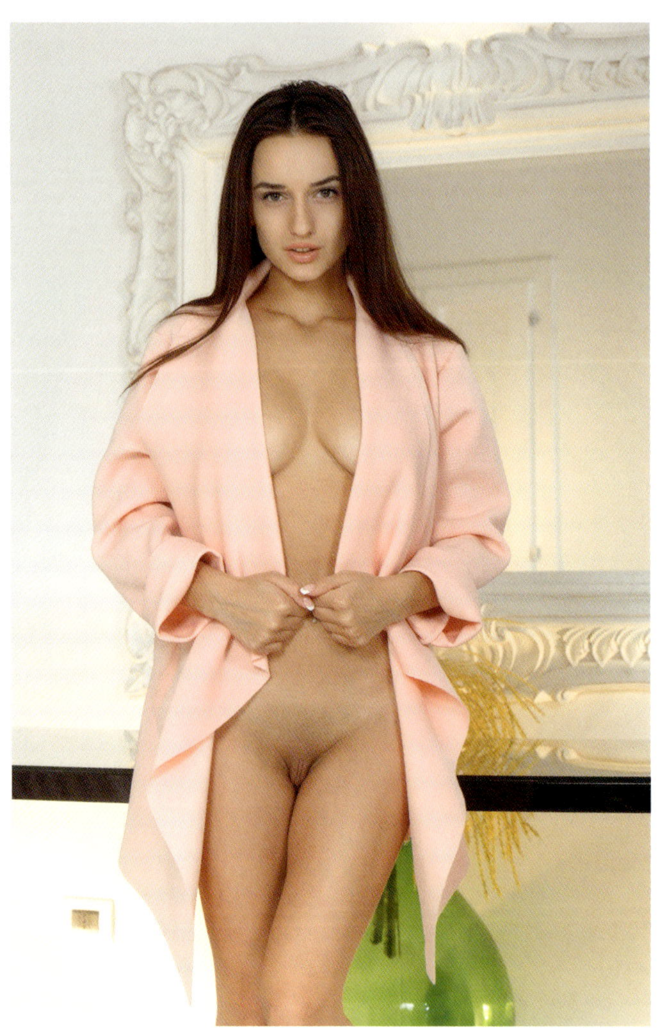

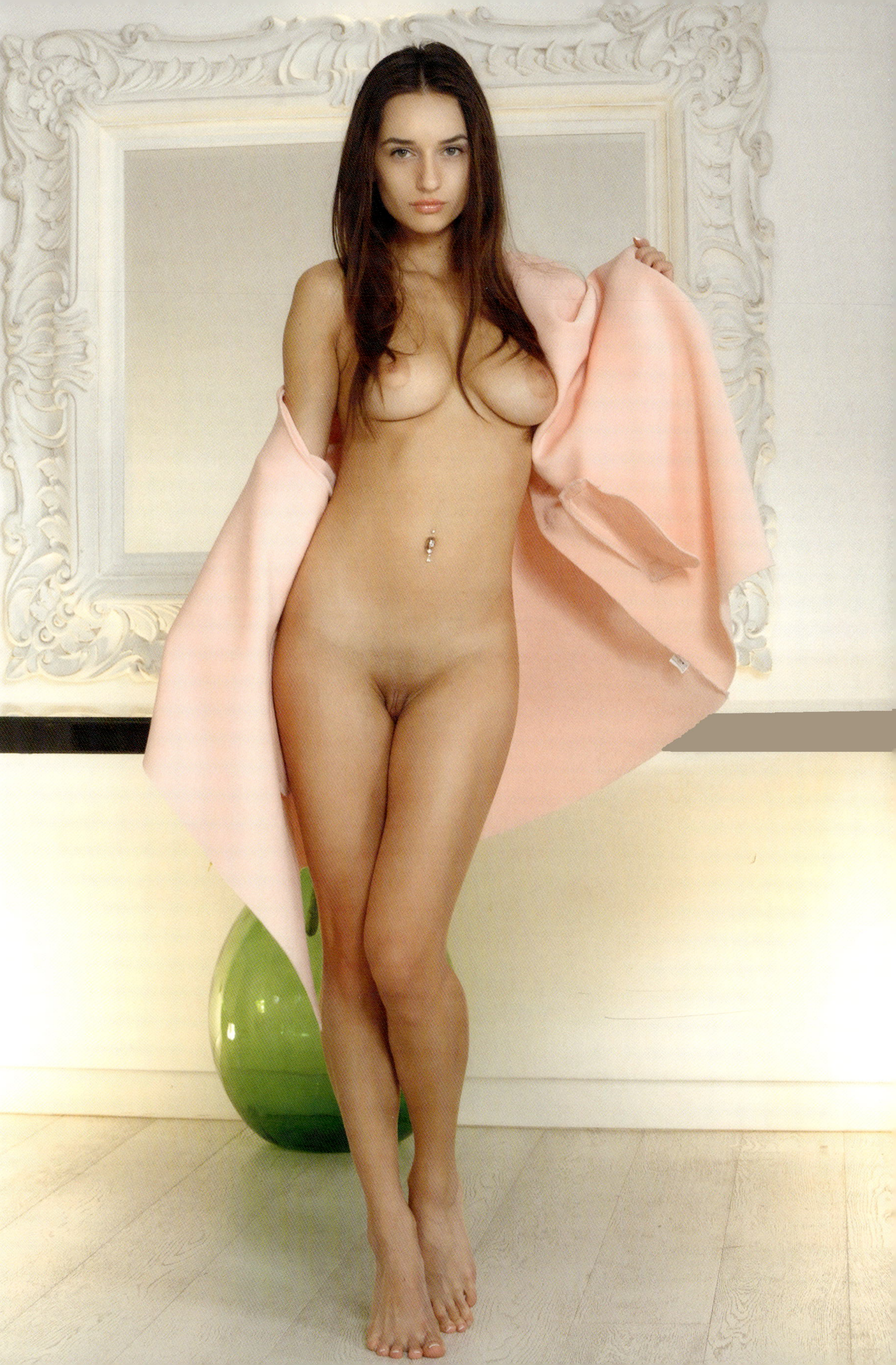

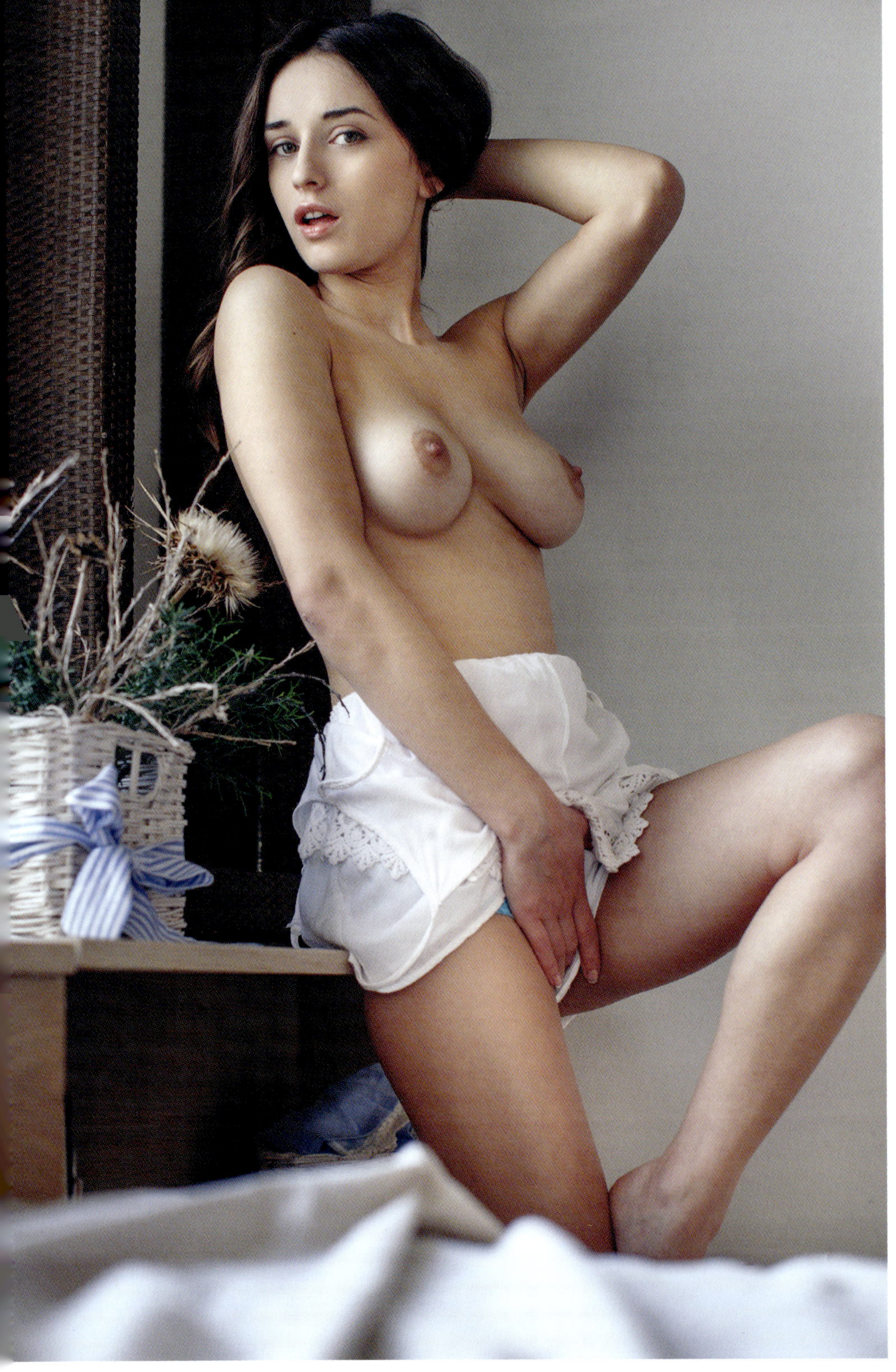

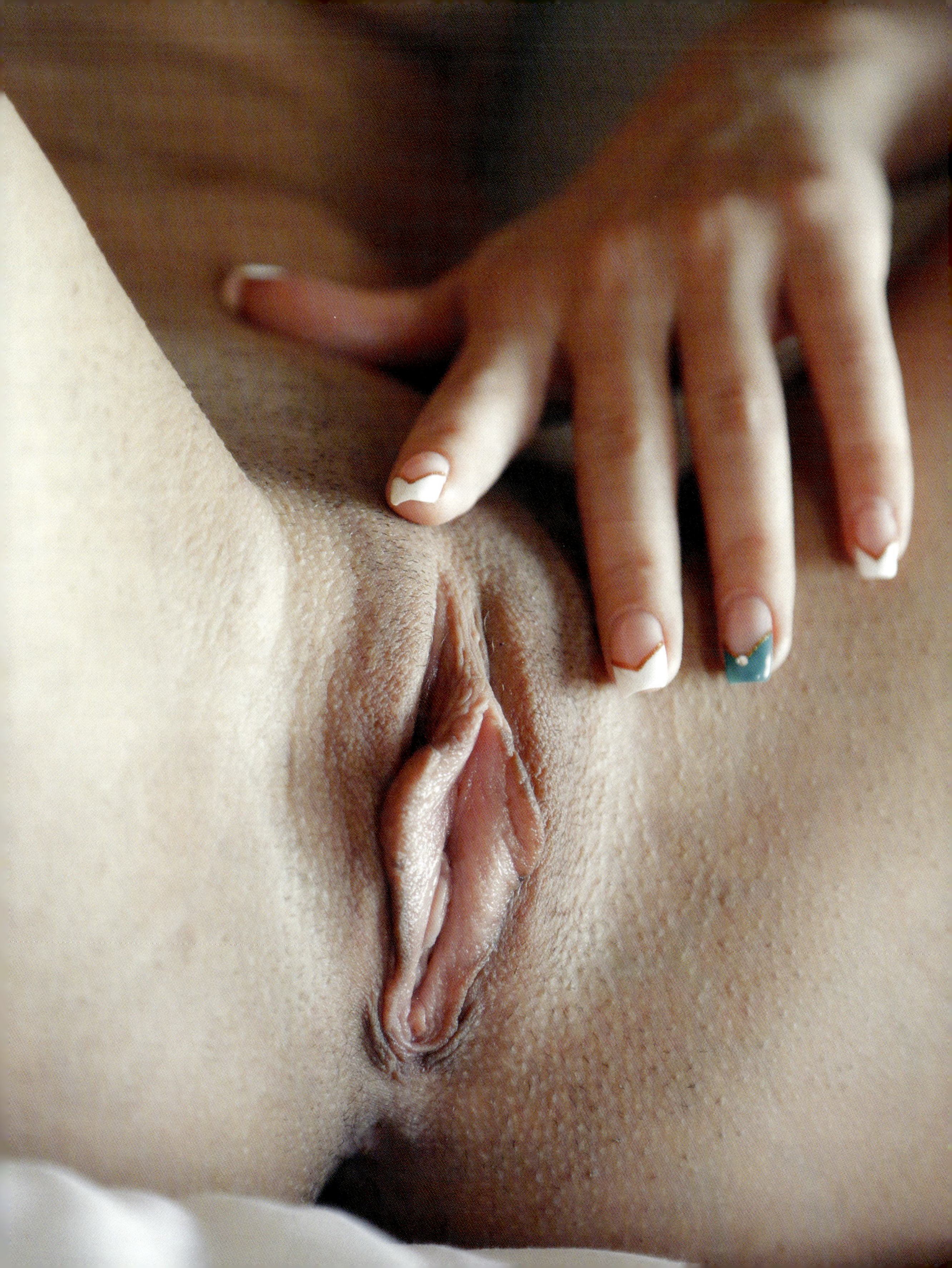

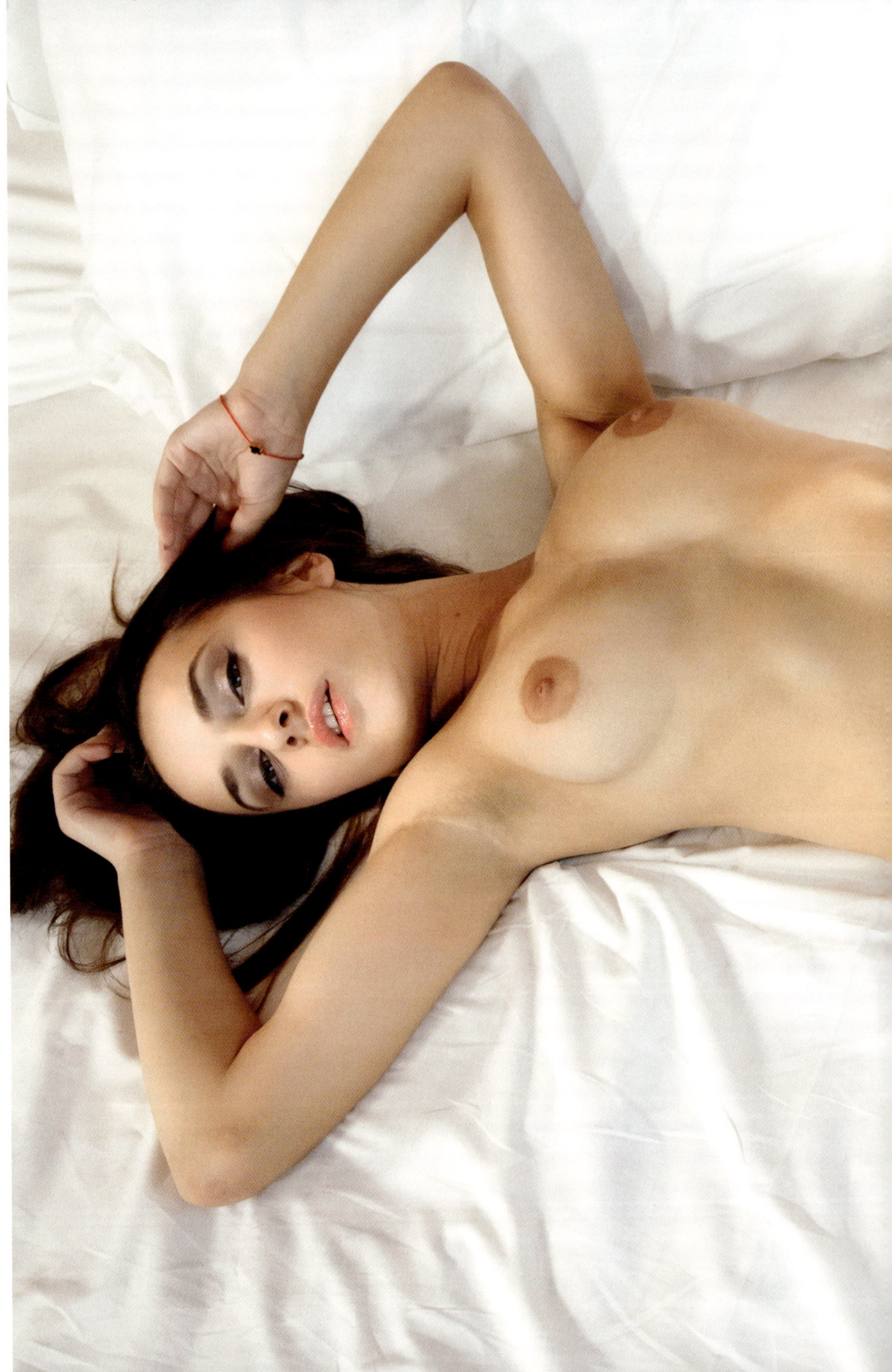

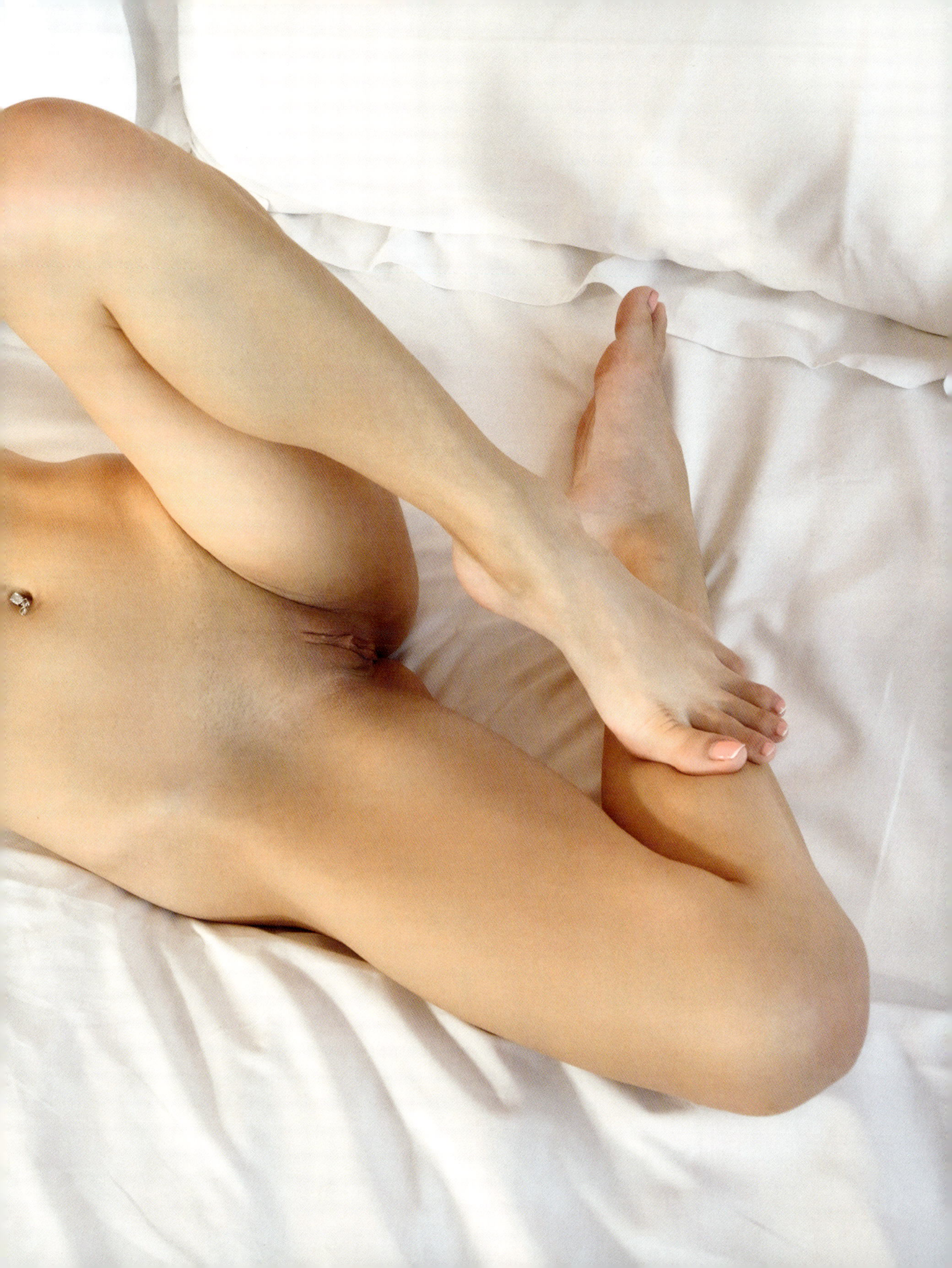

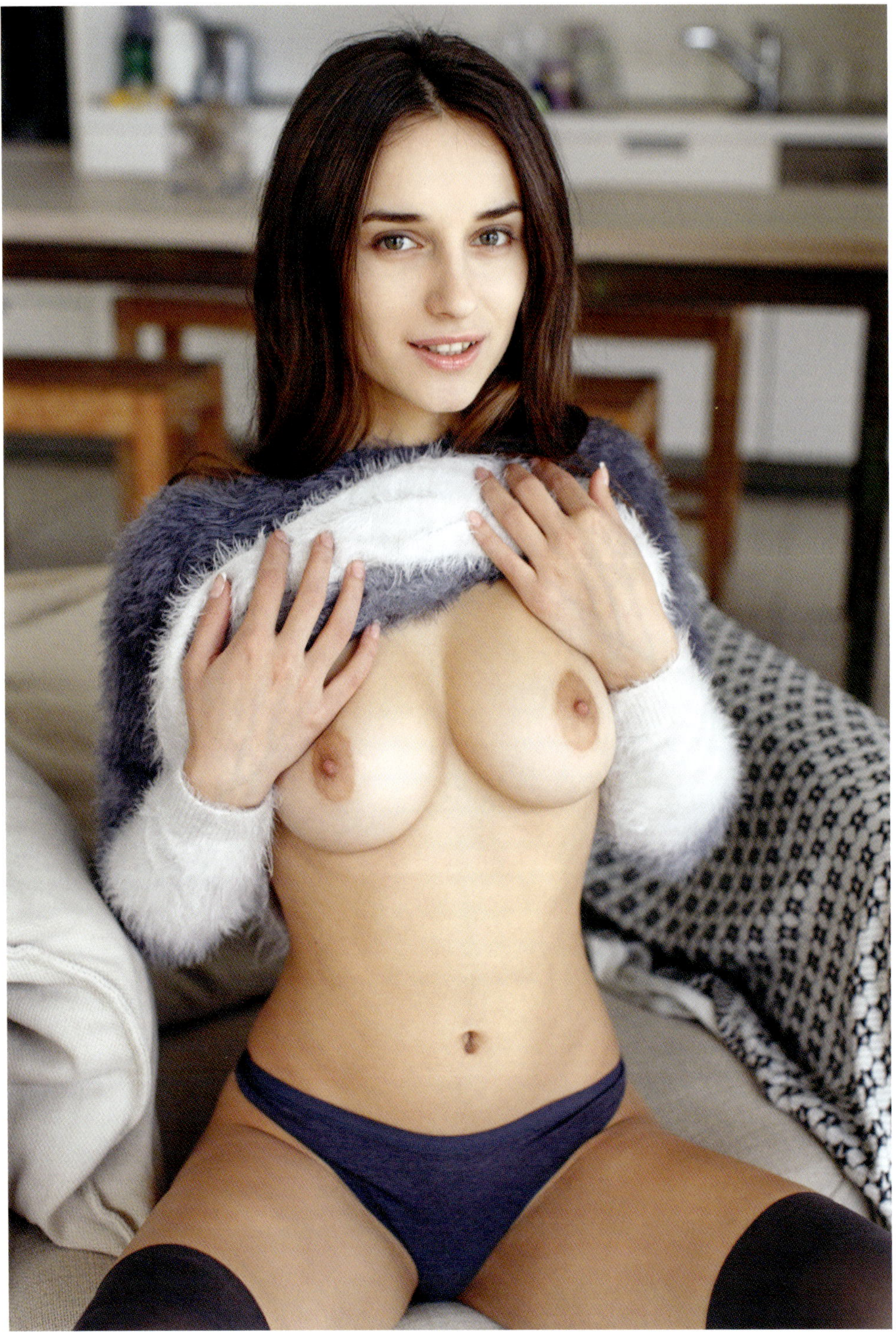

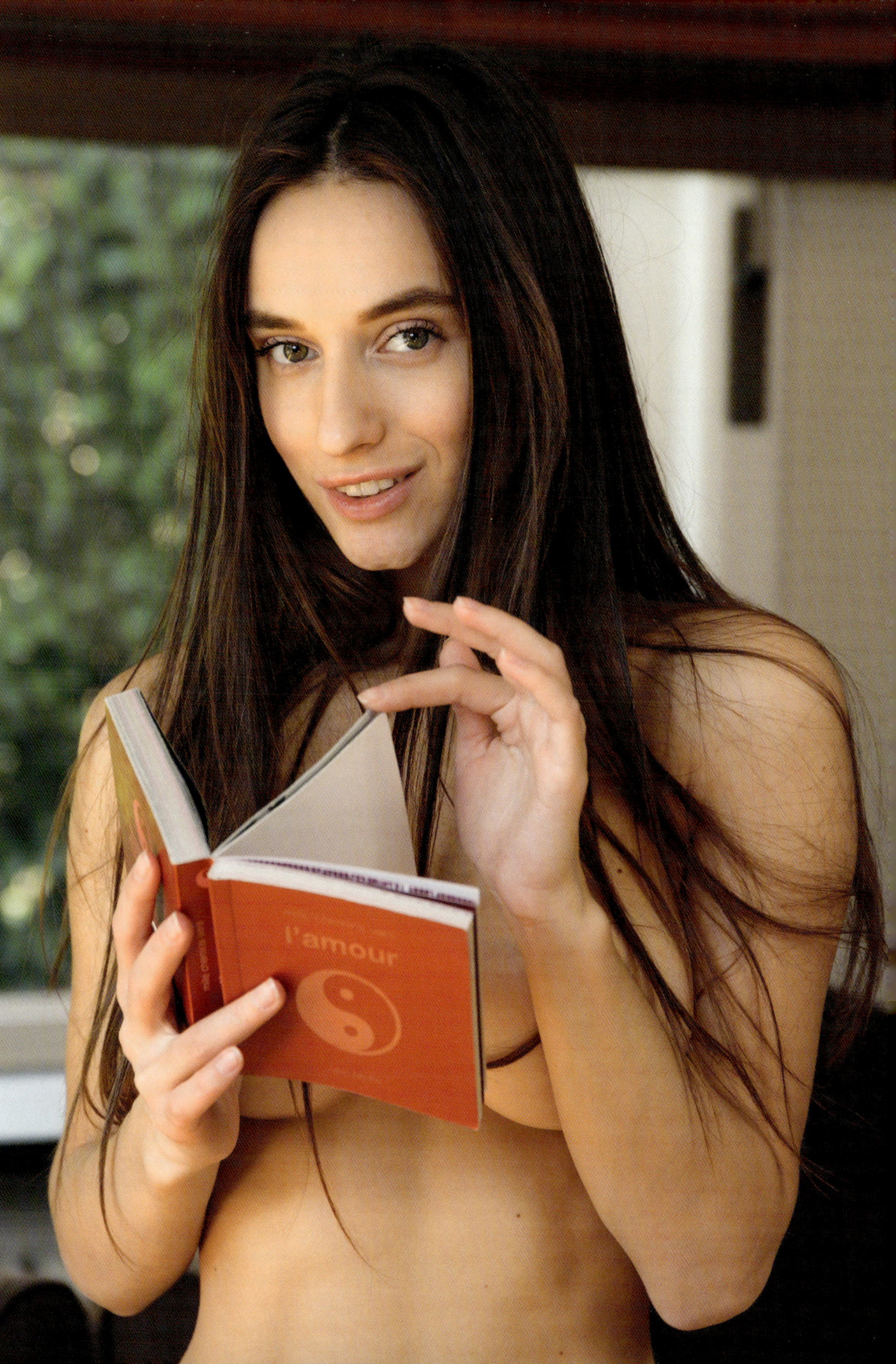
l'amour

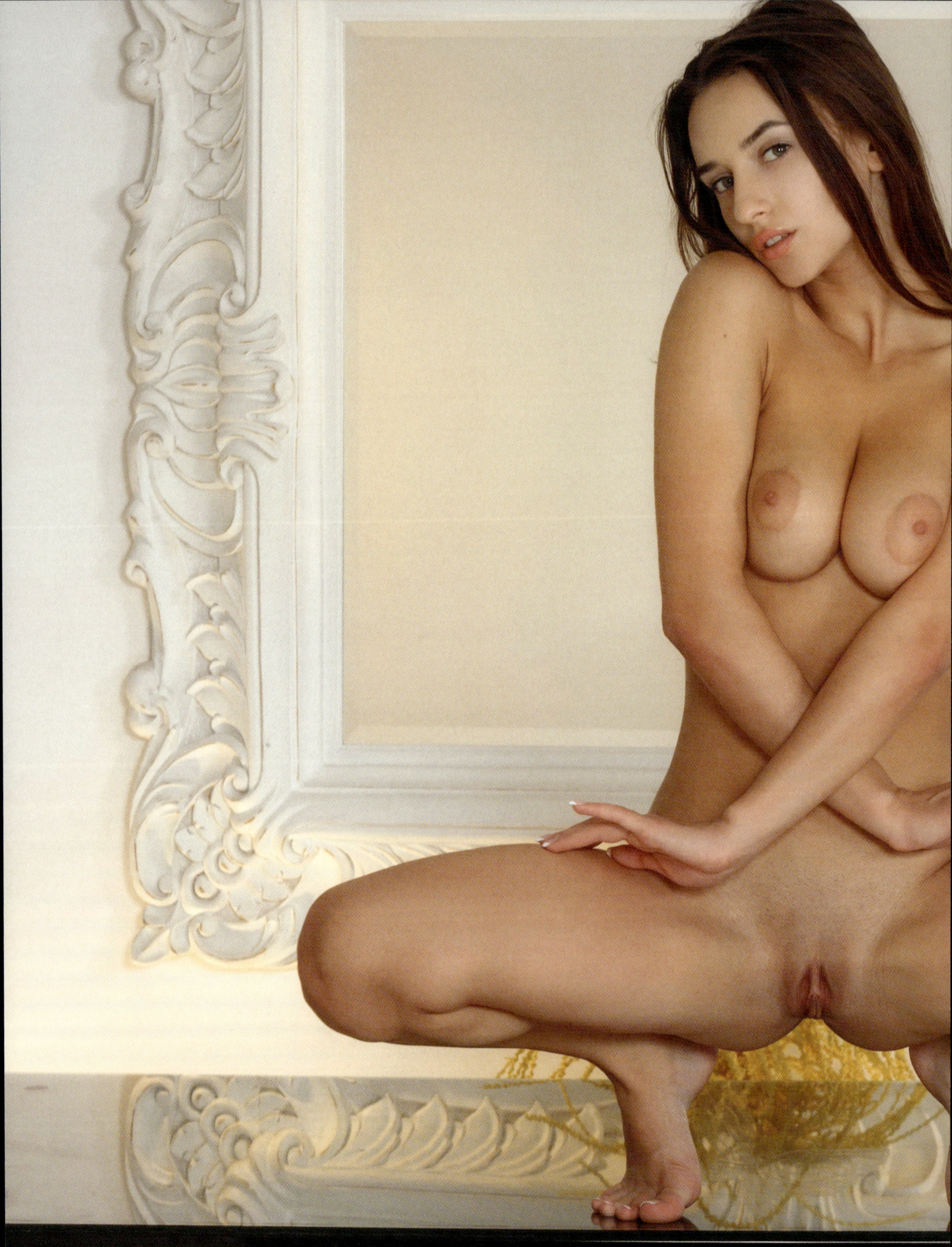

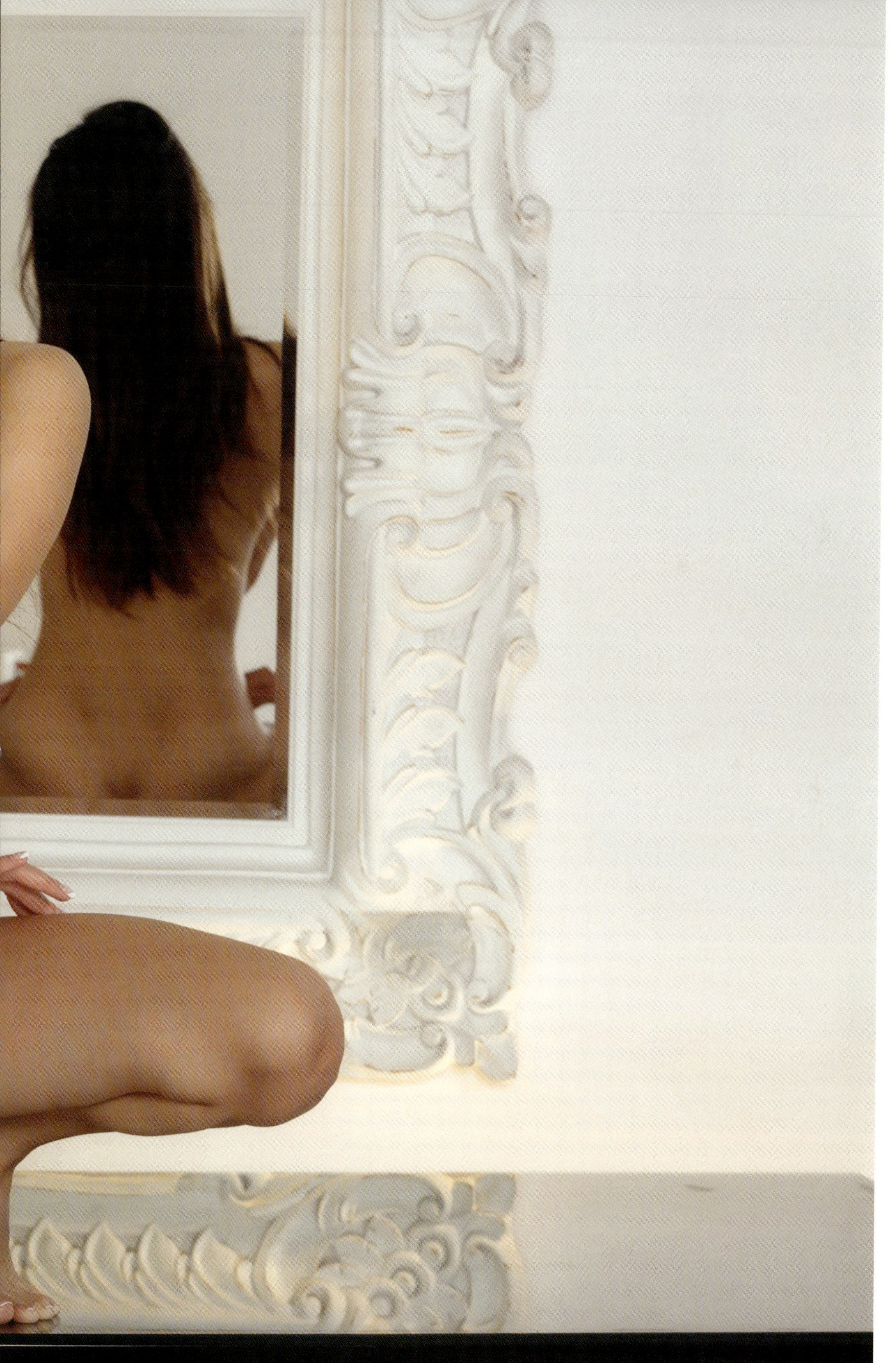

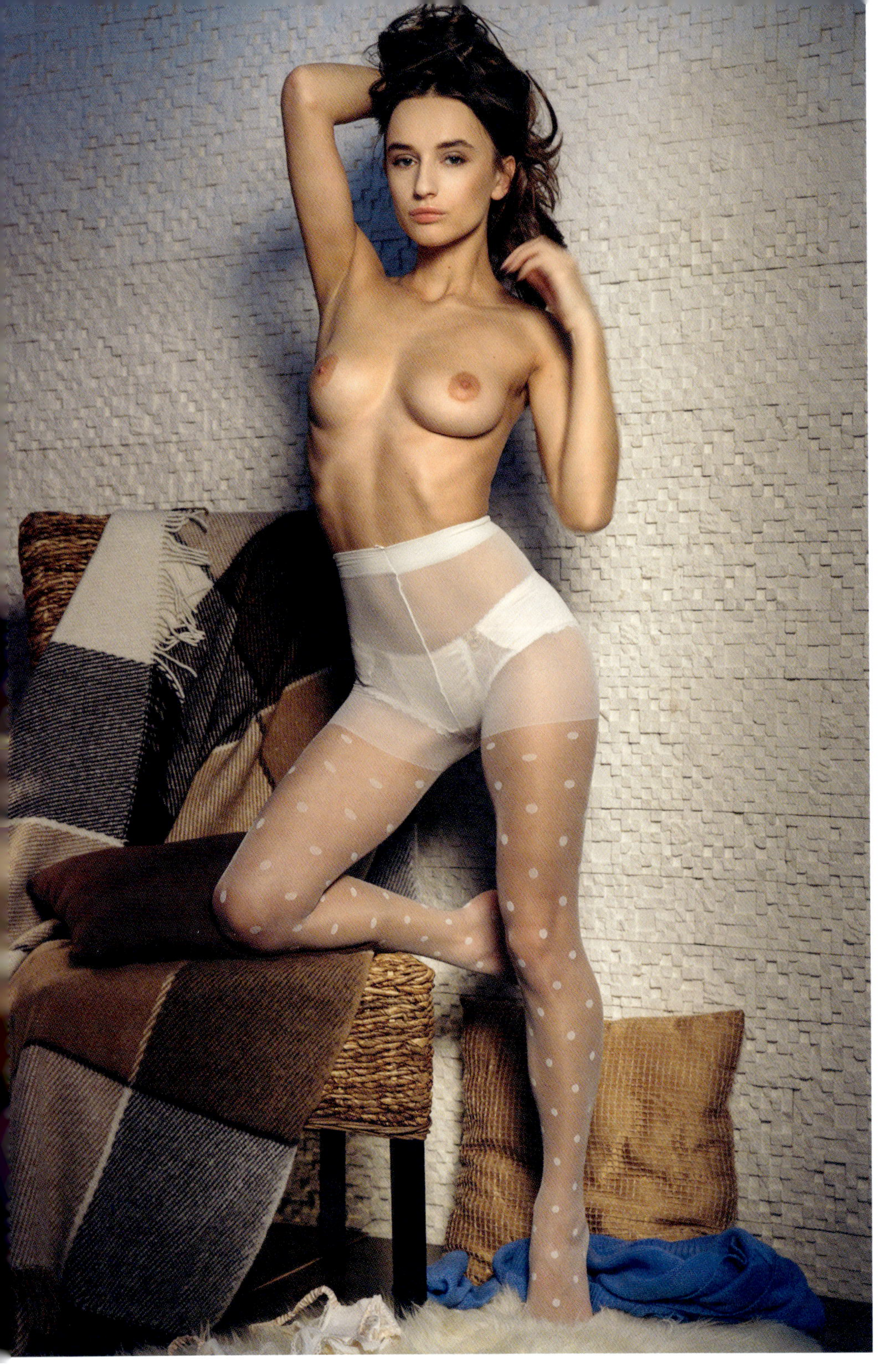

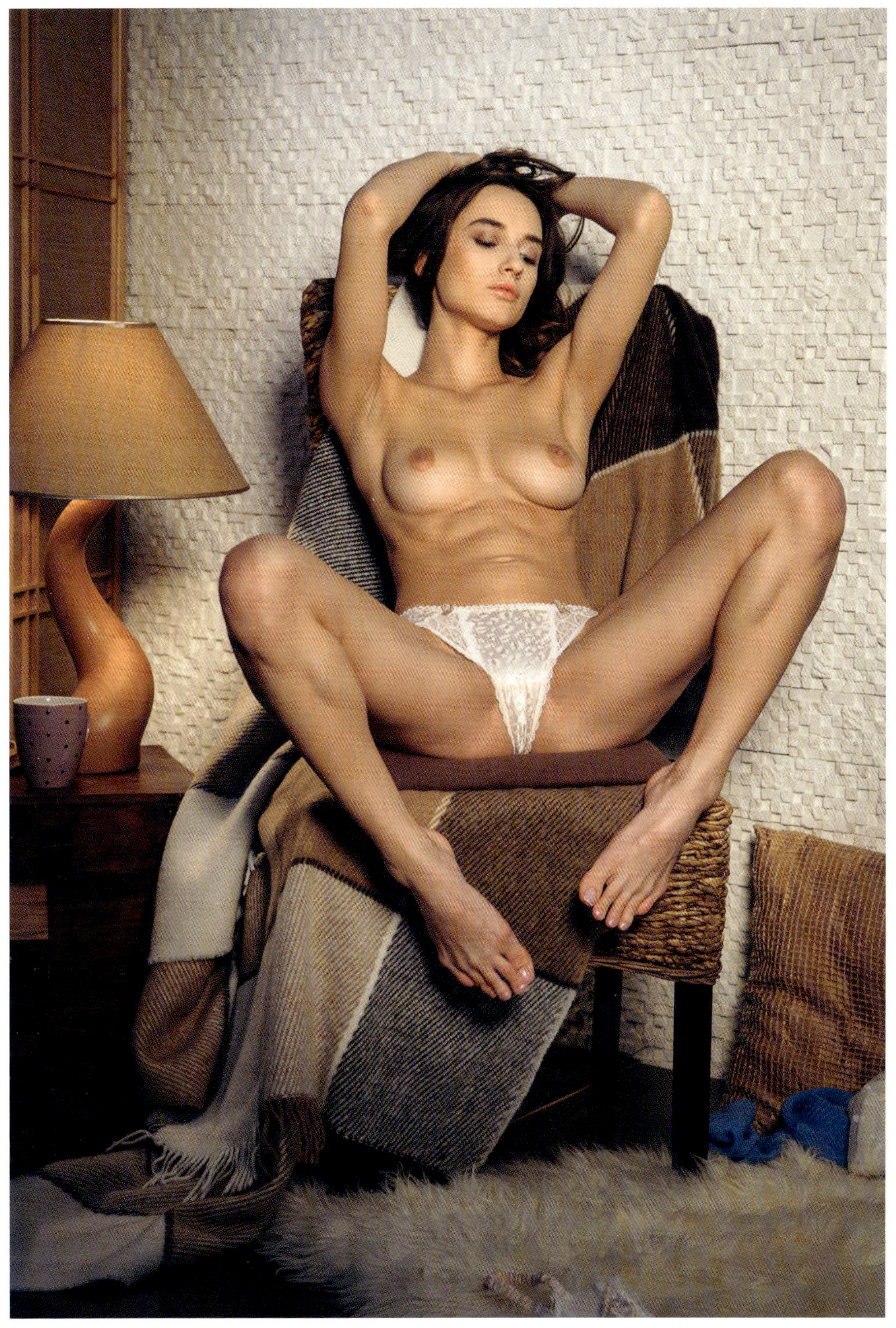

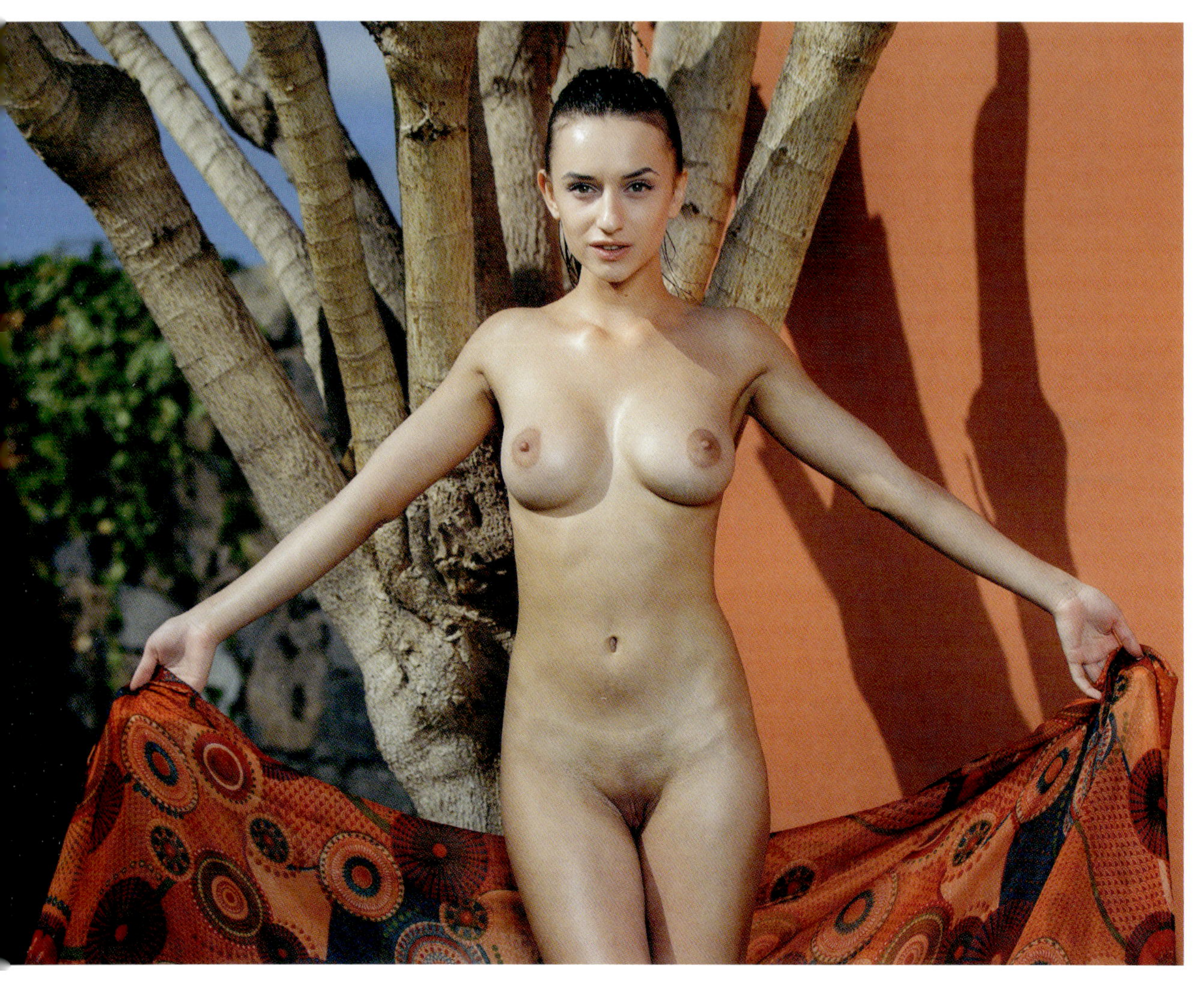

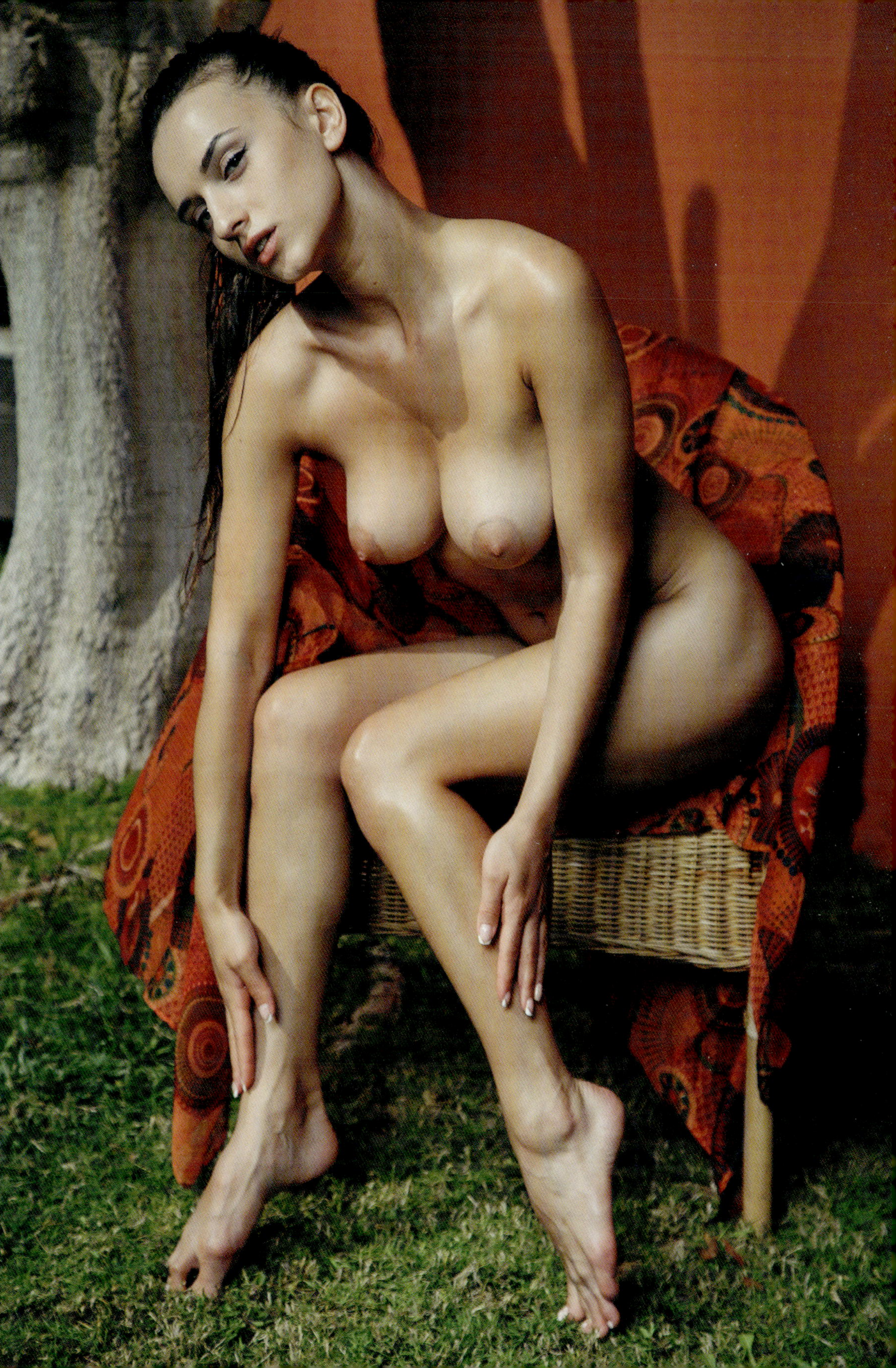

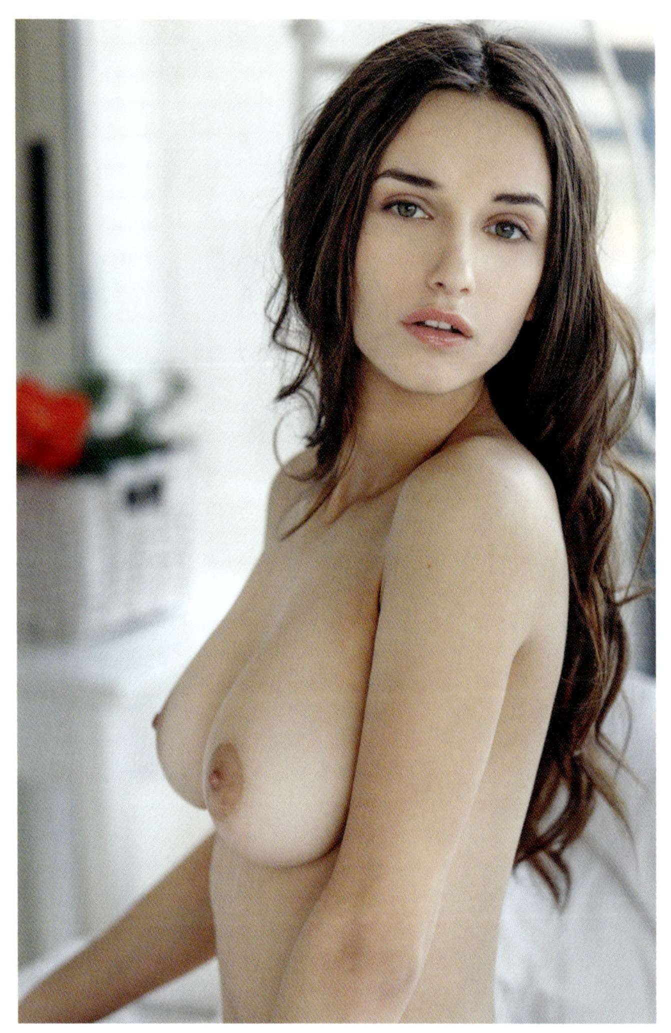

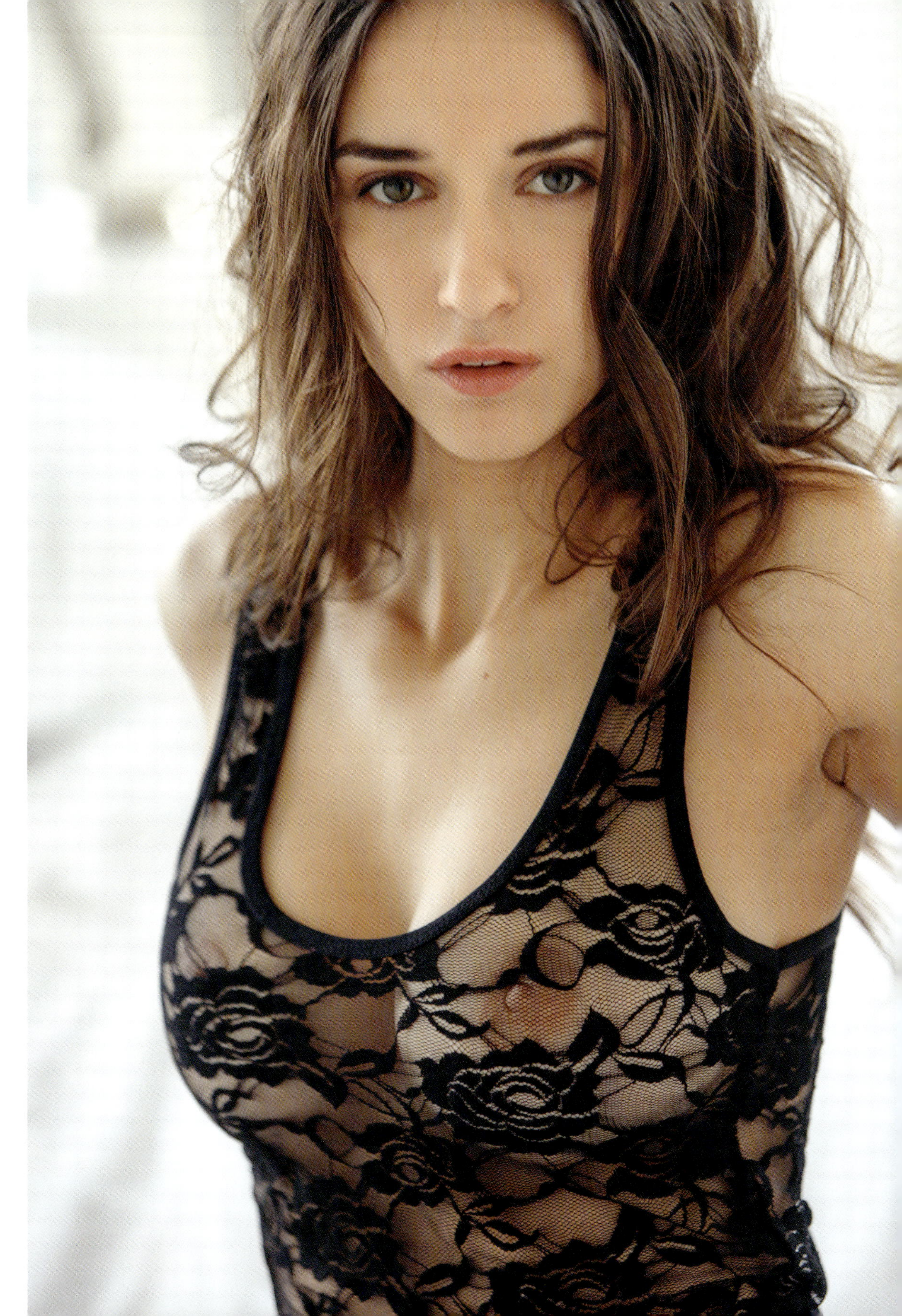

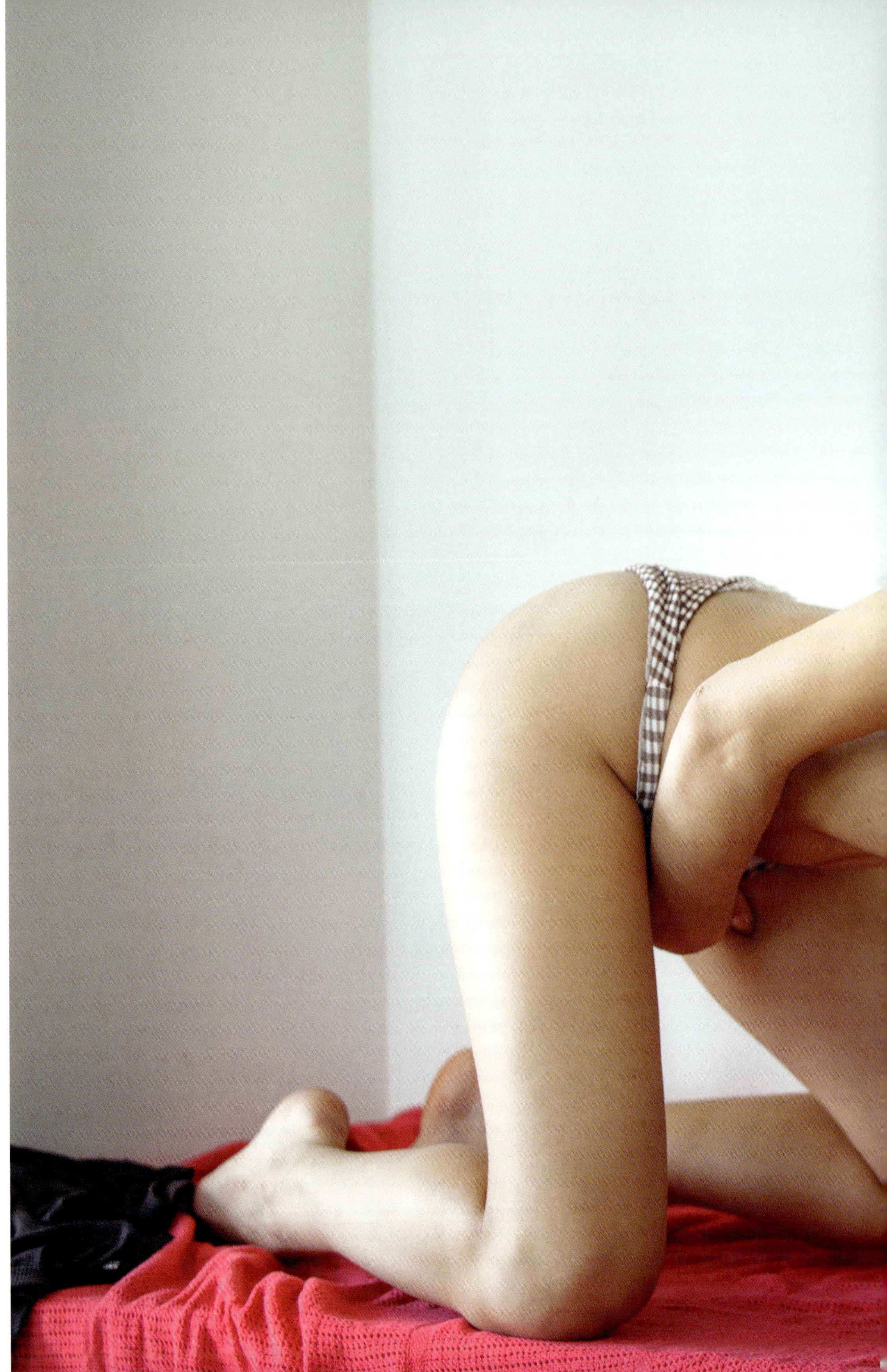

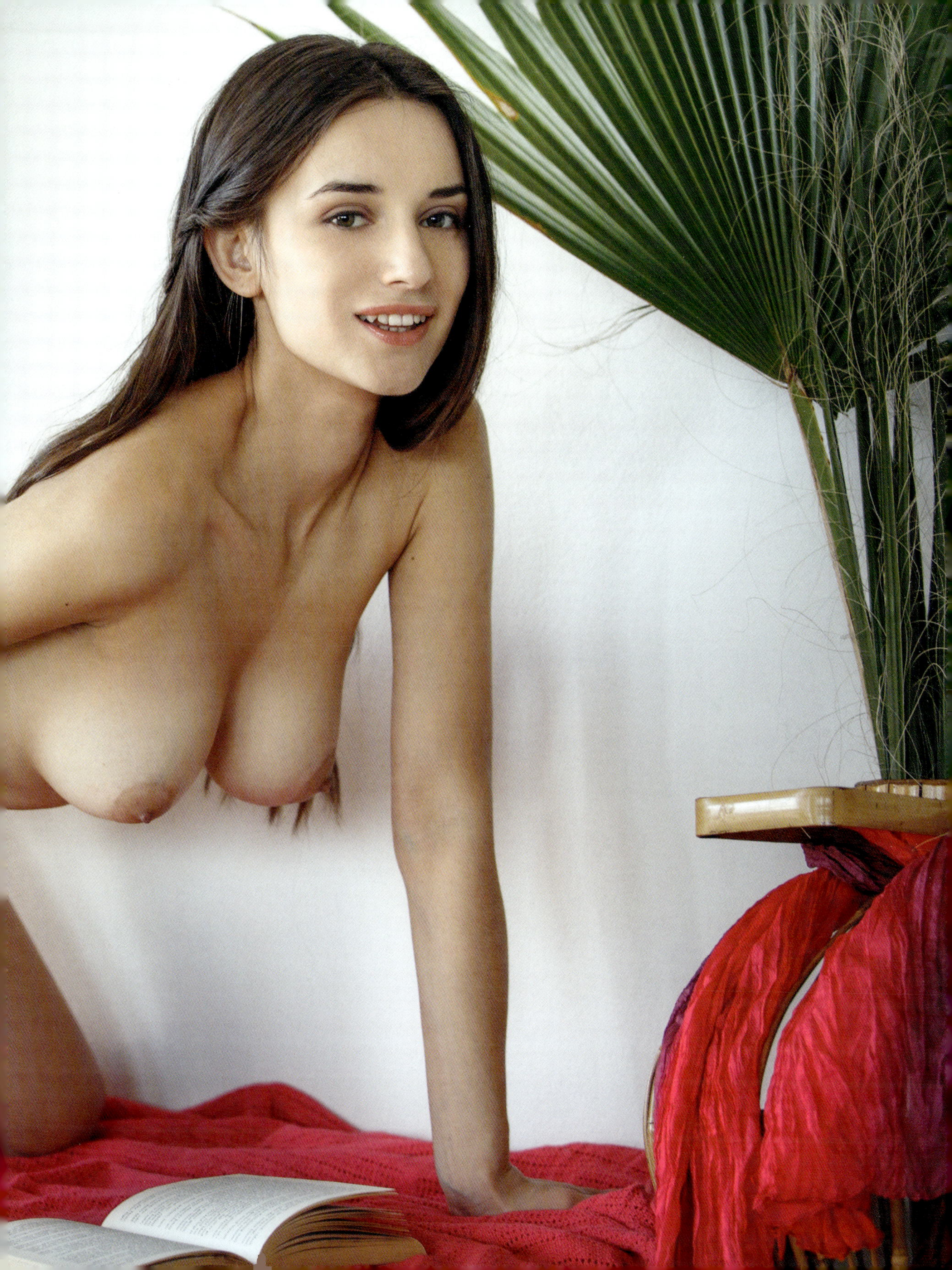

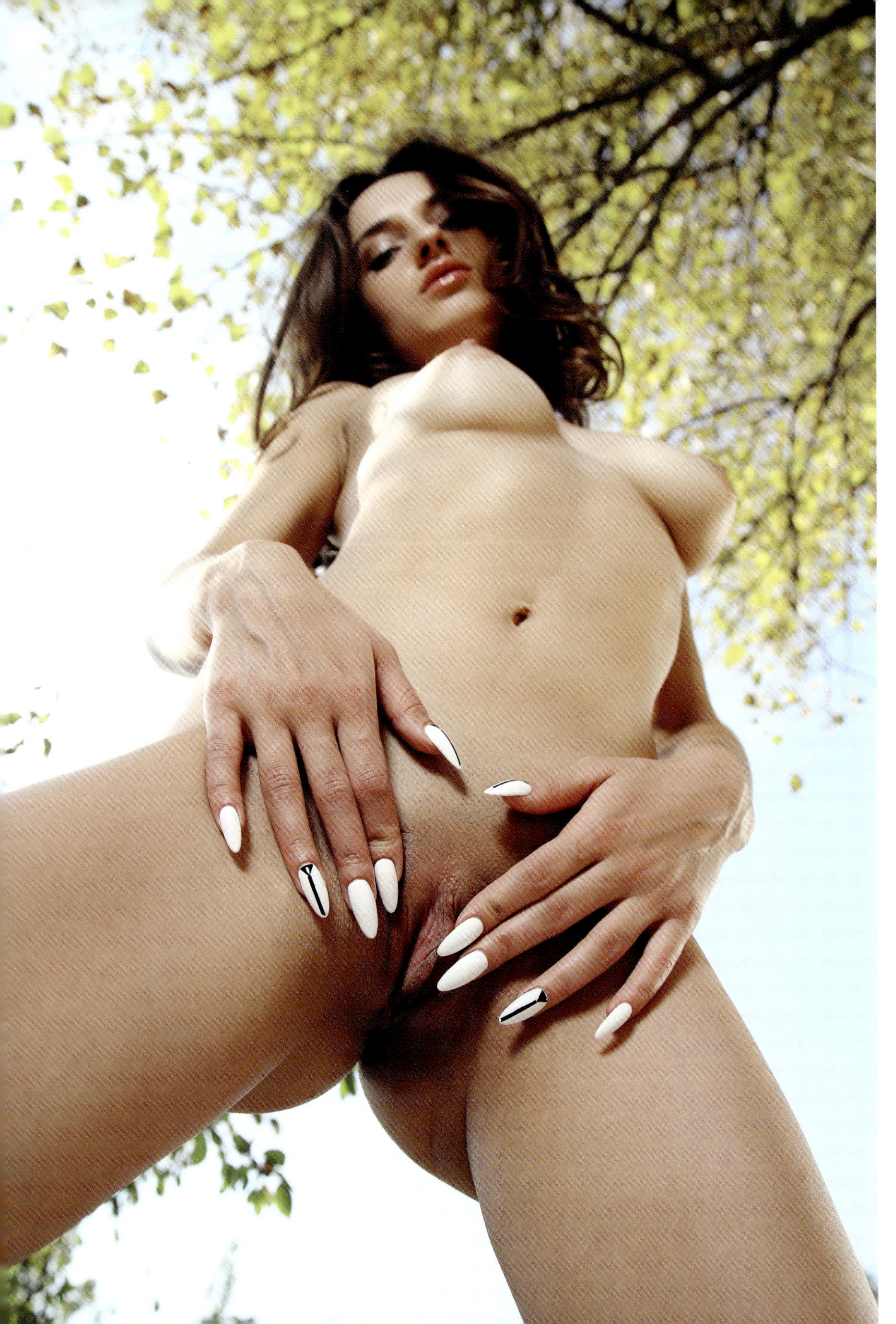

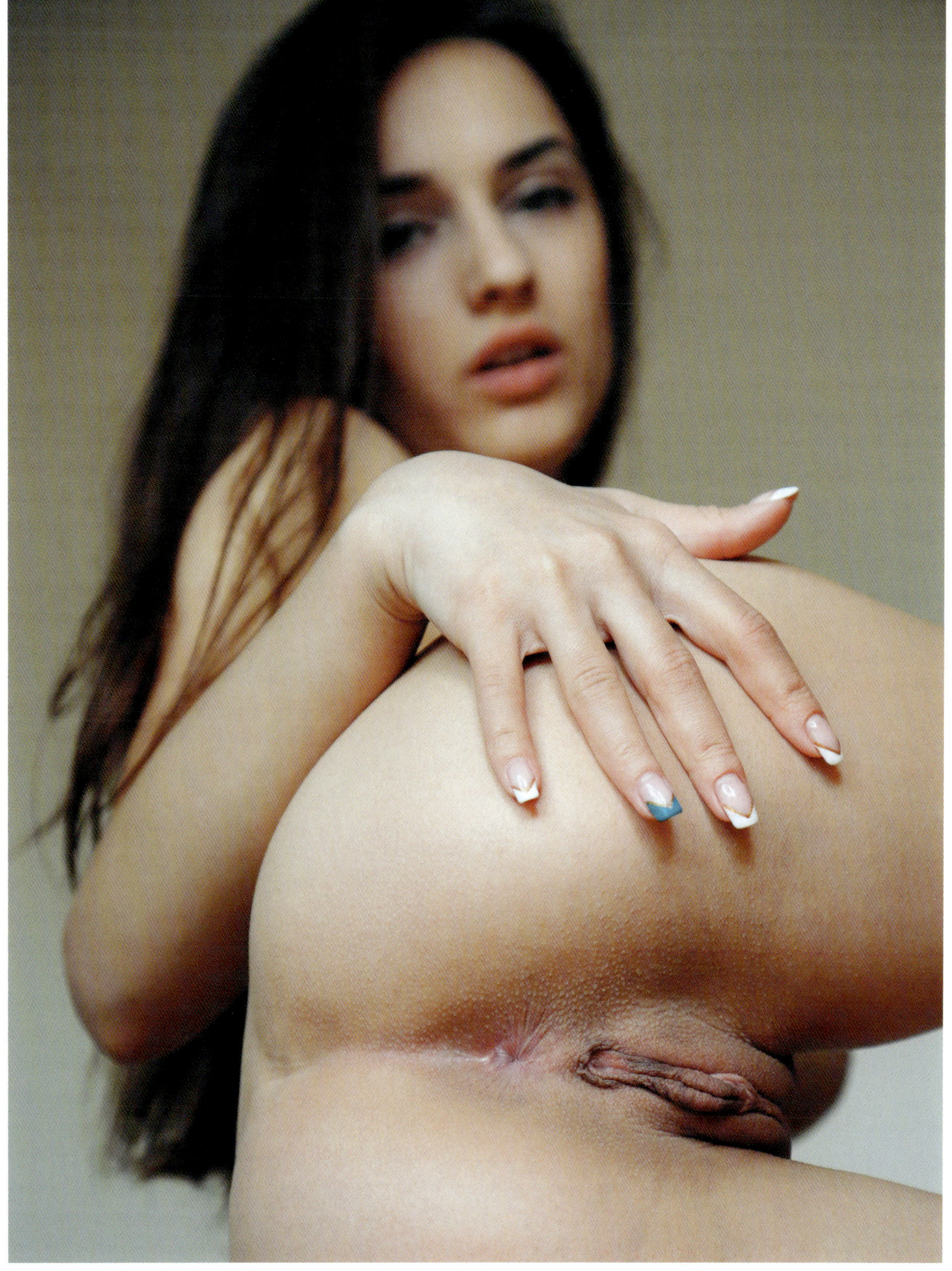

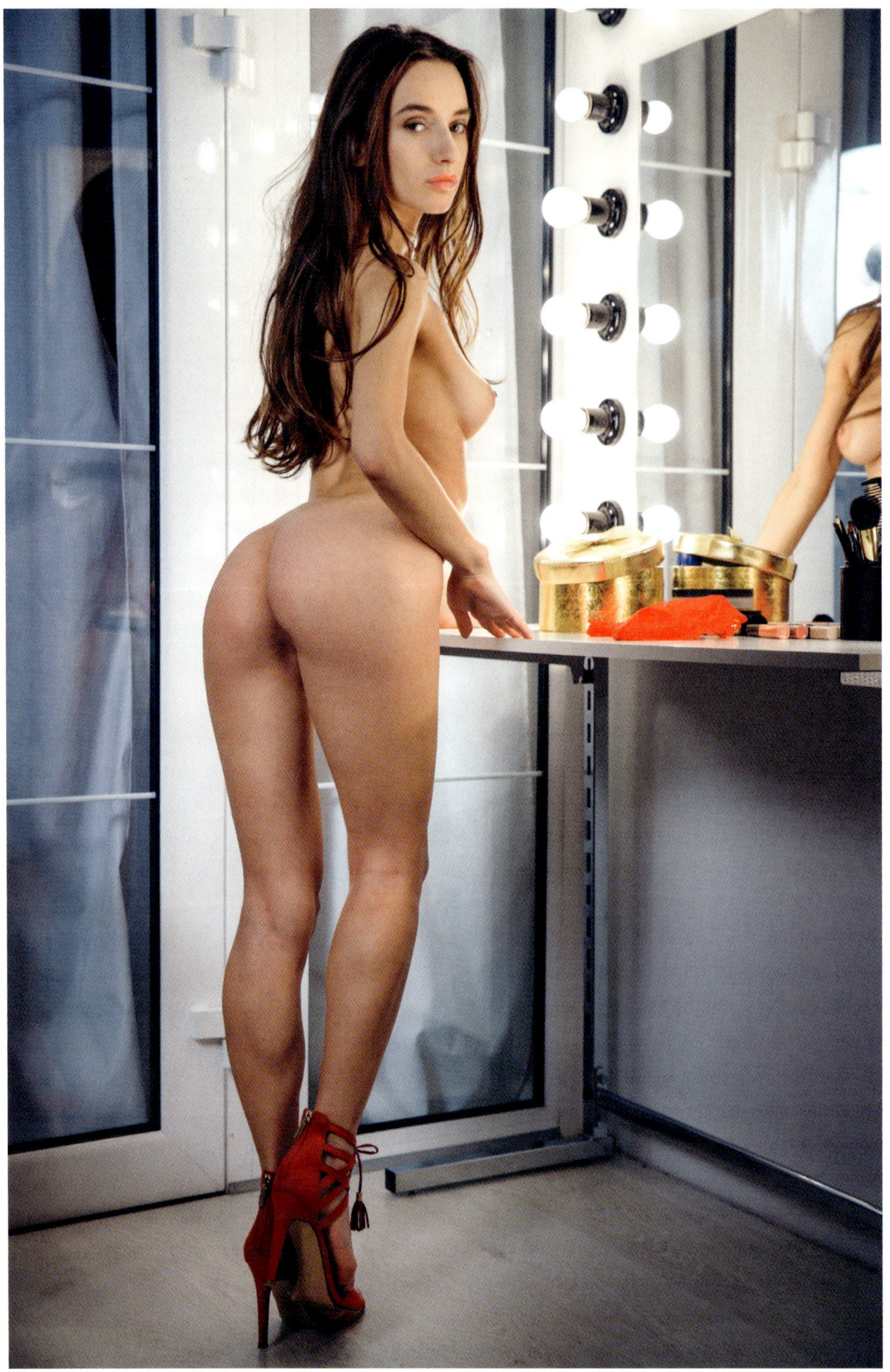

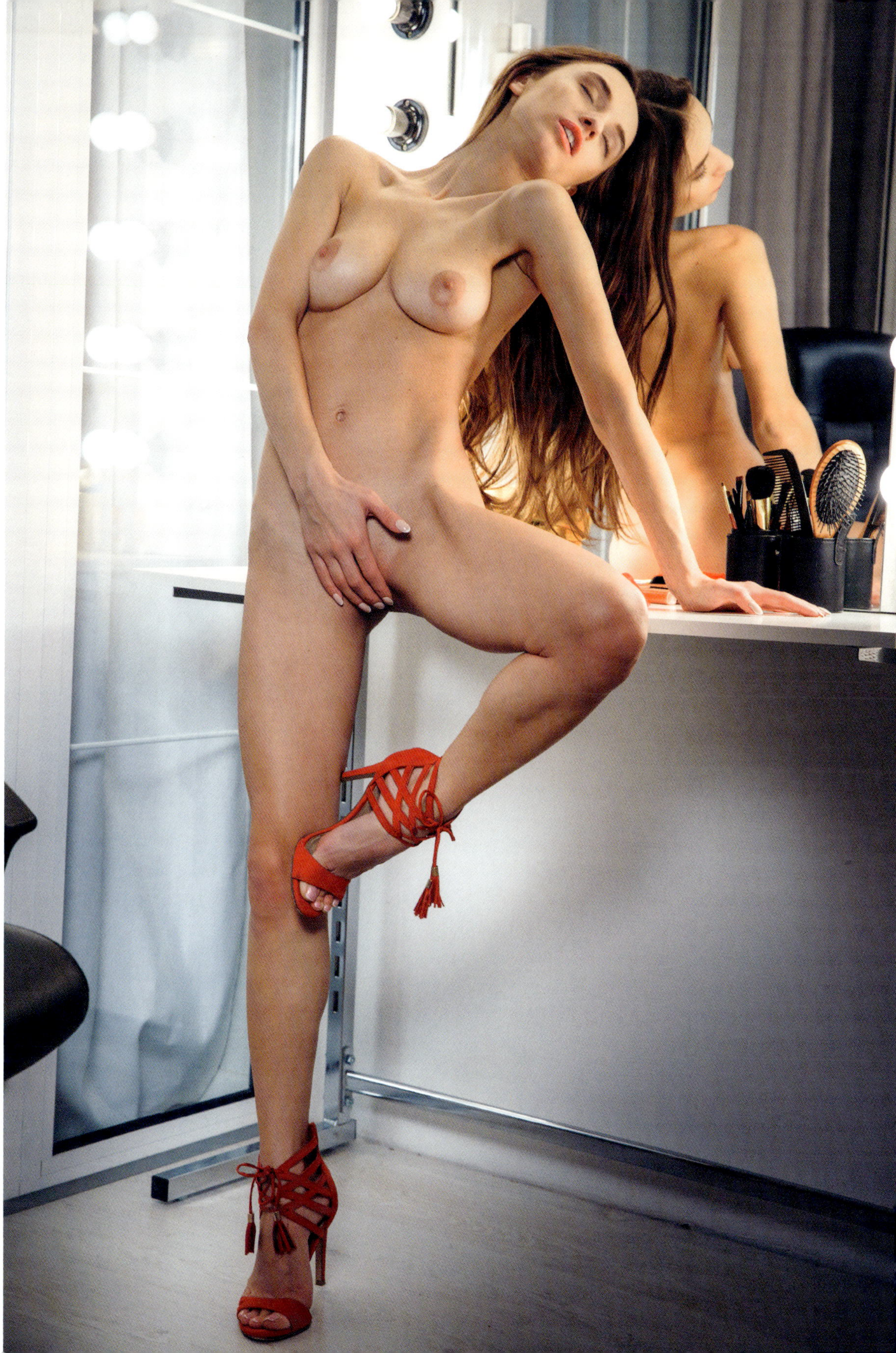

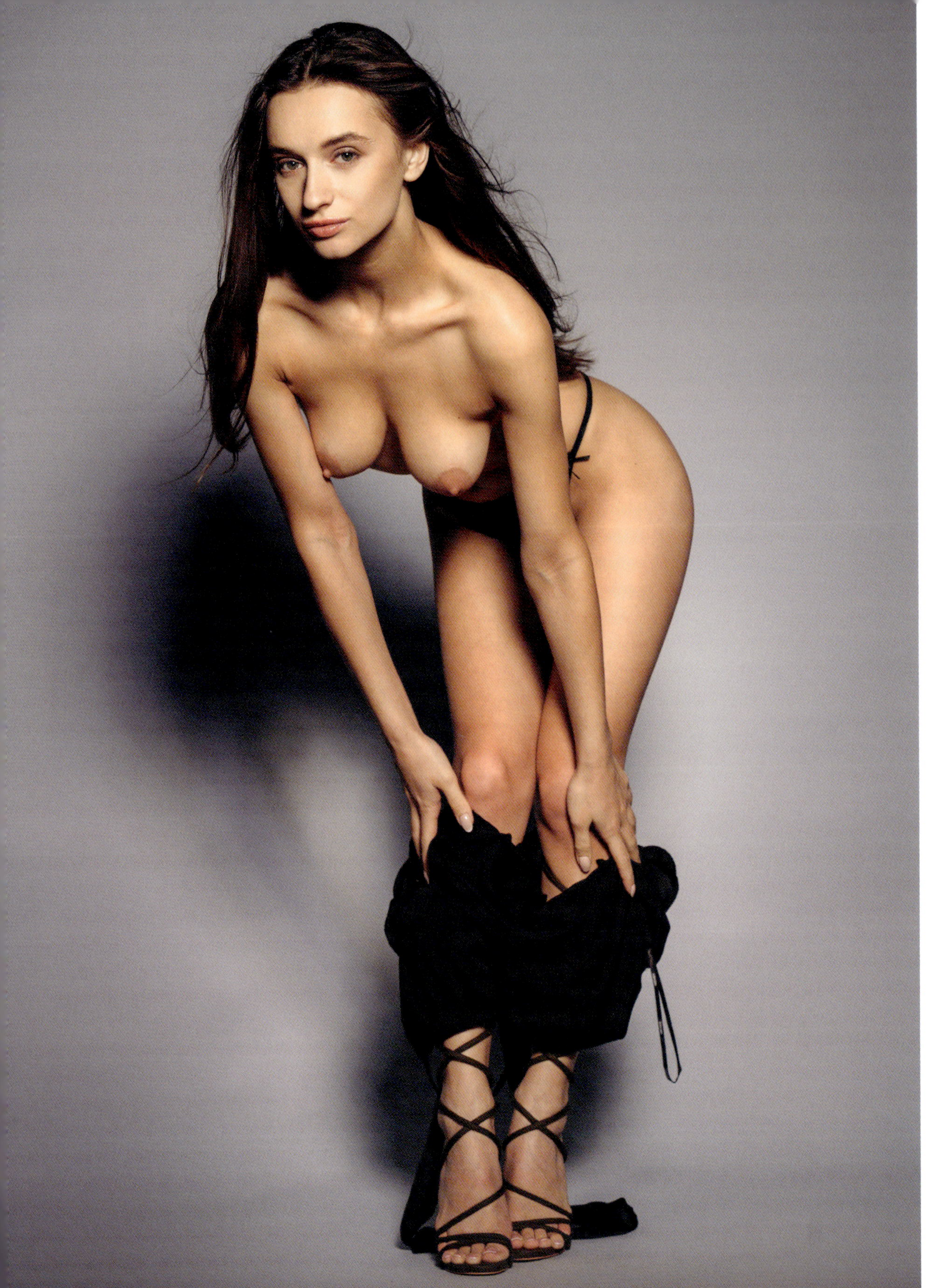

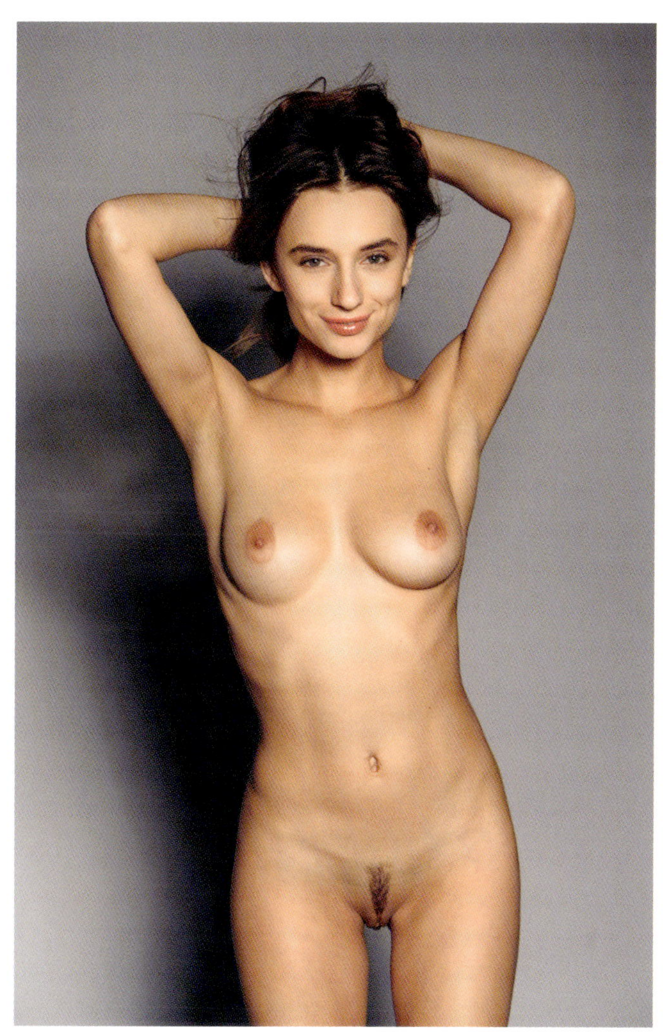

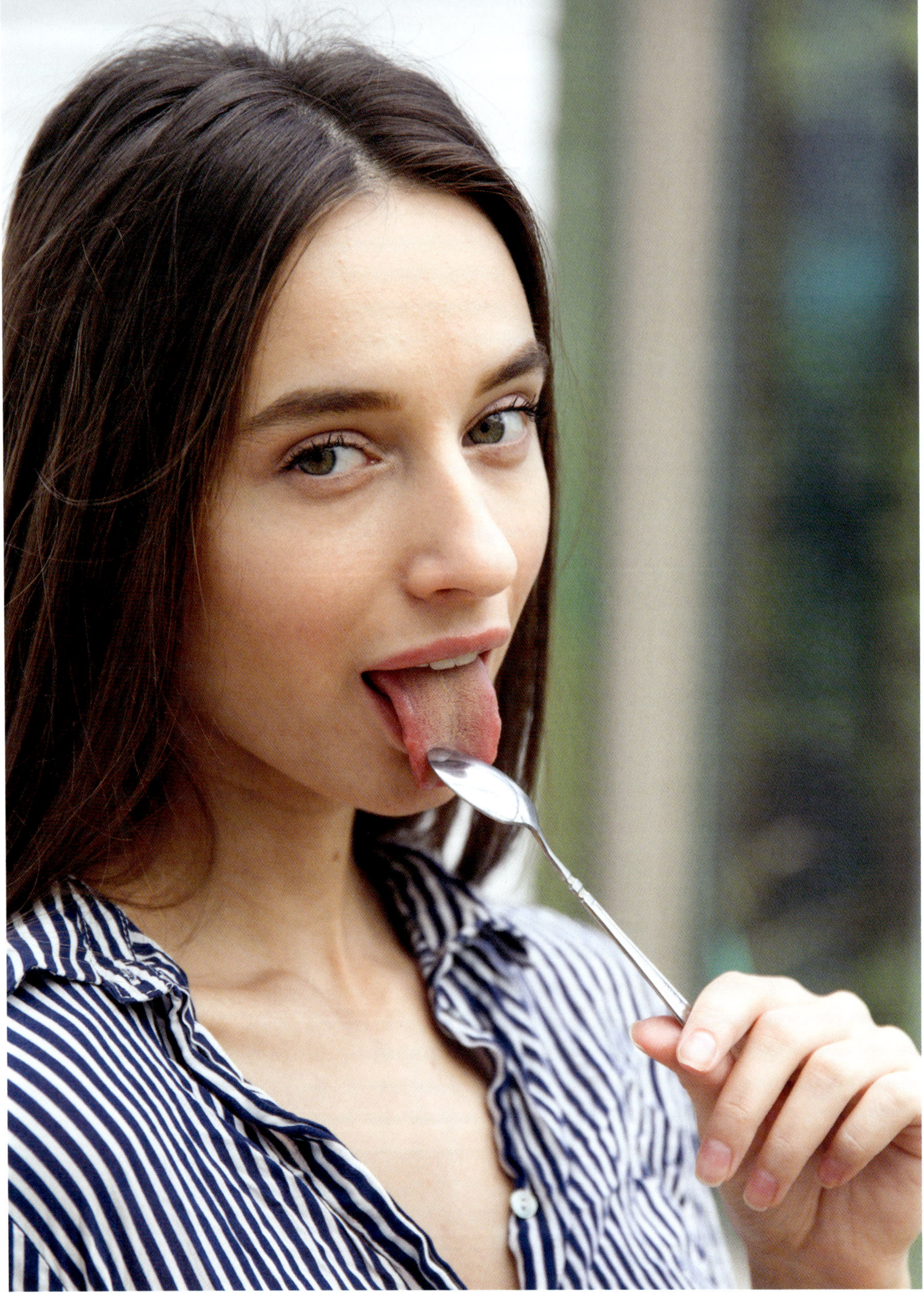

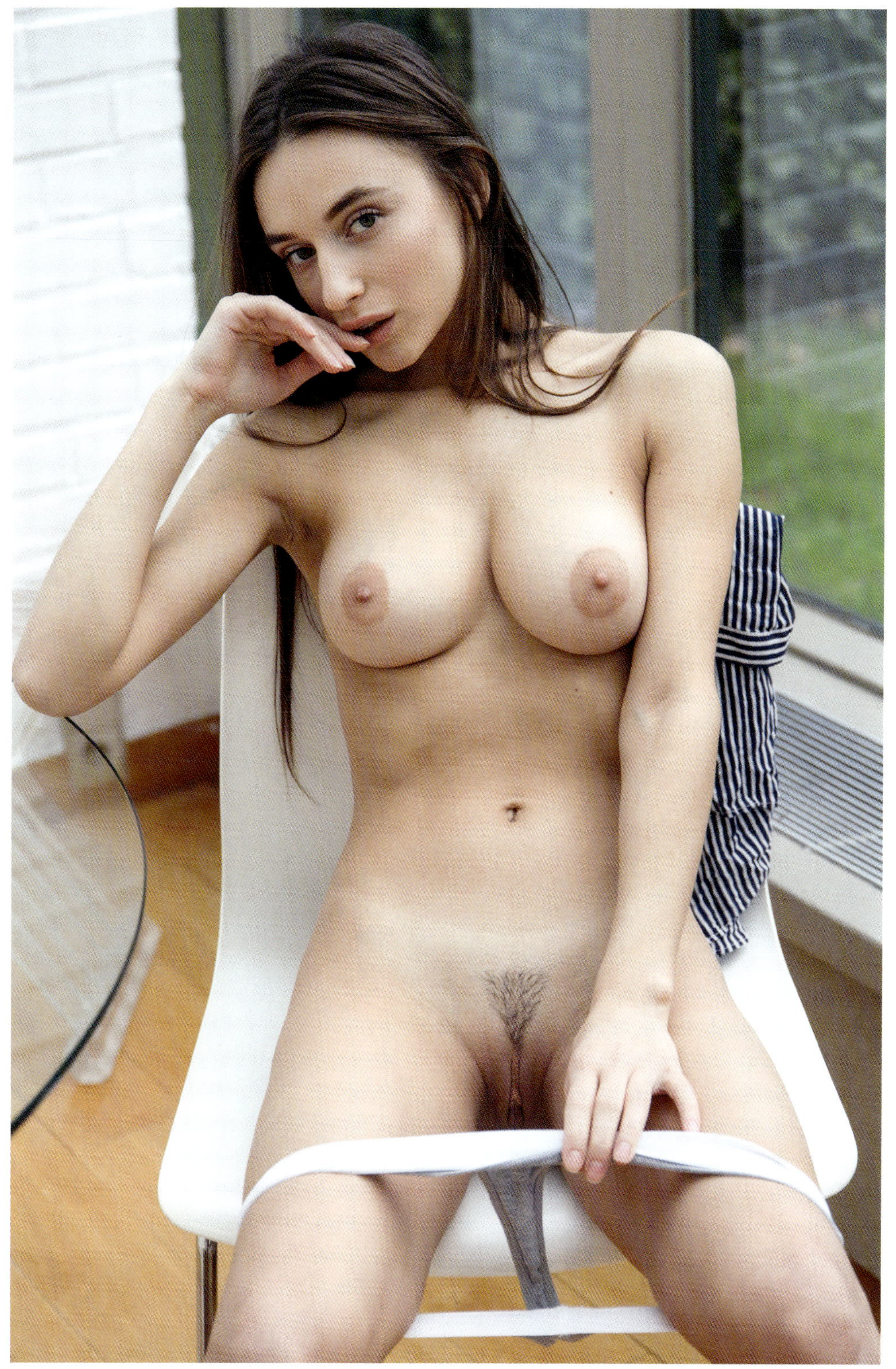

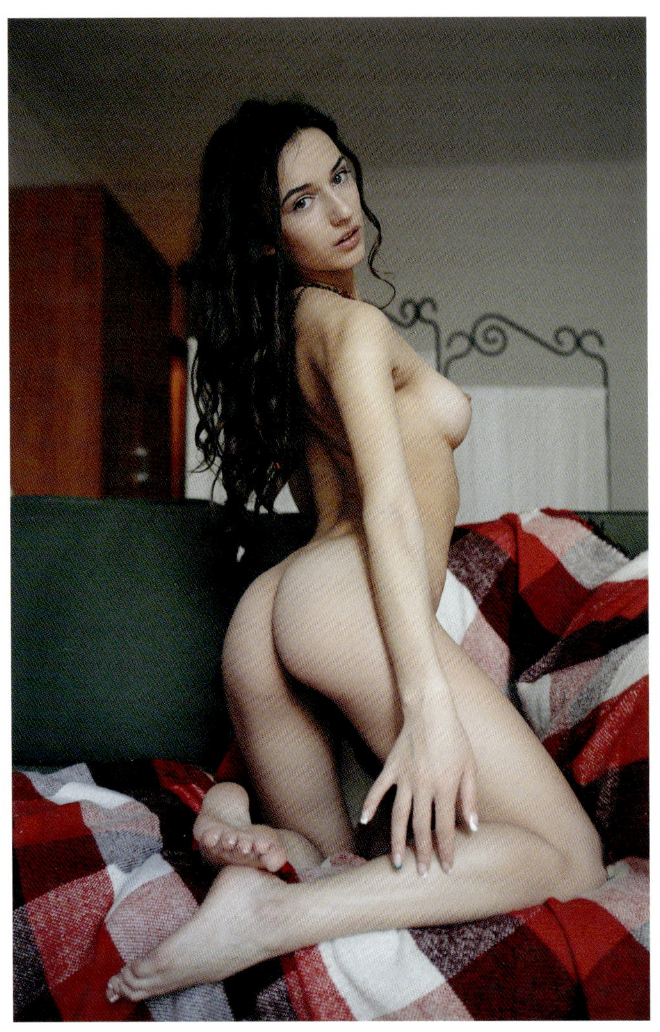

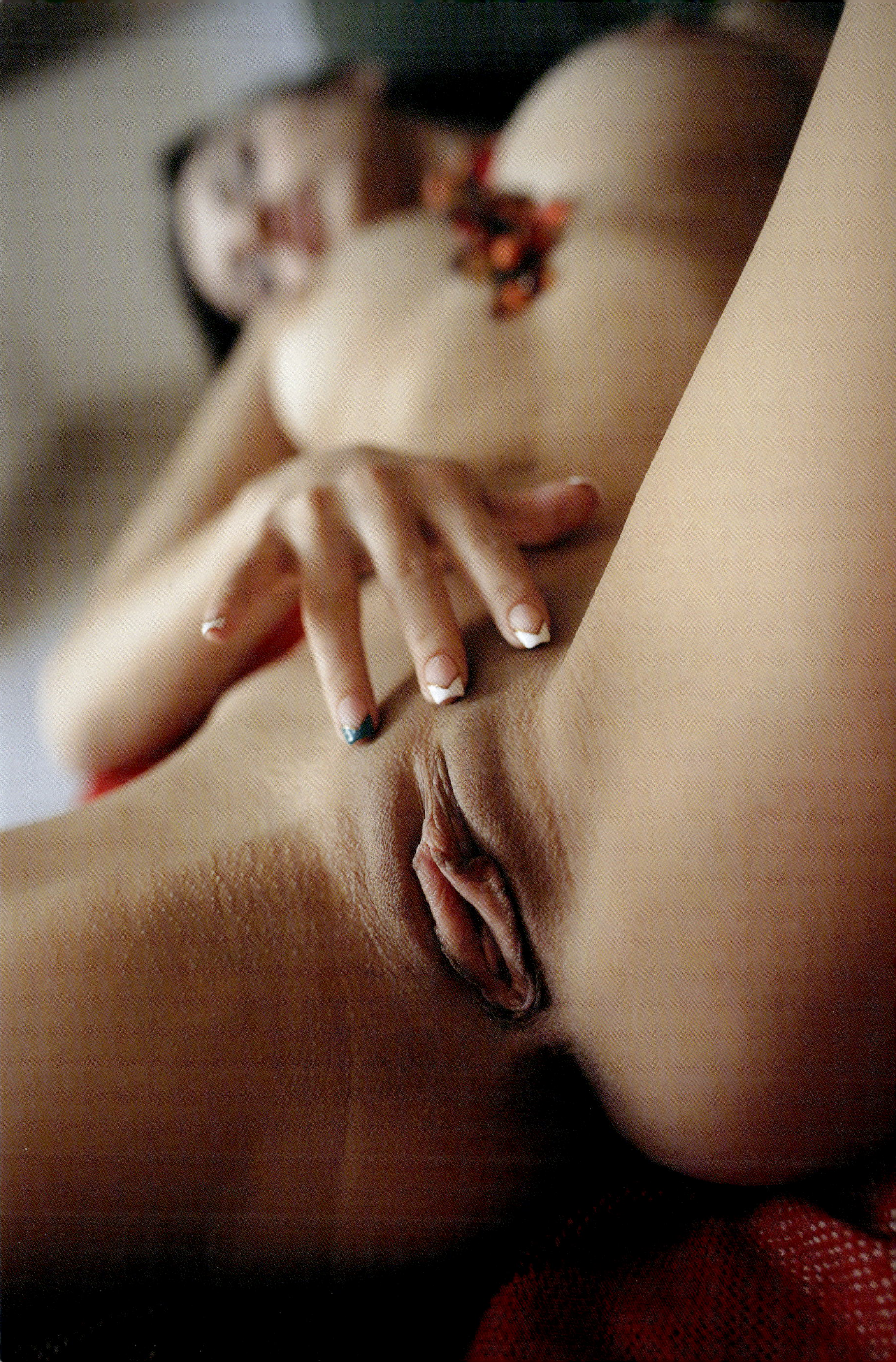

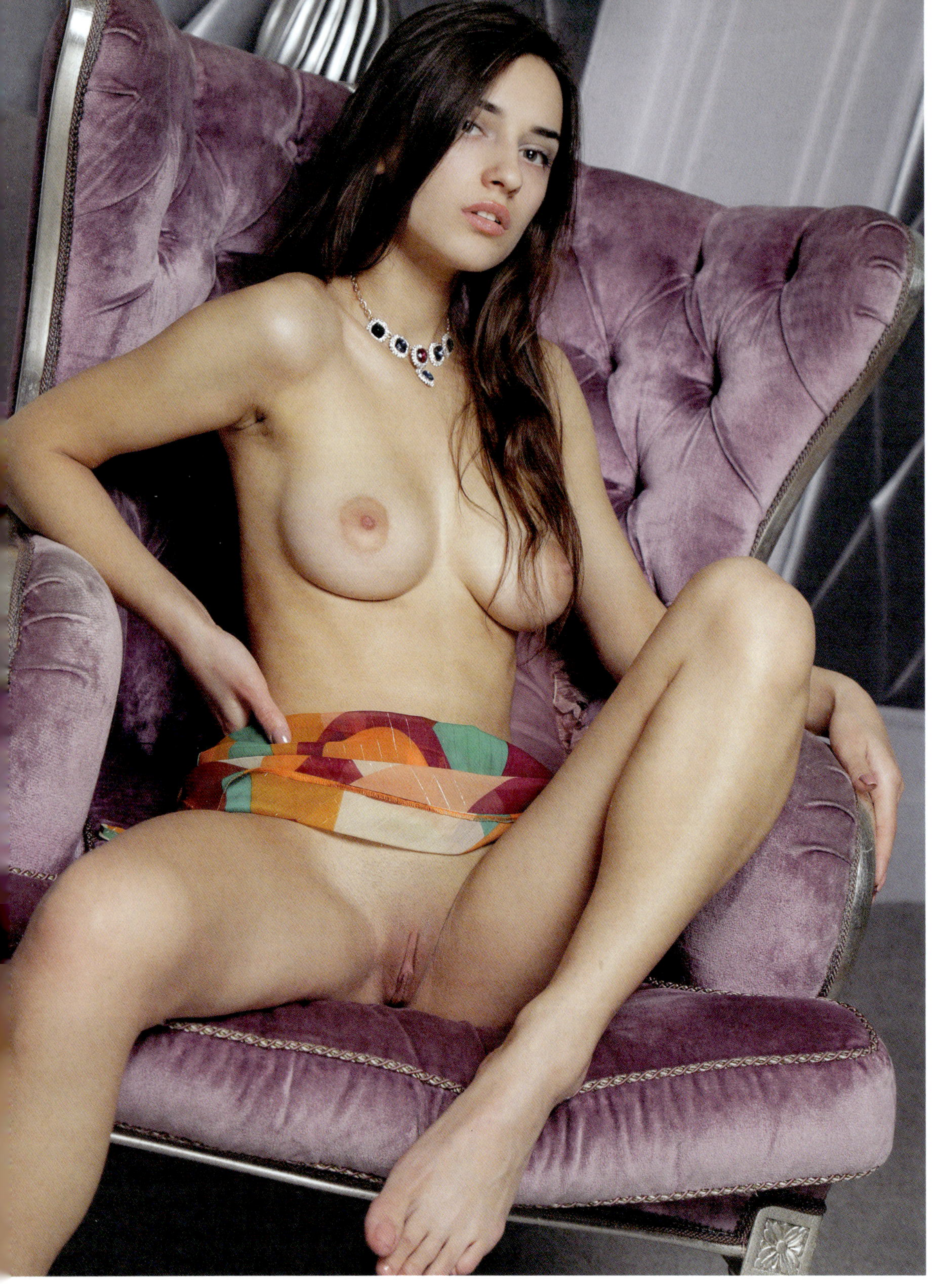

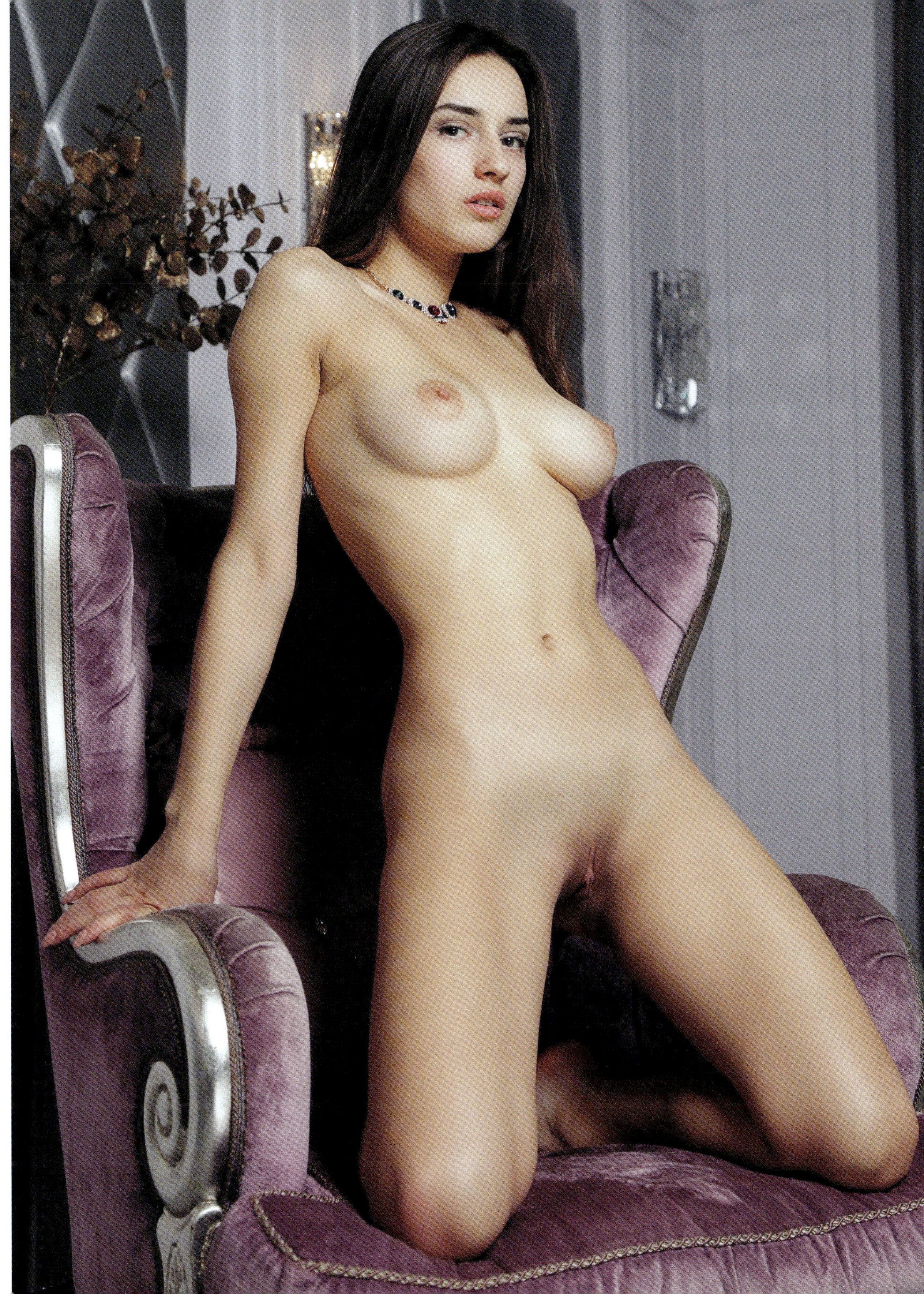

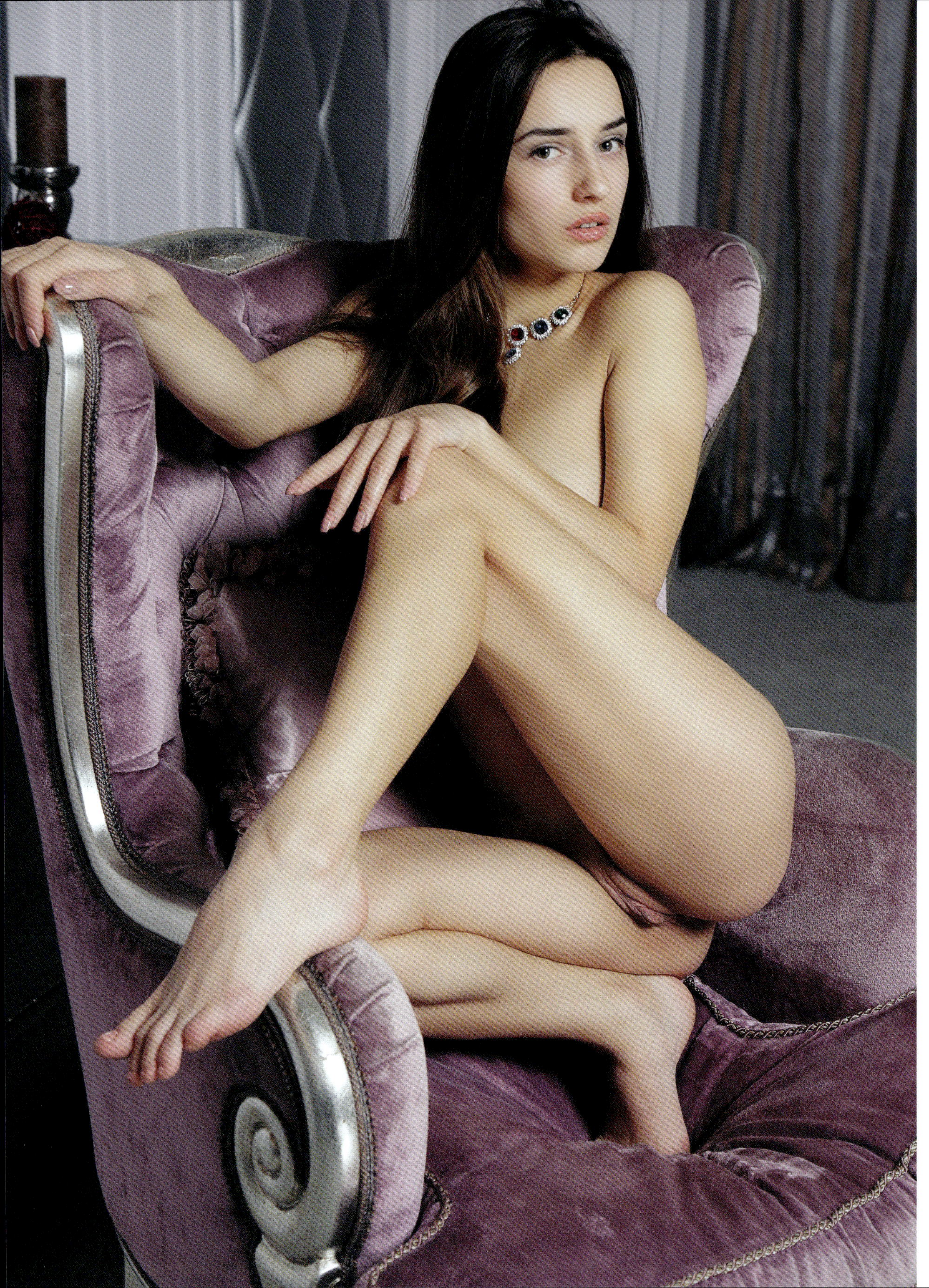

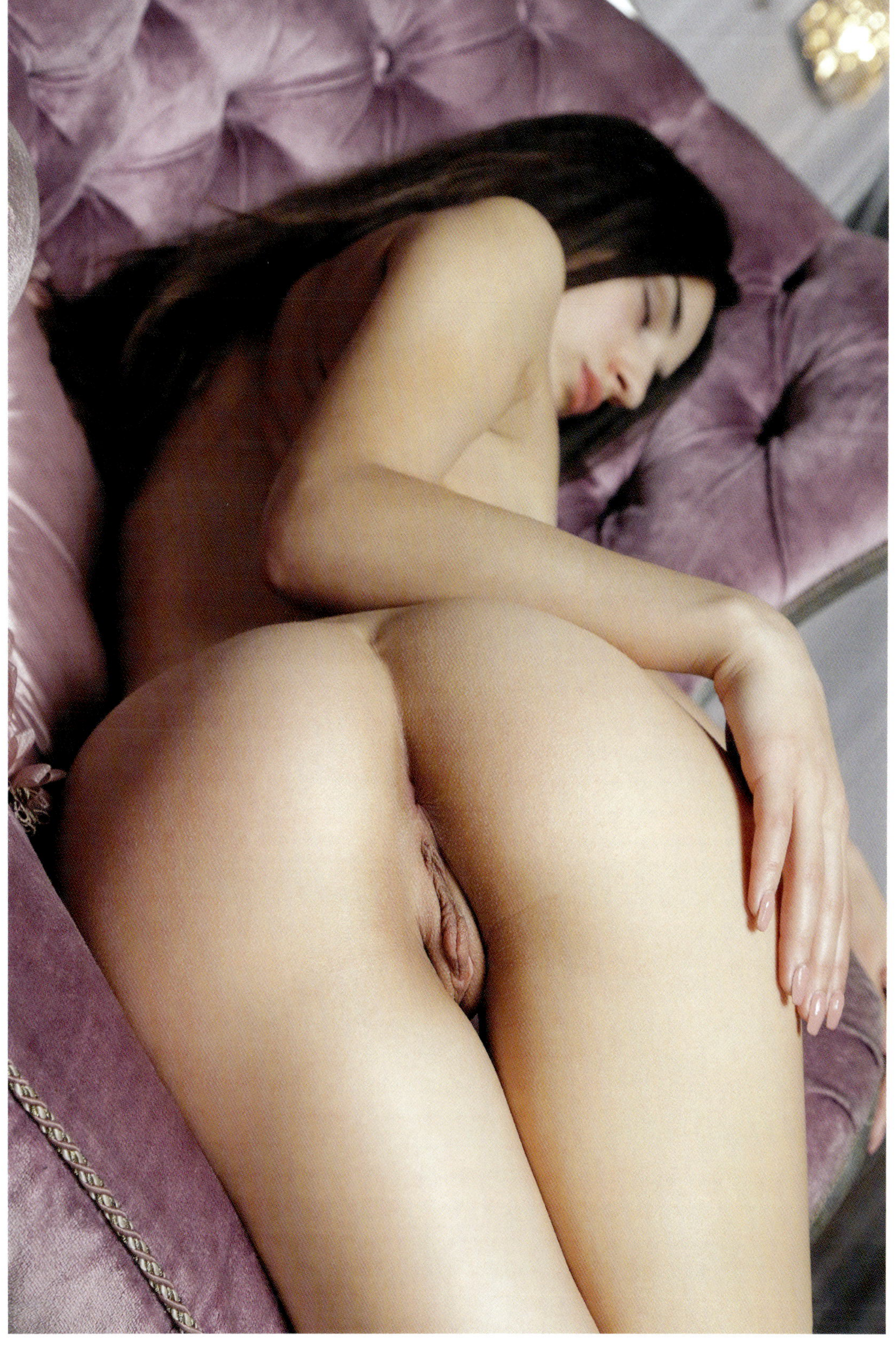

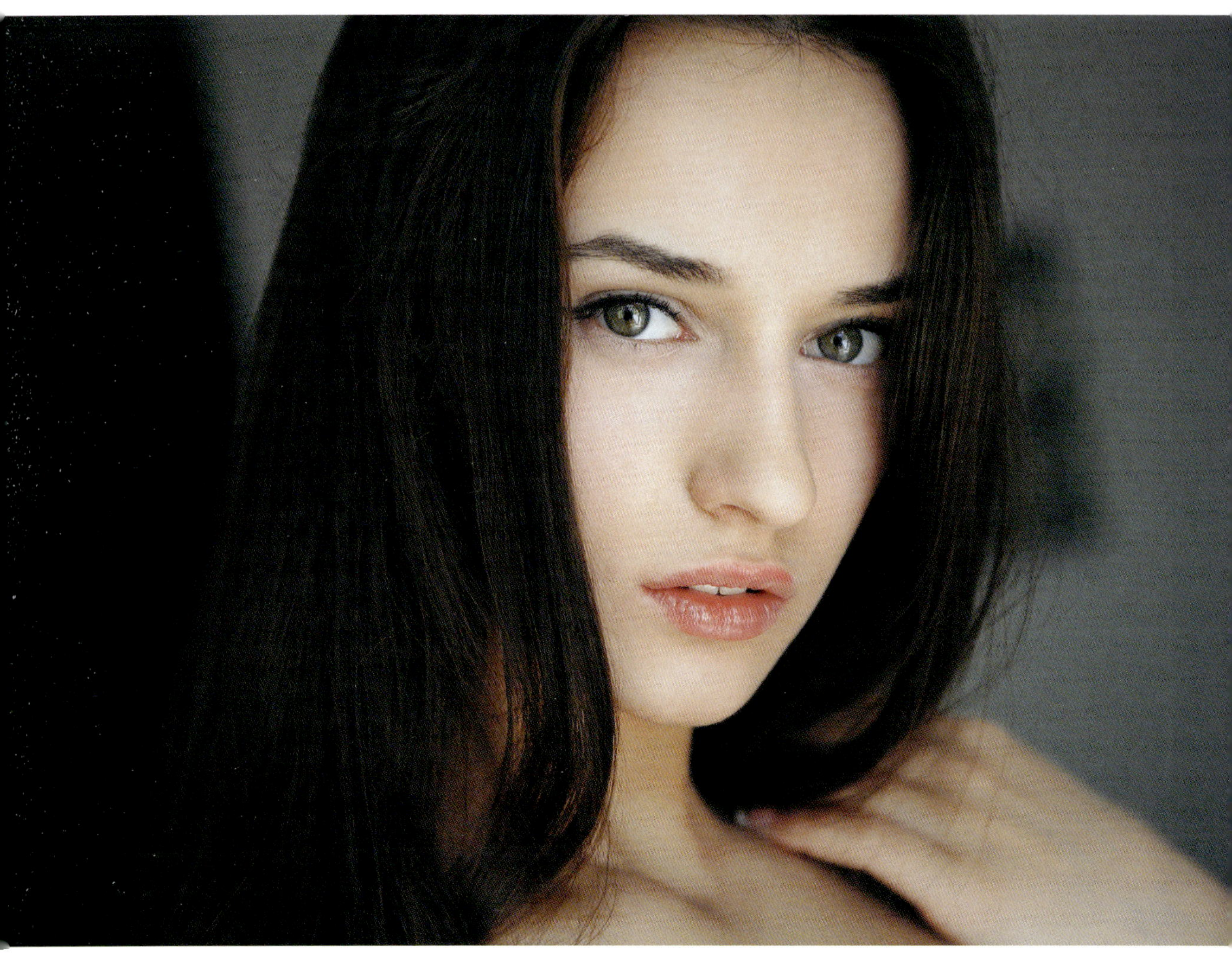

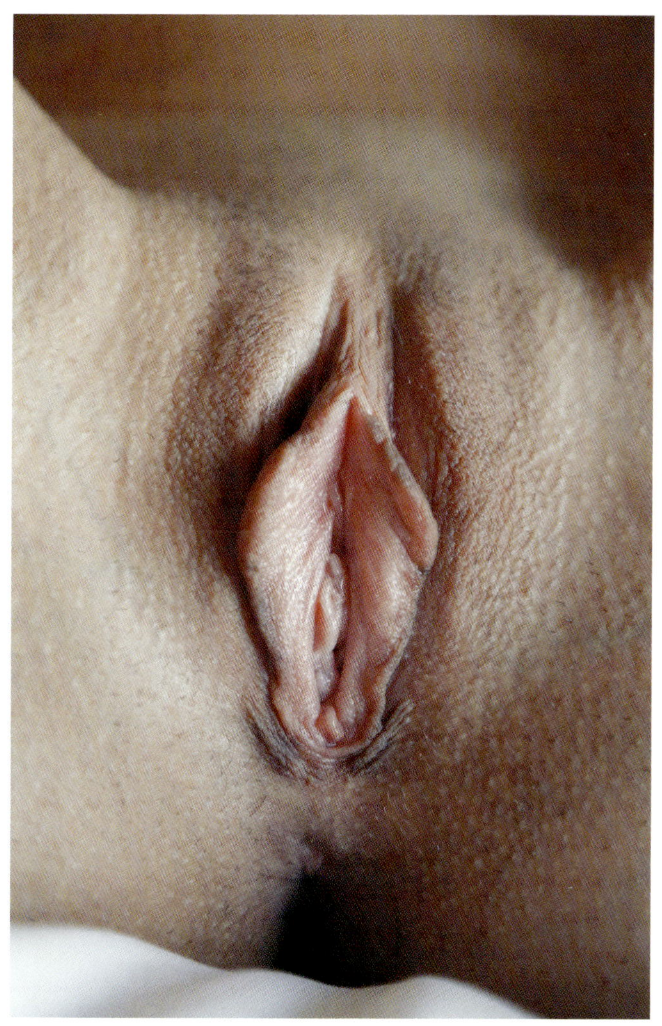

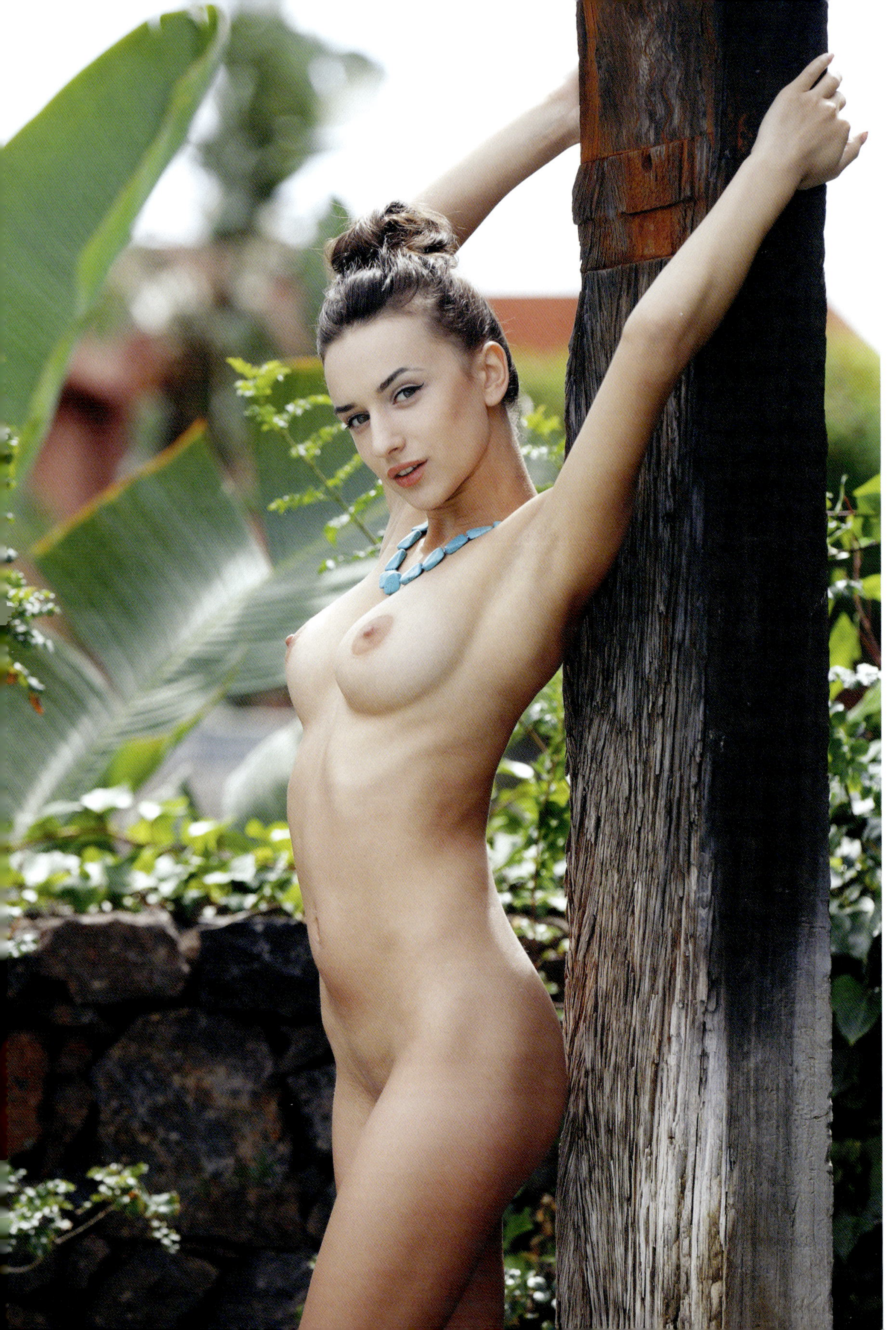

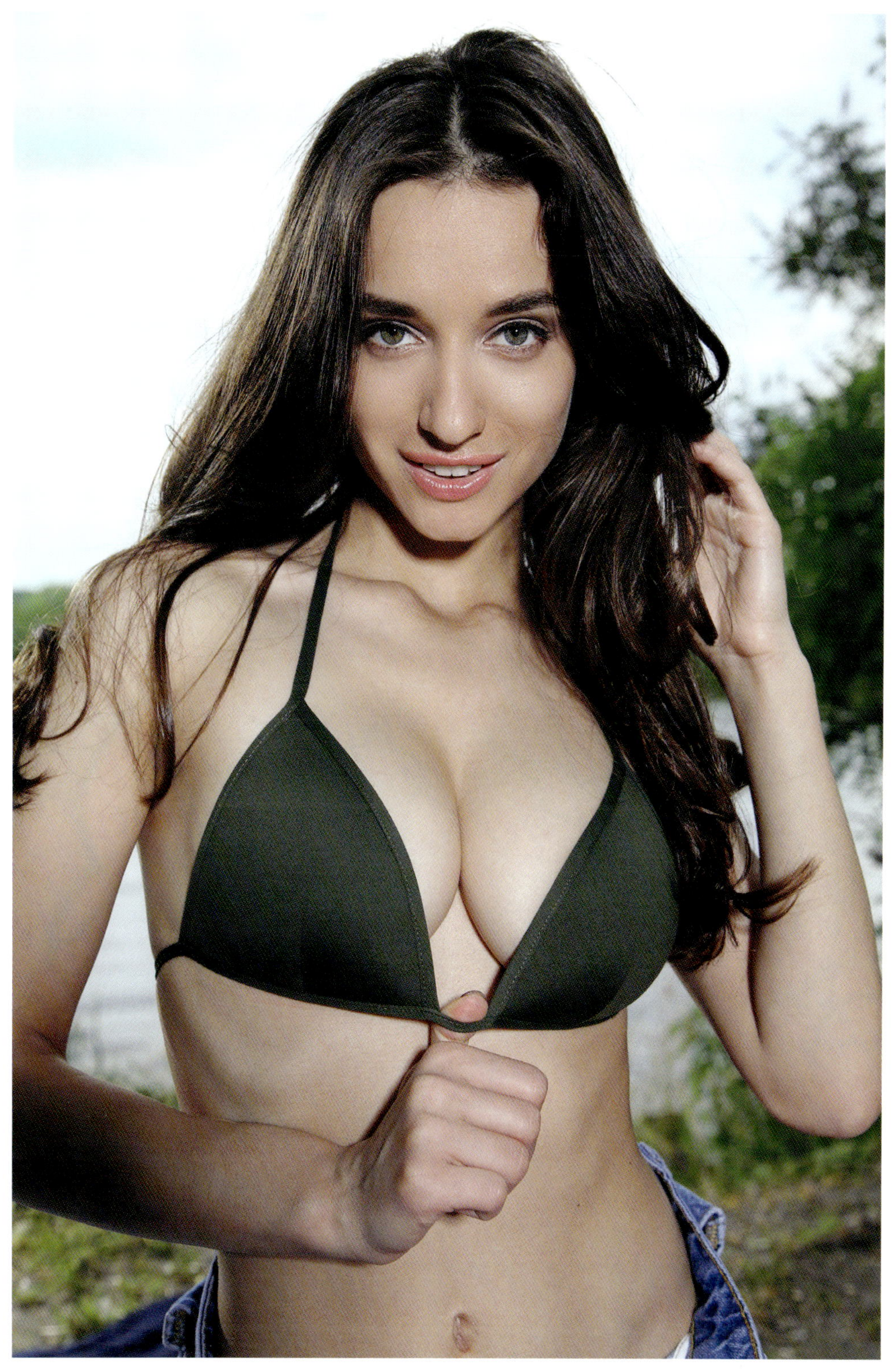

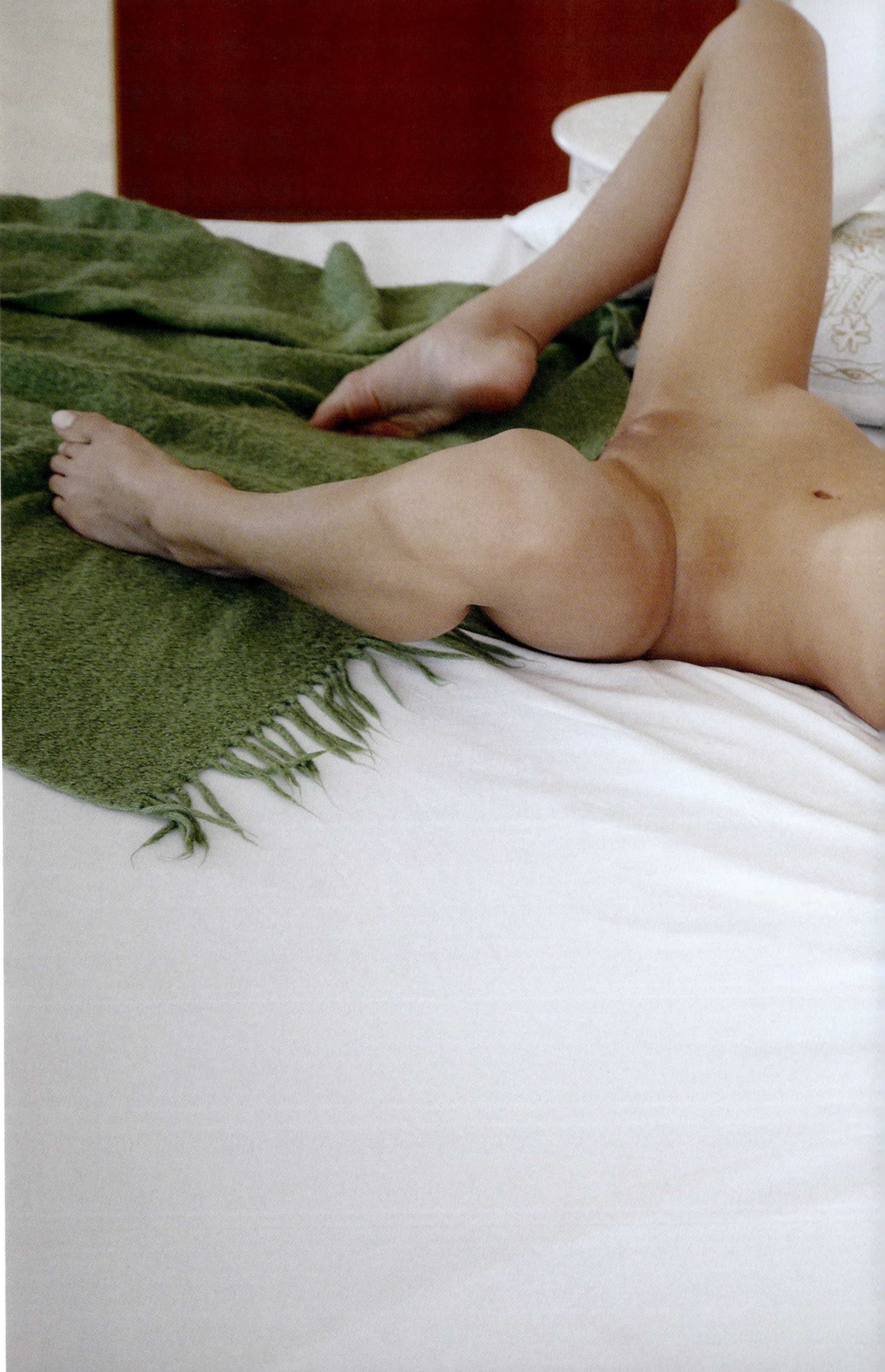

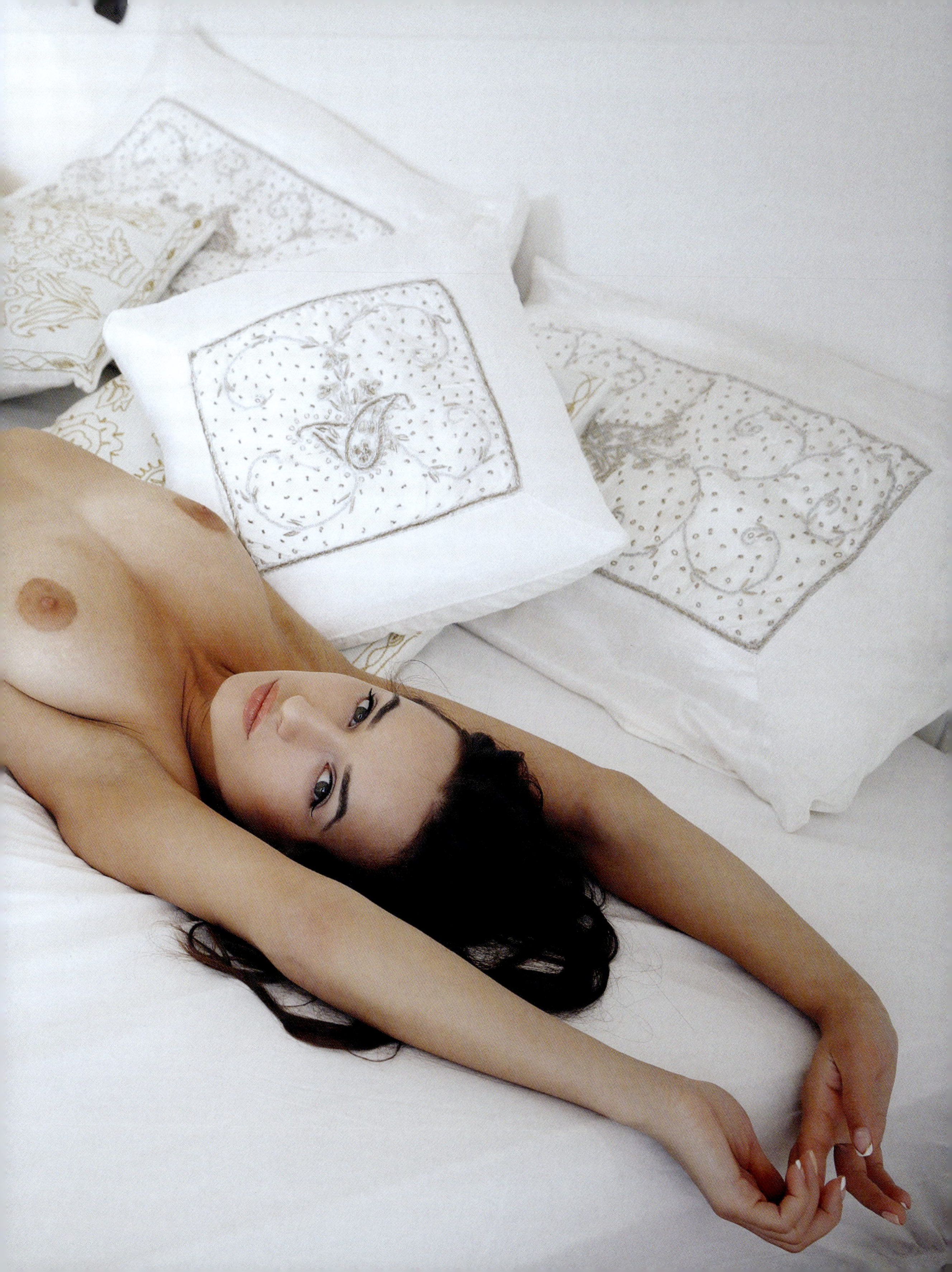

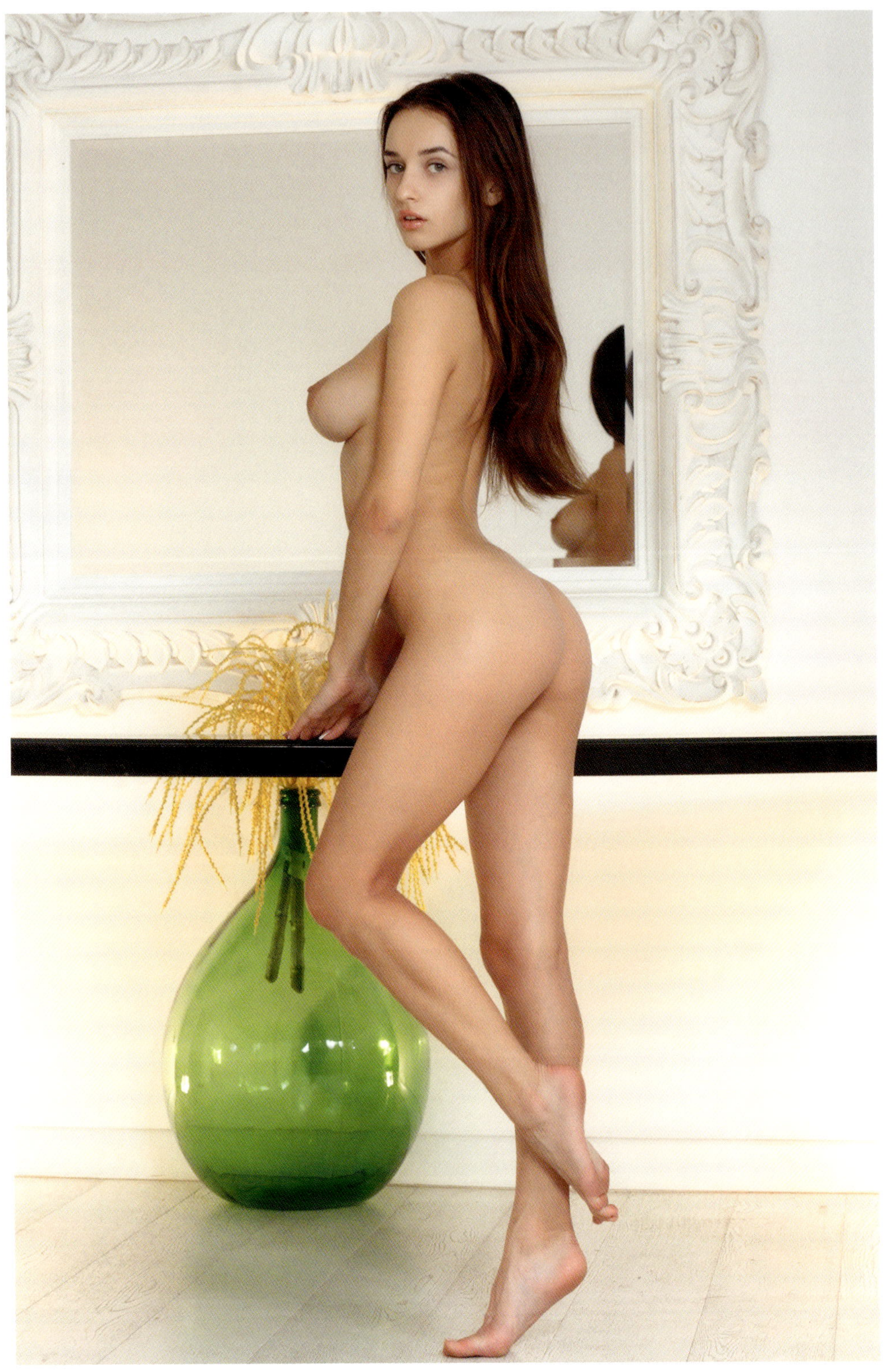

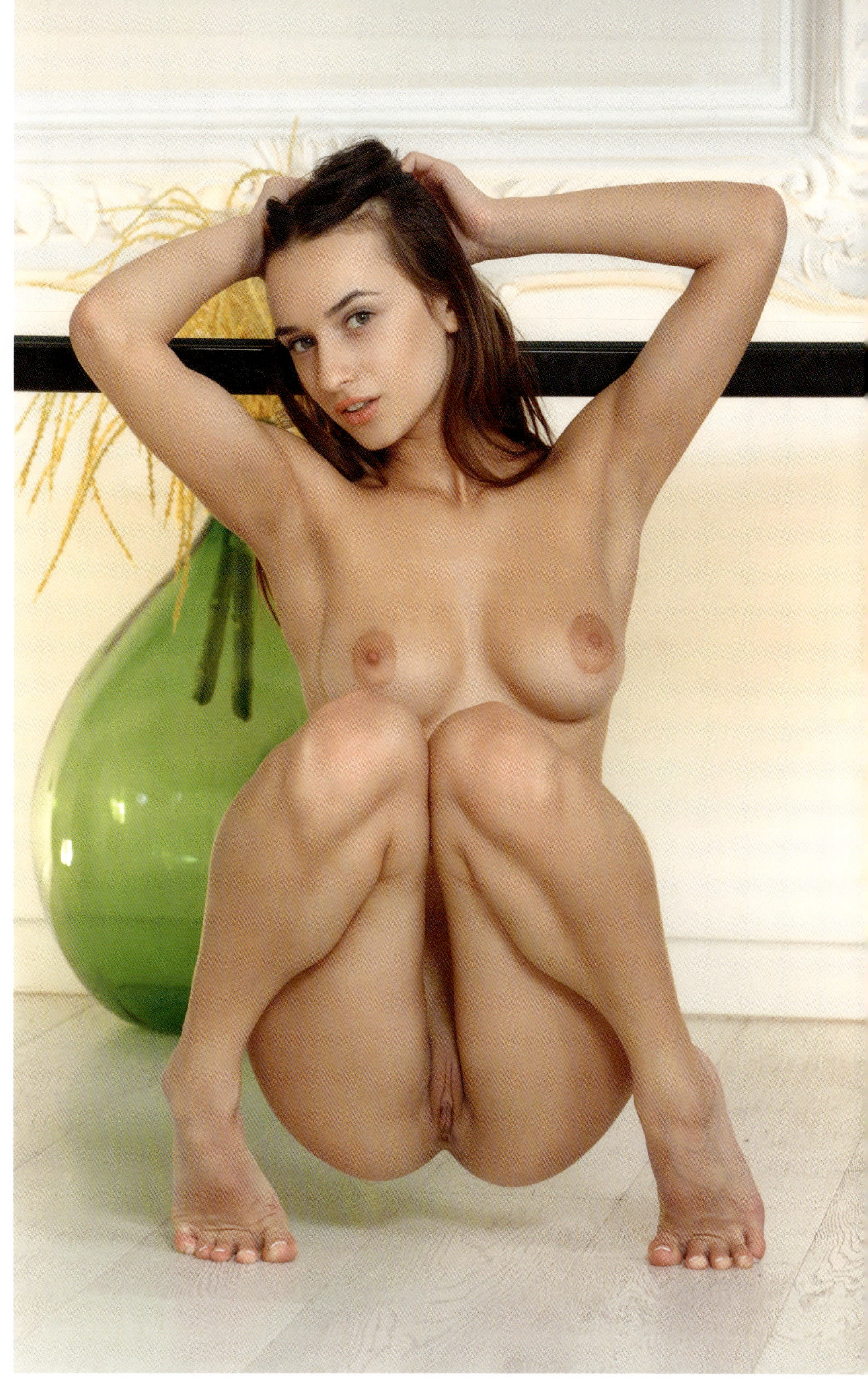

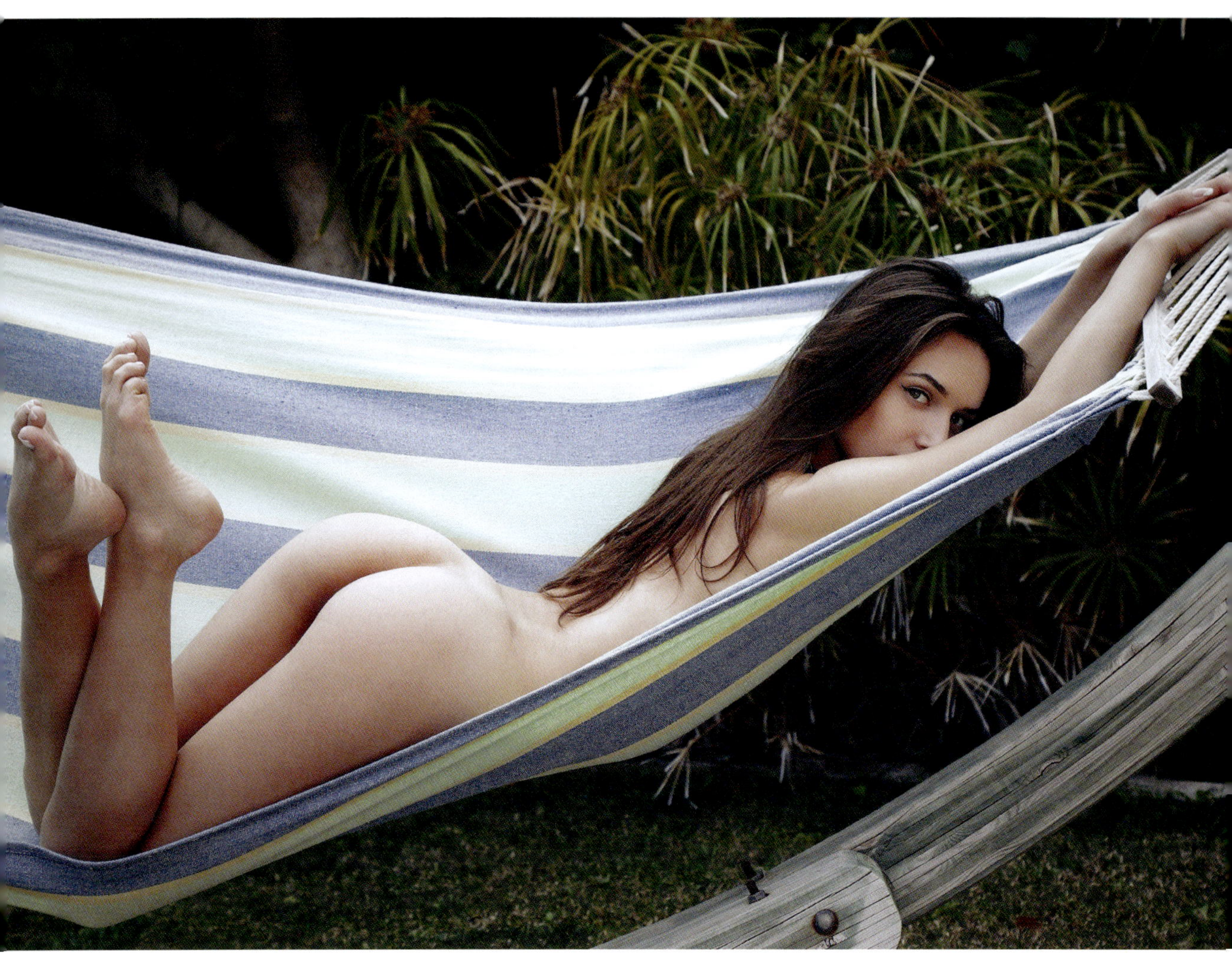

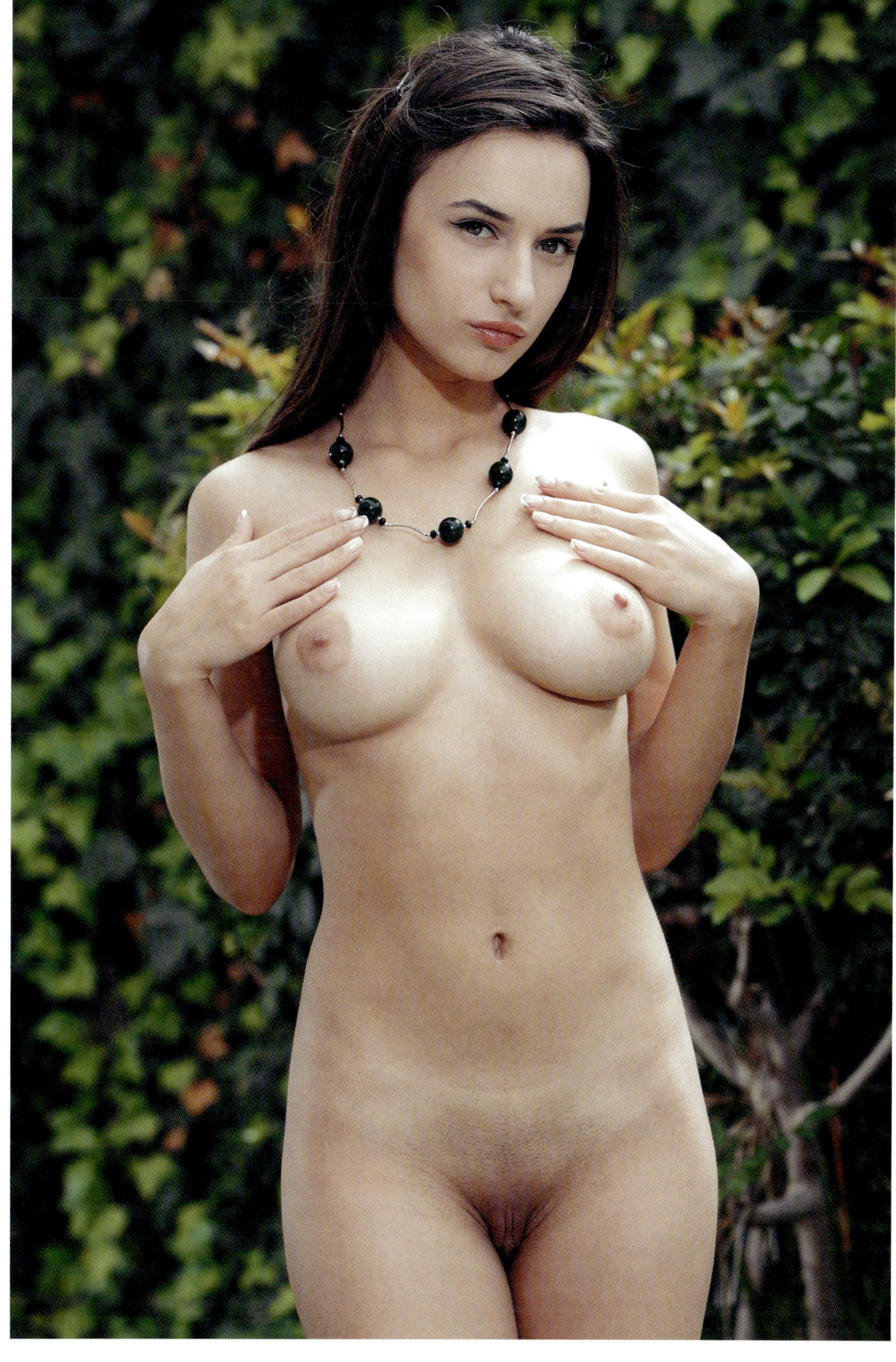

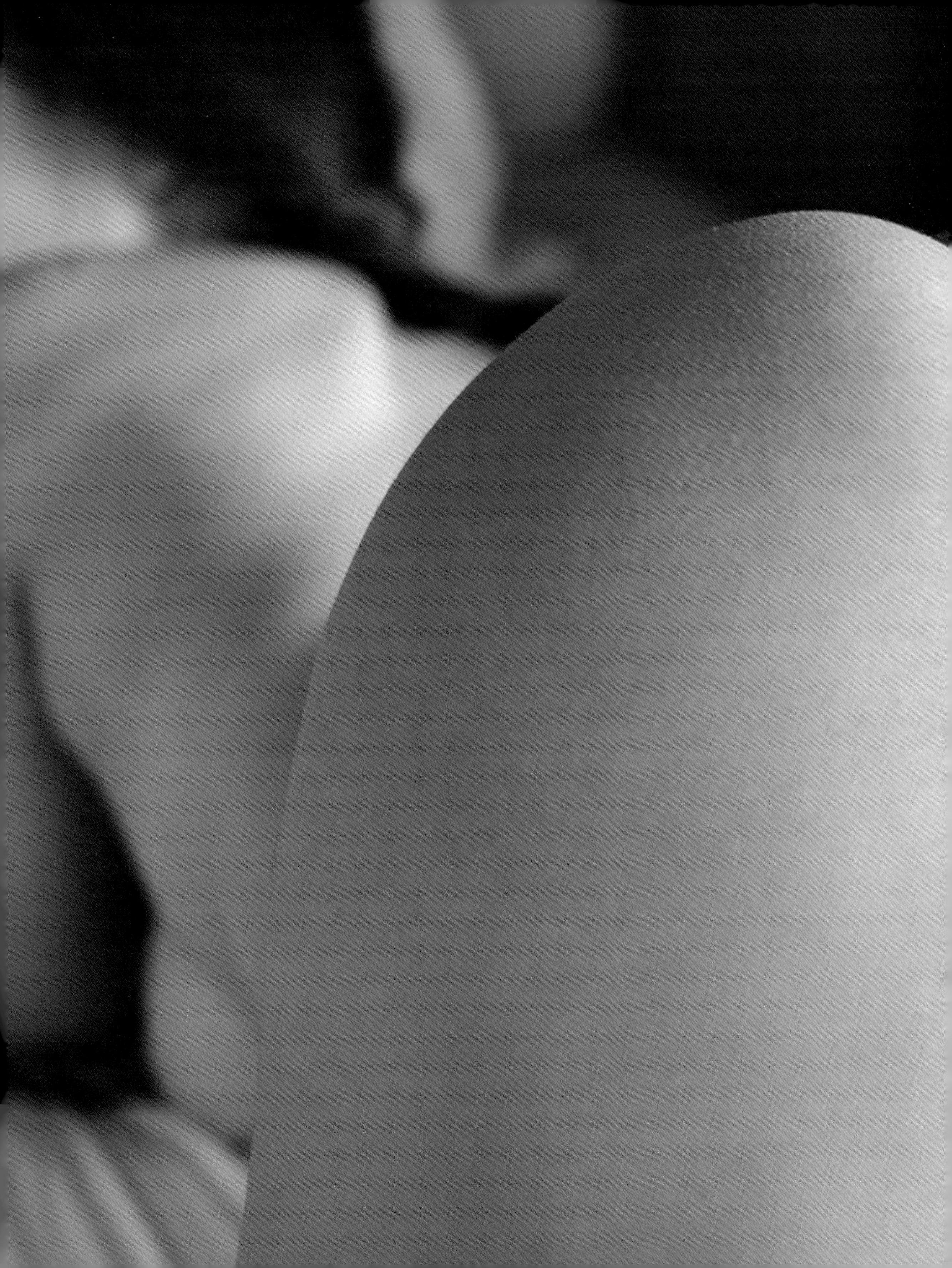

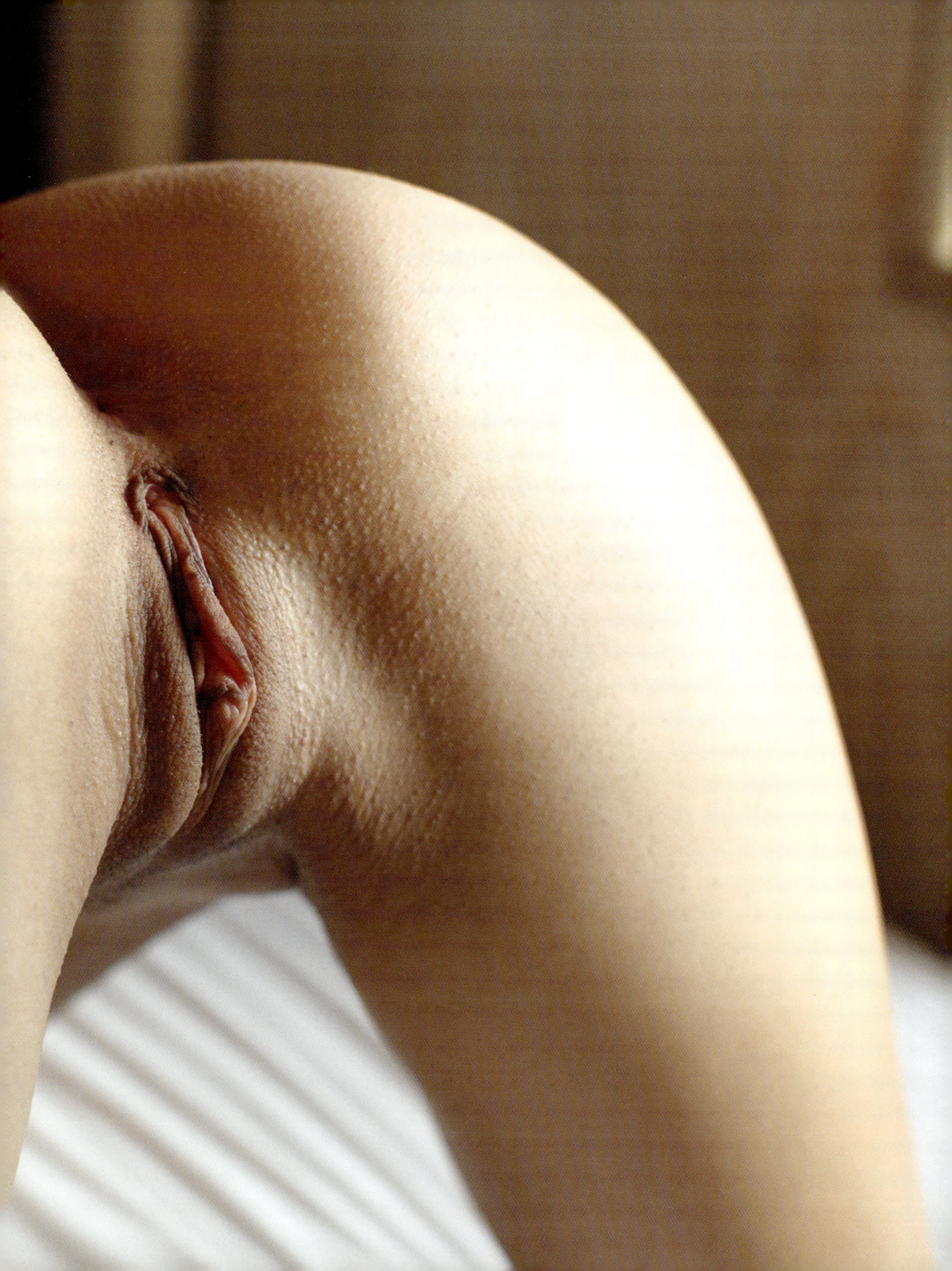

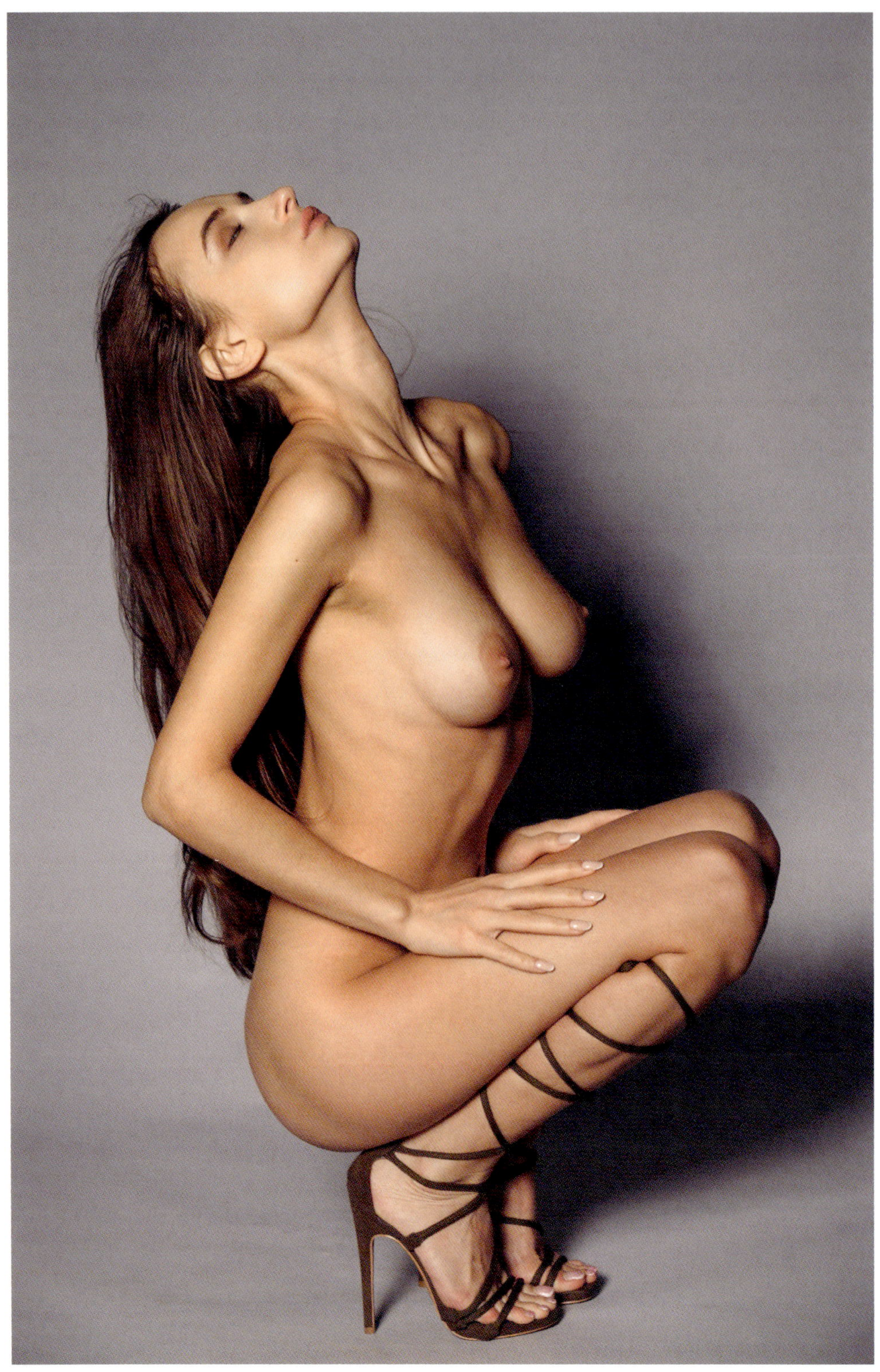

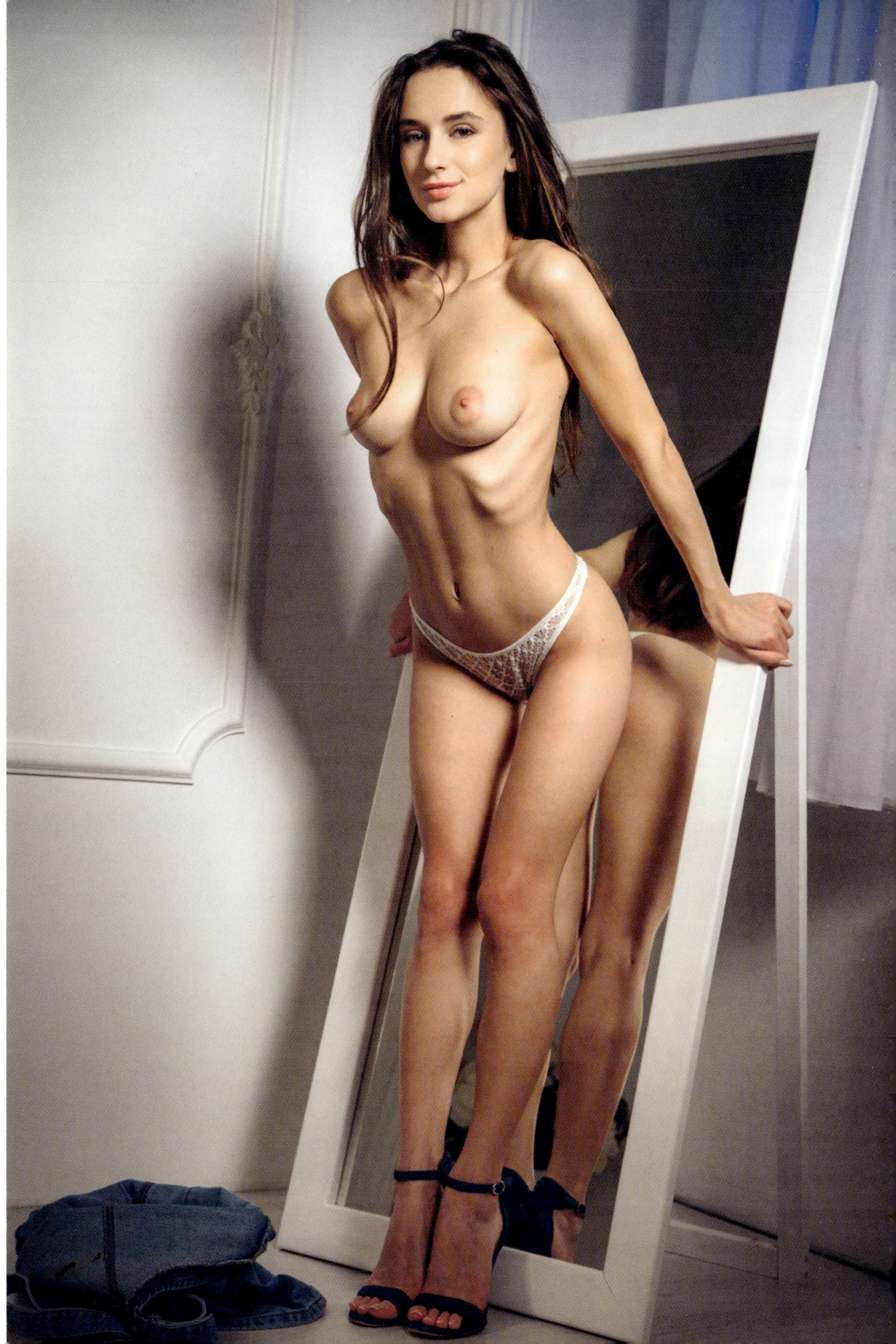

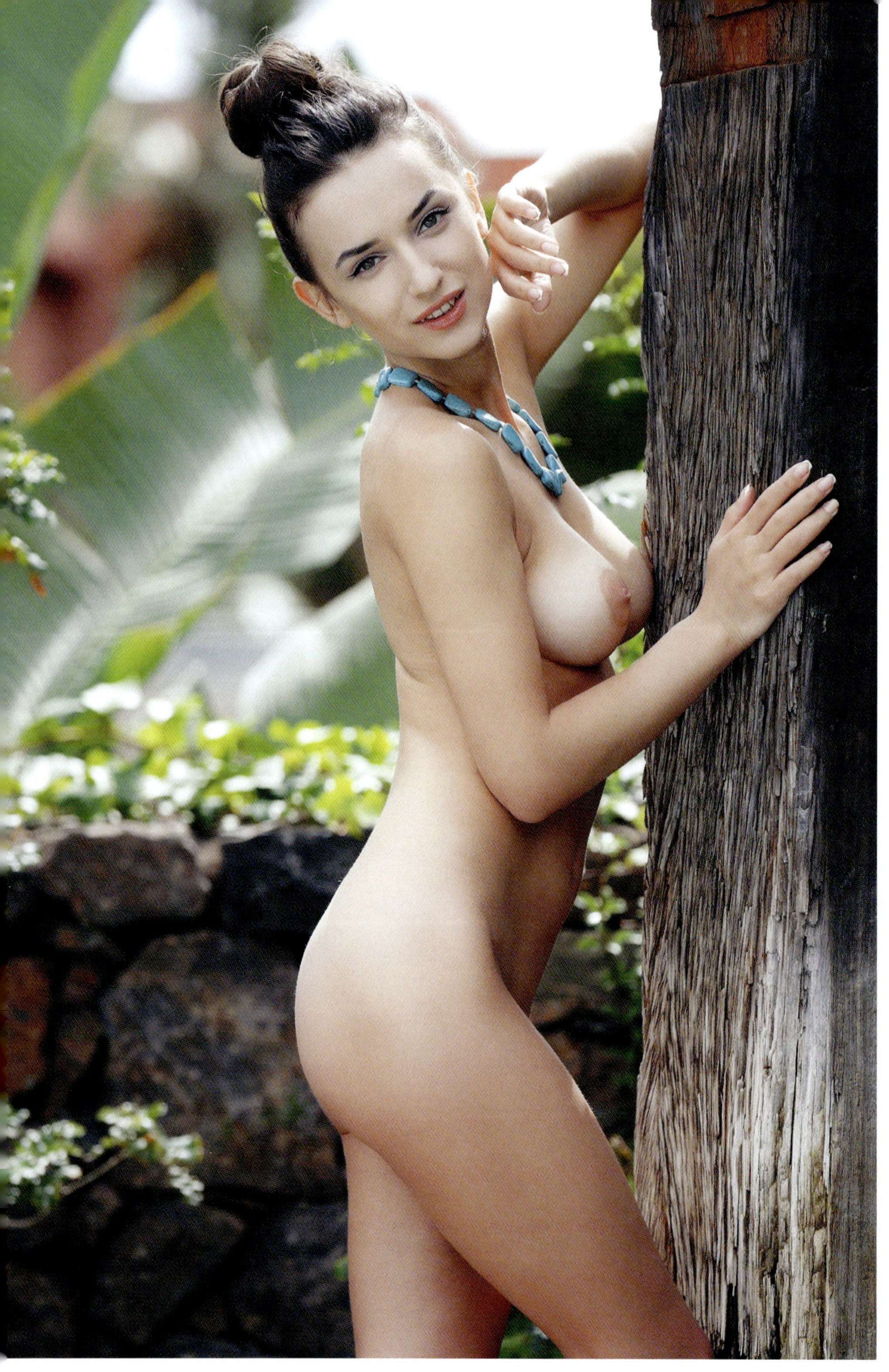

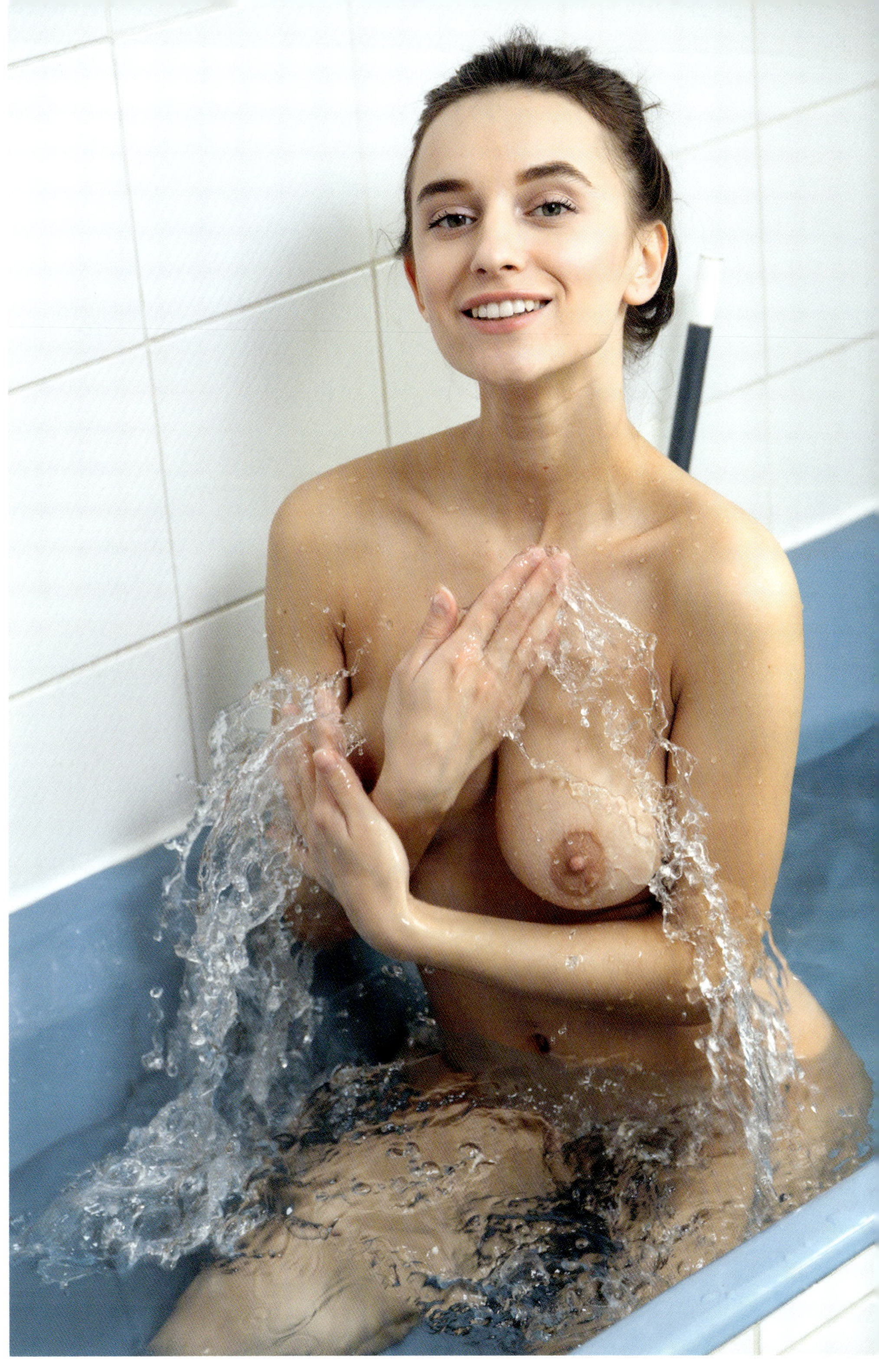

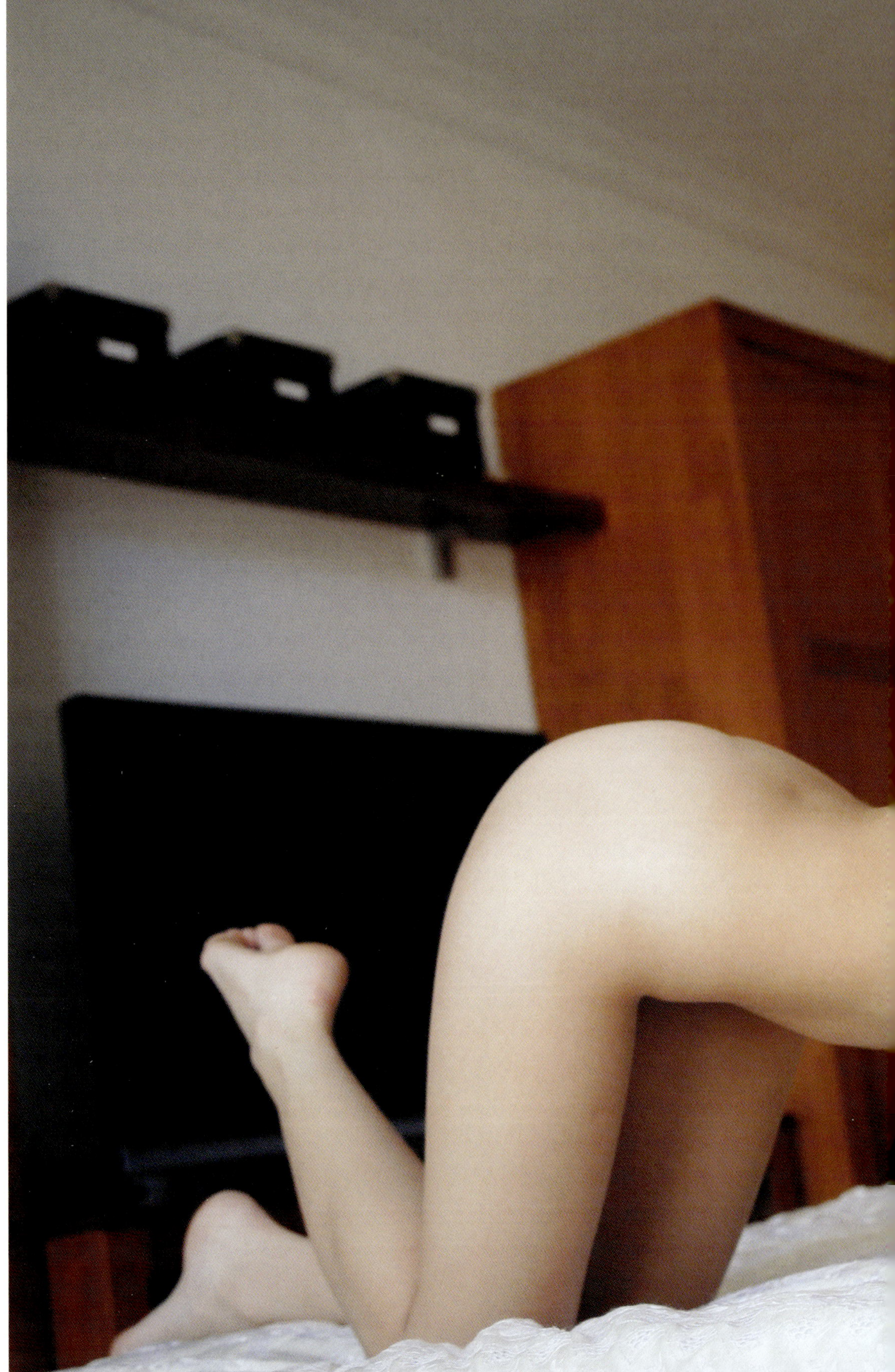

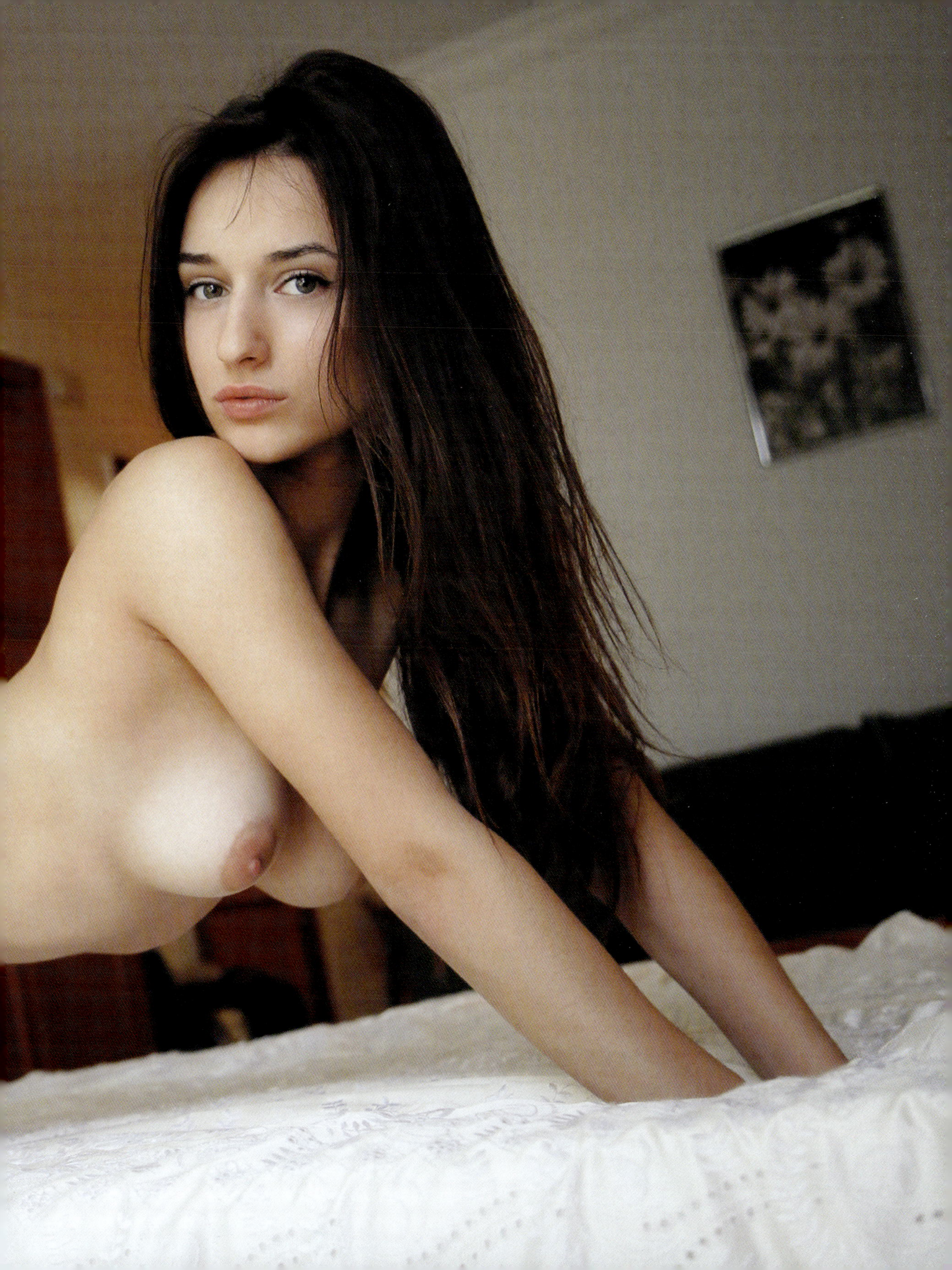

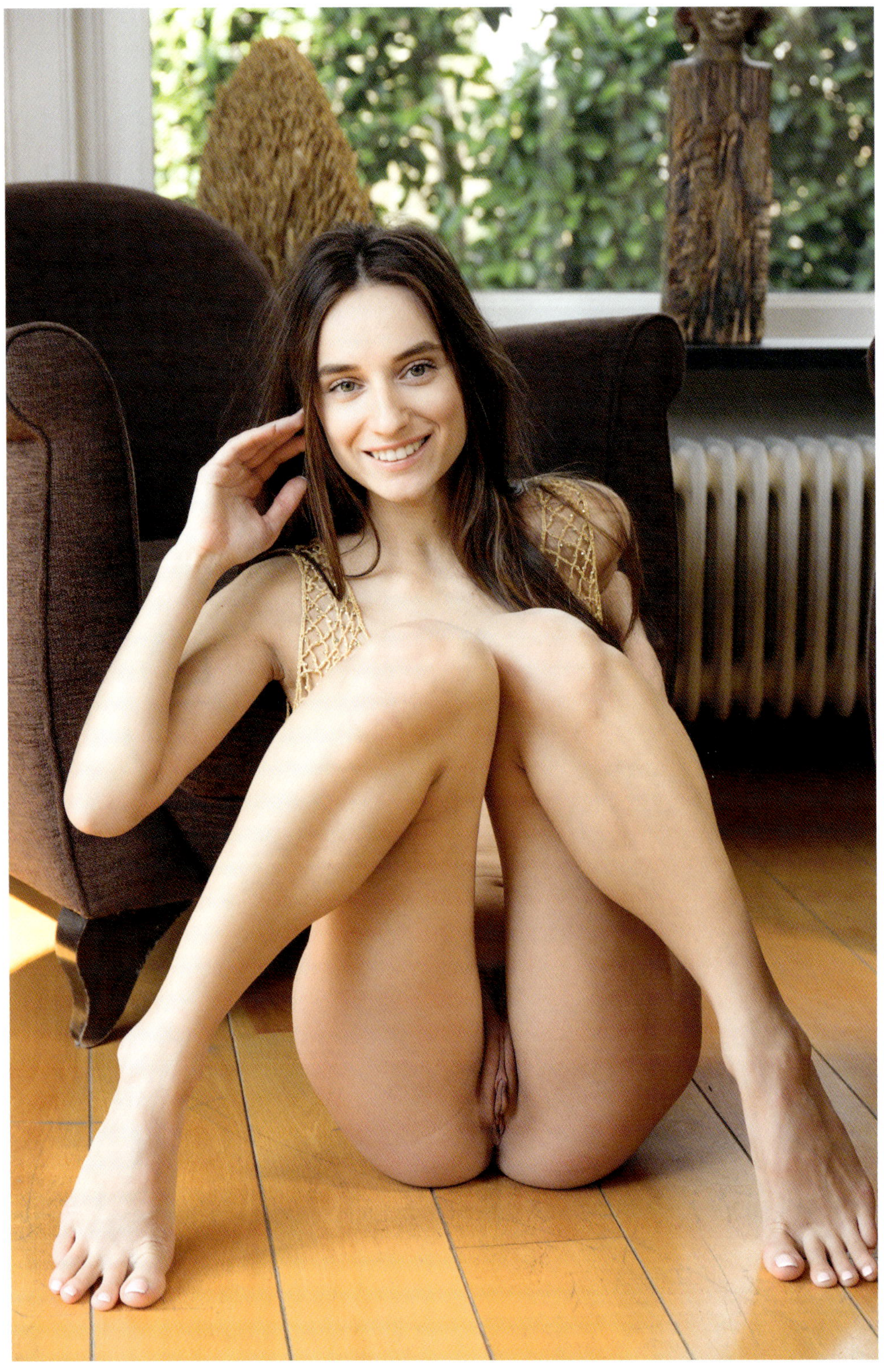

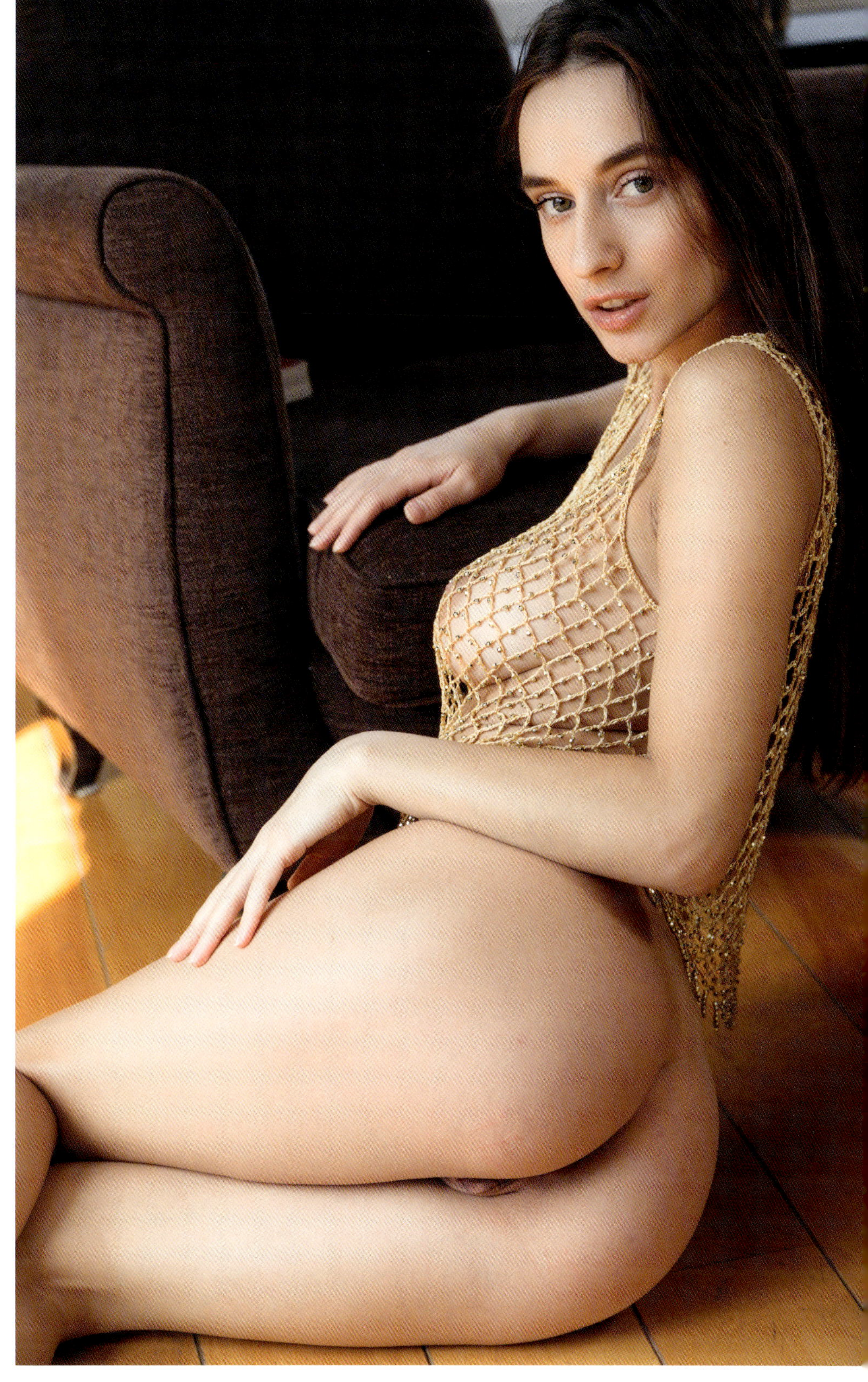

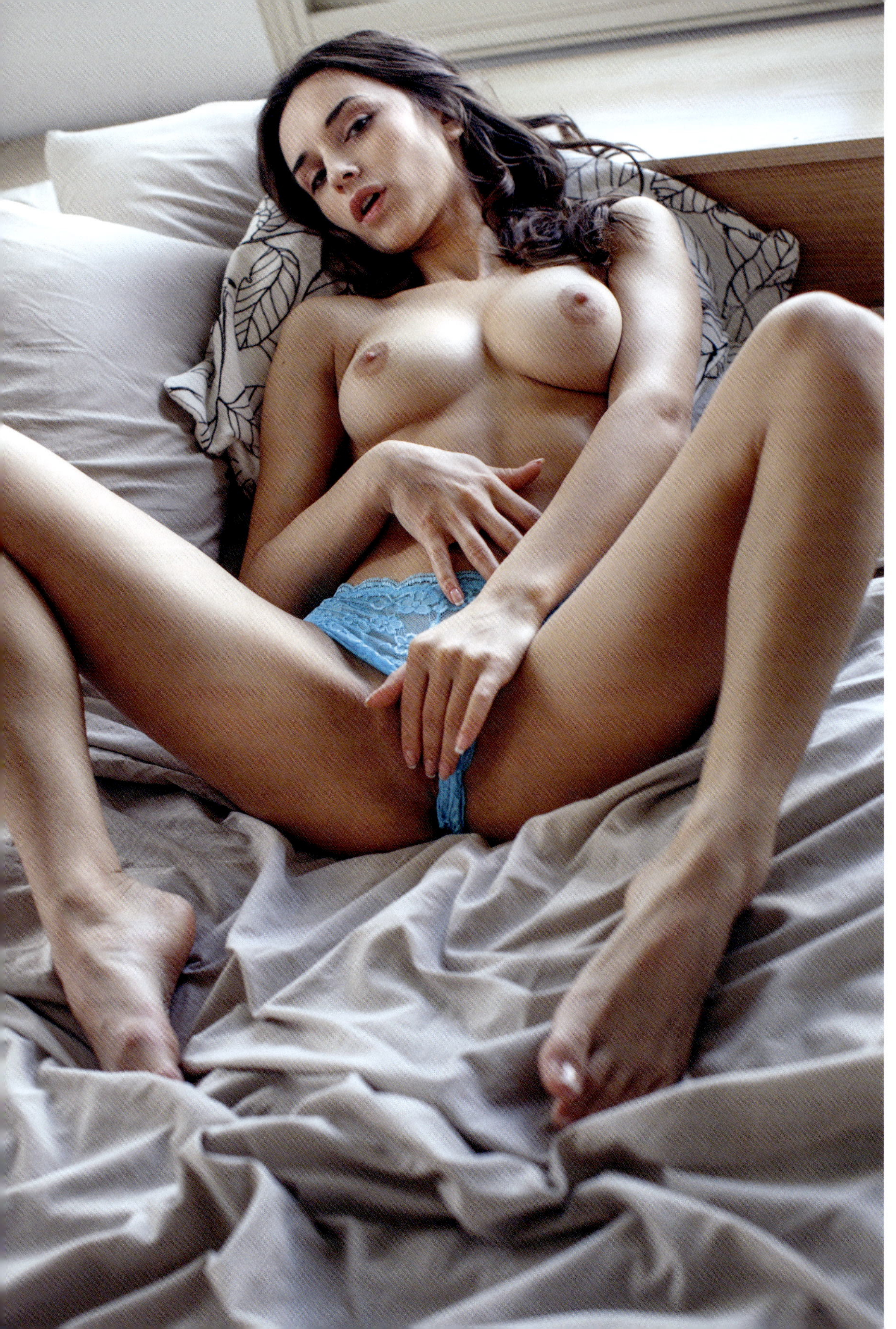

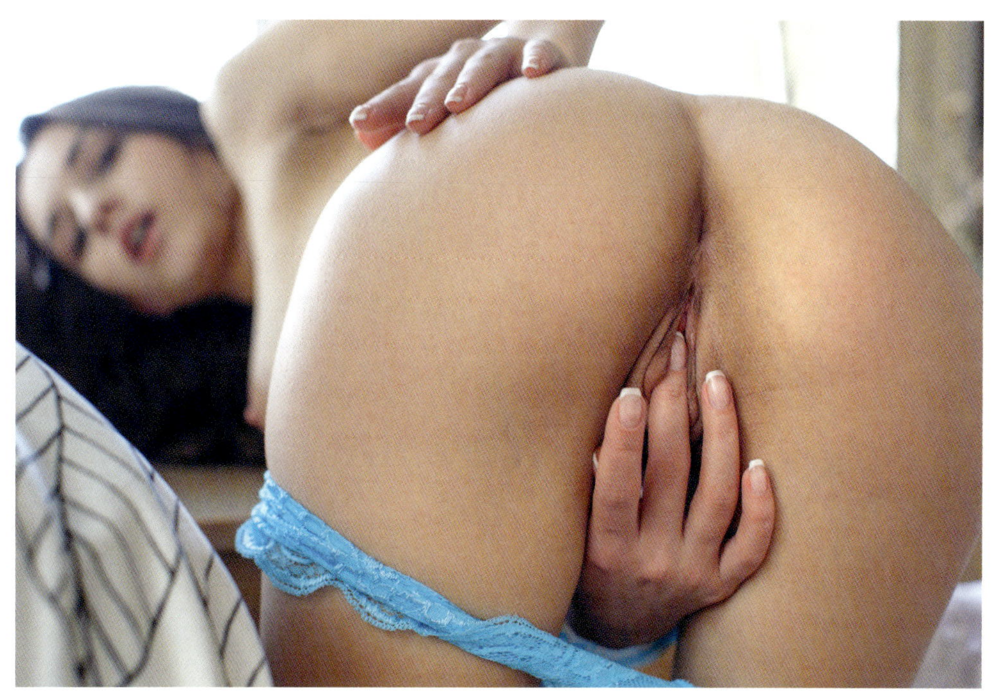

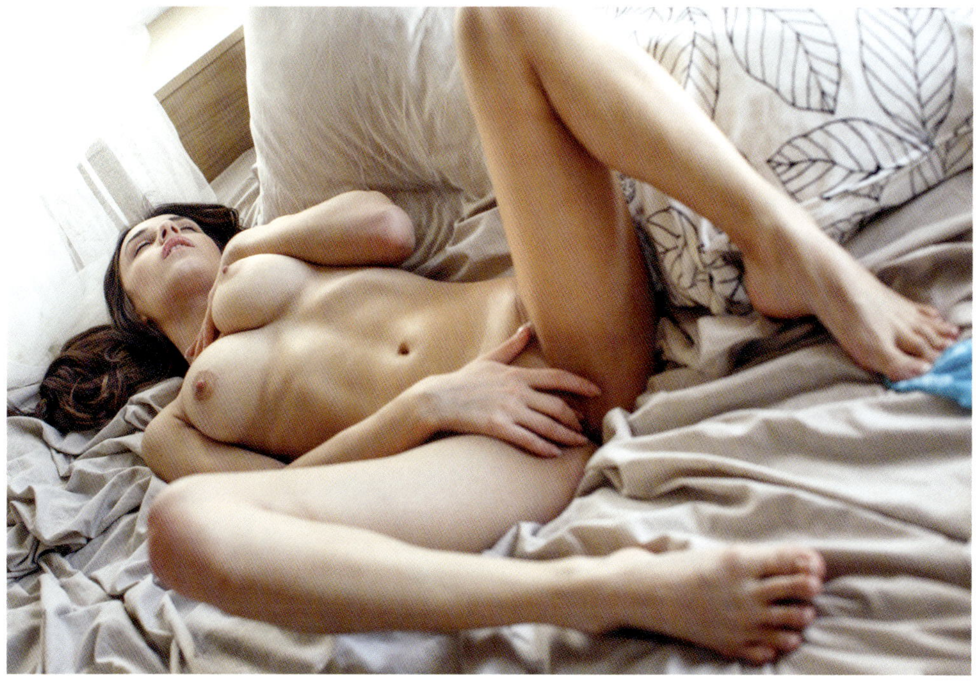

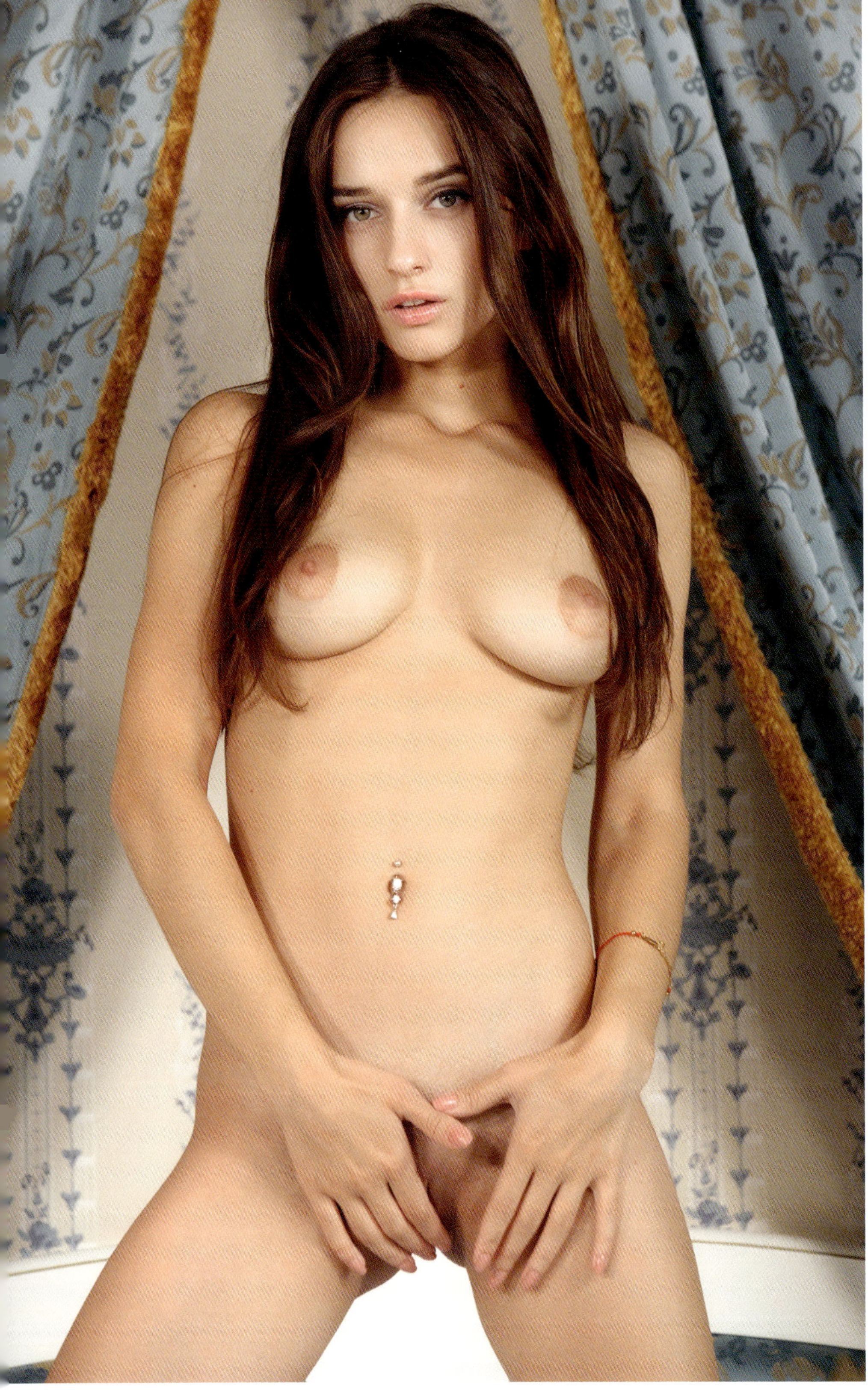

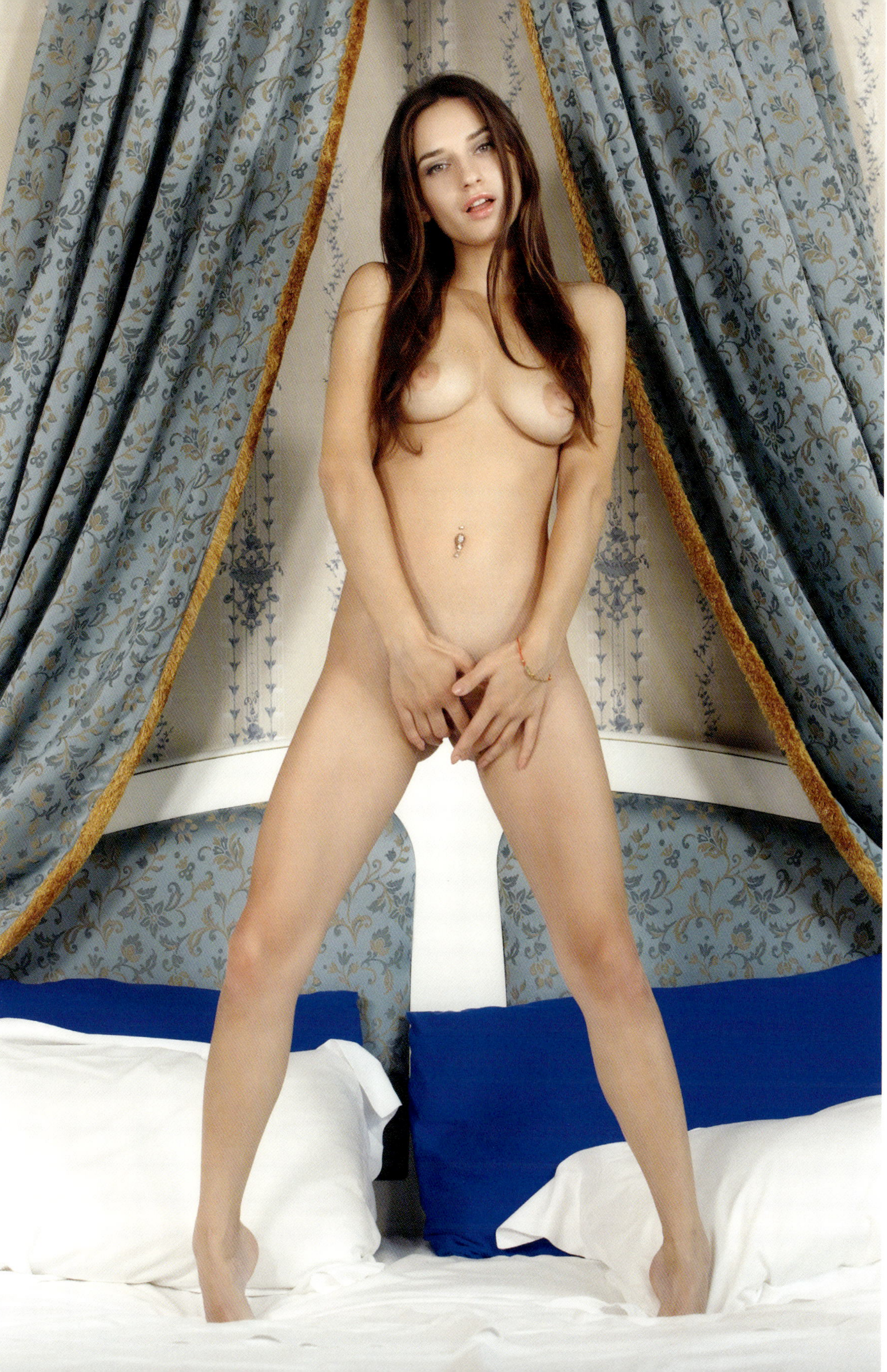

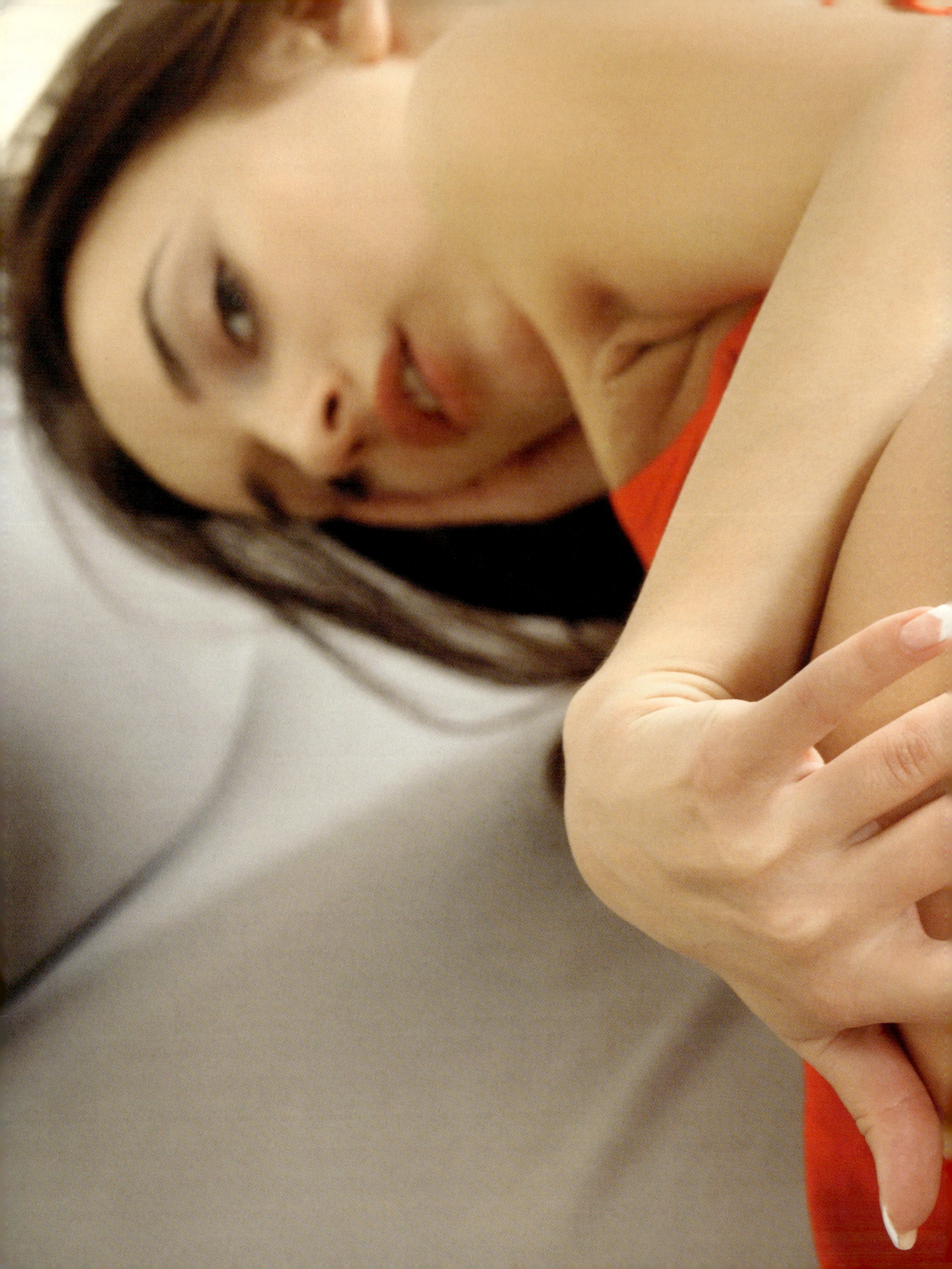

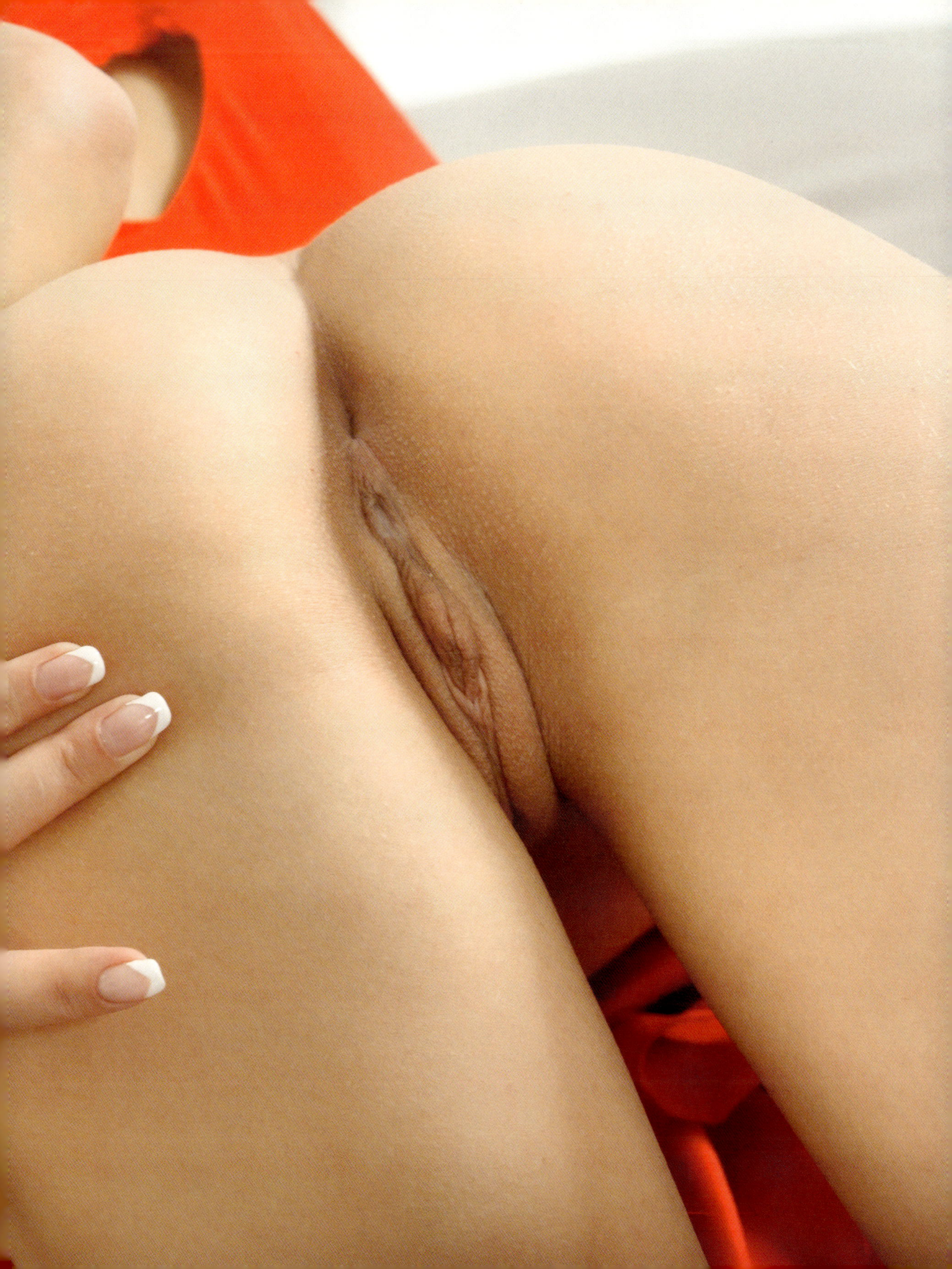

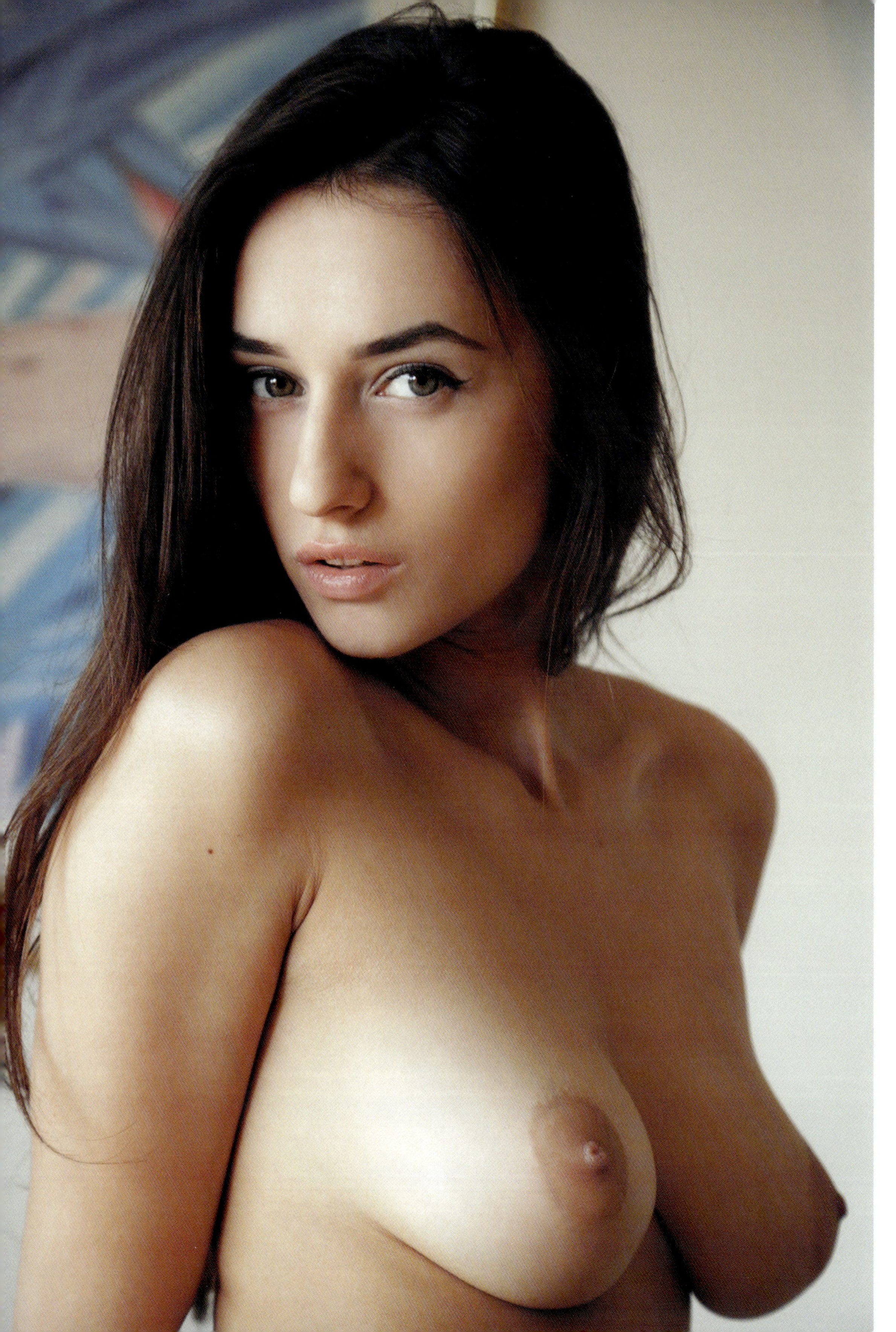

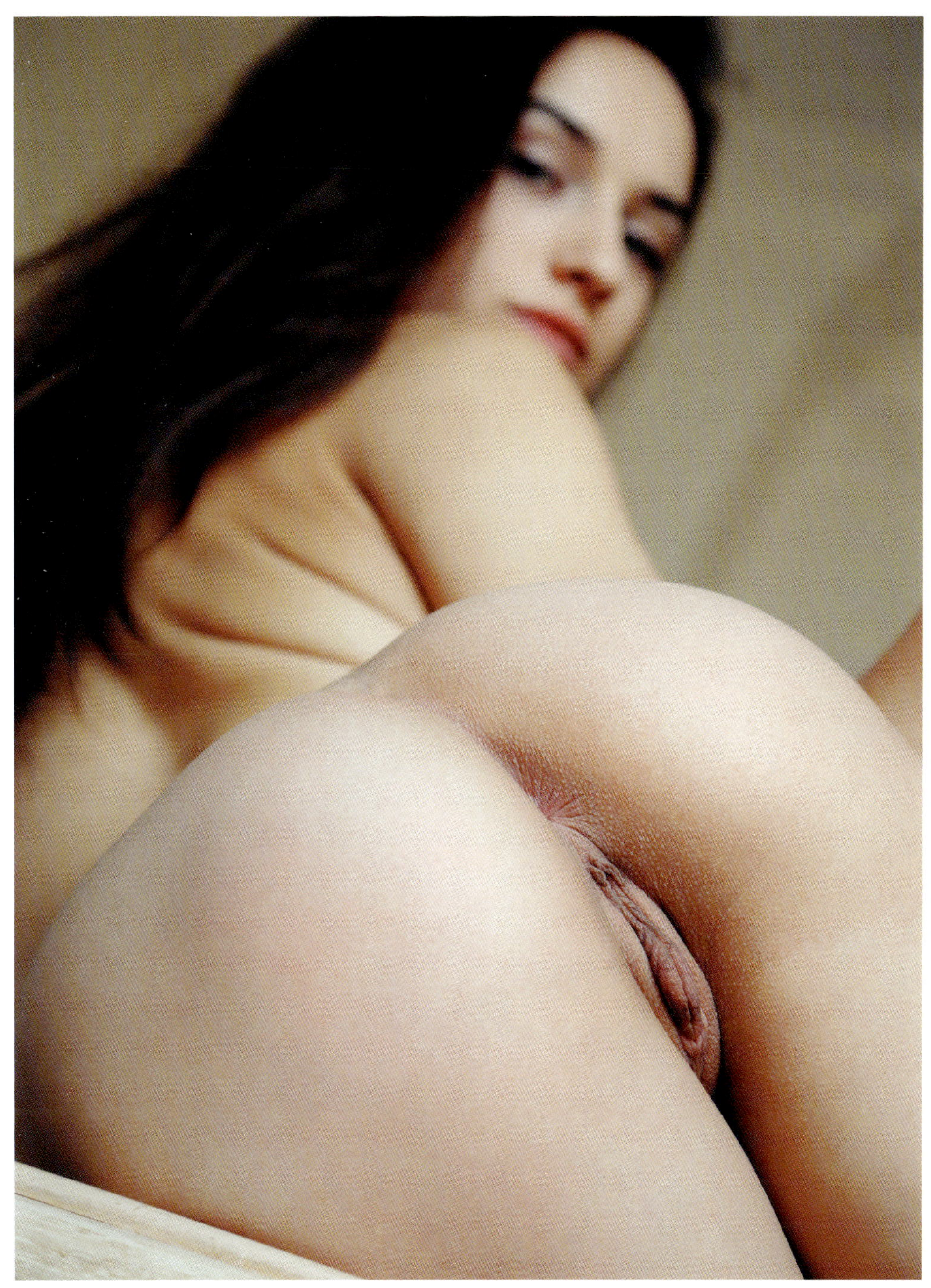

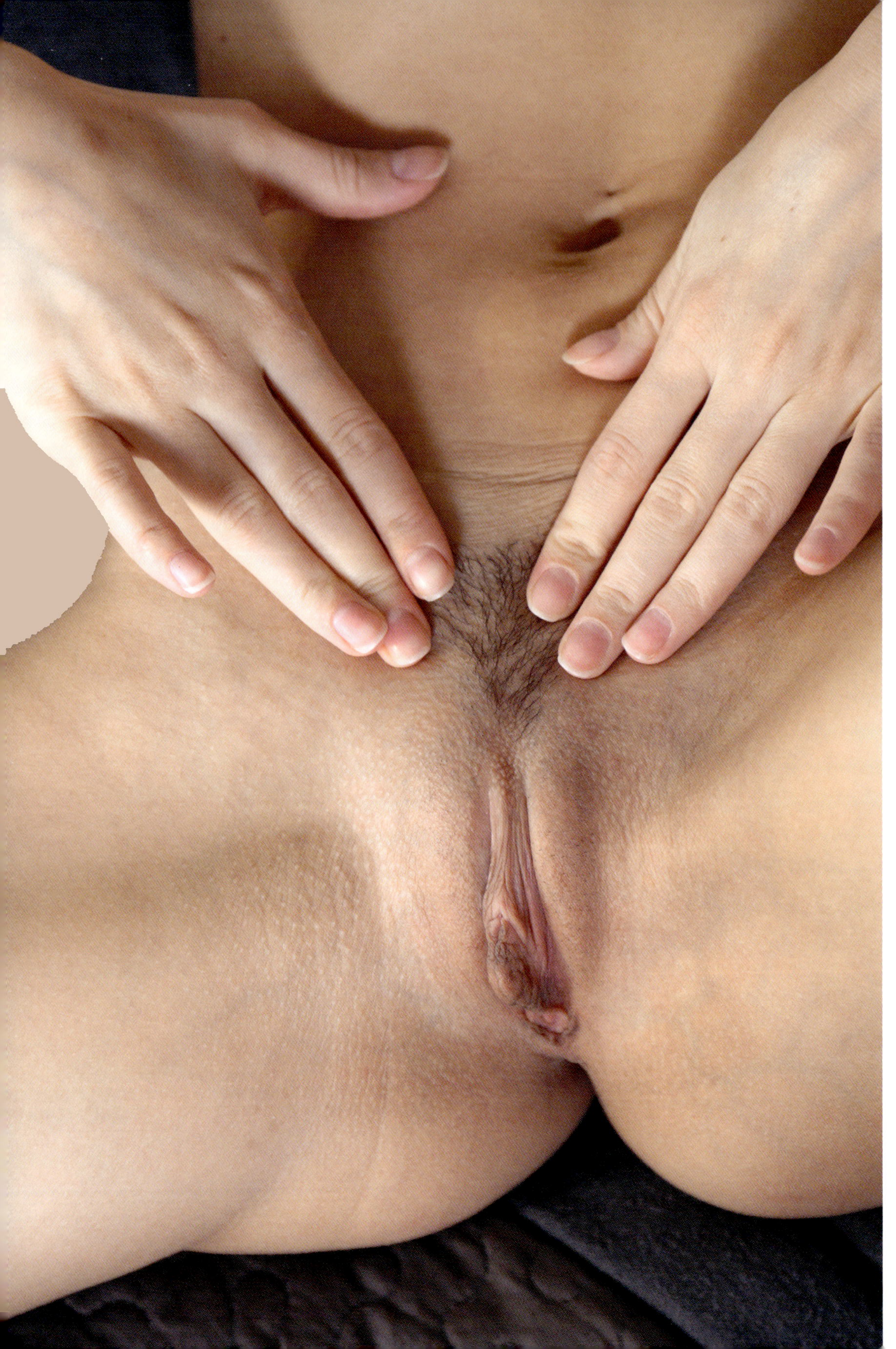

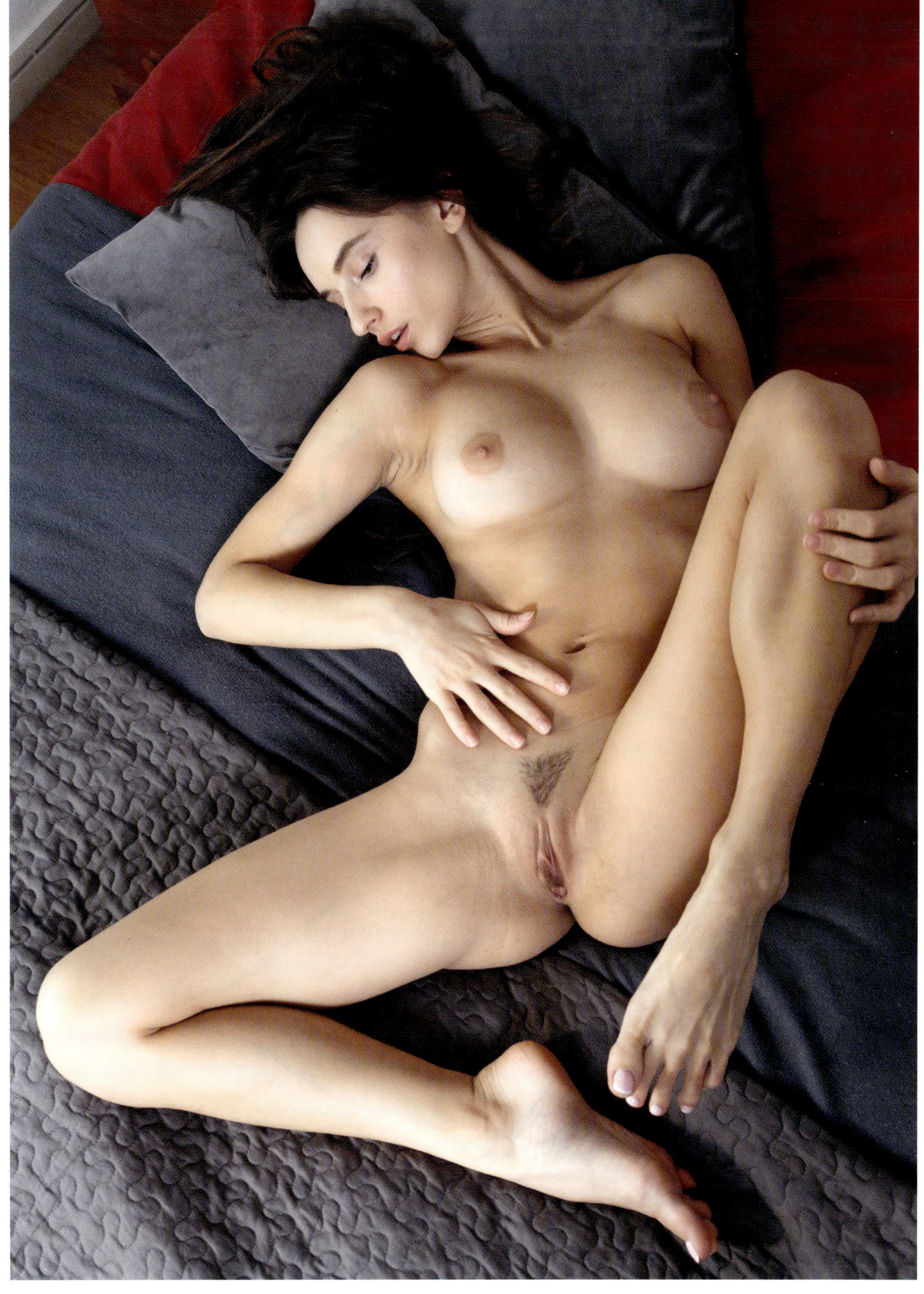

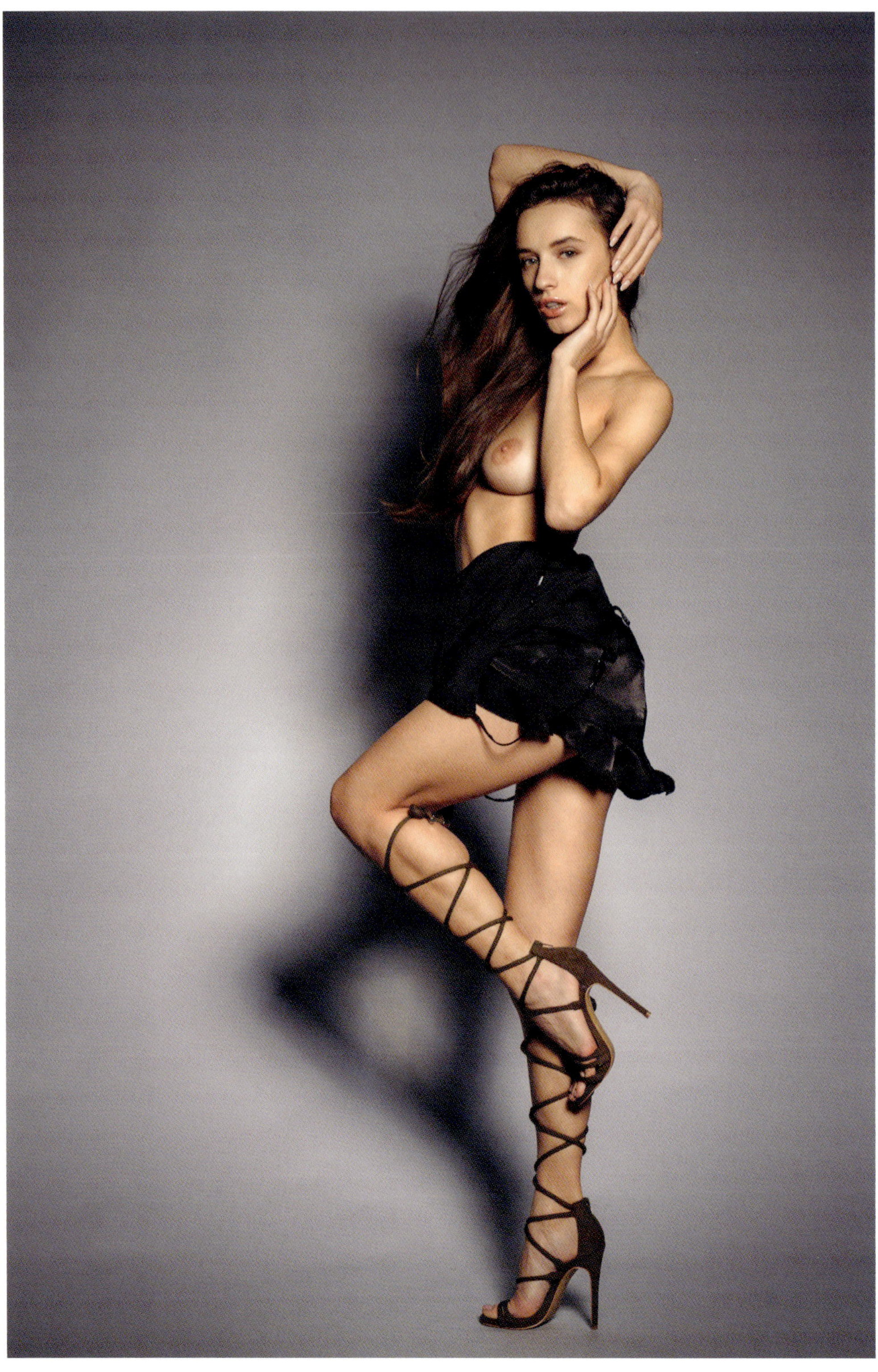

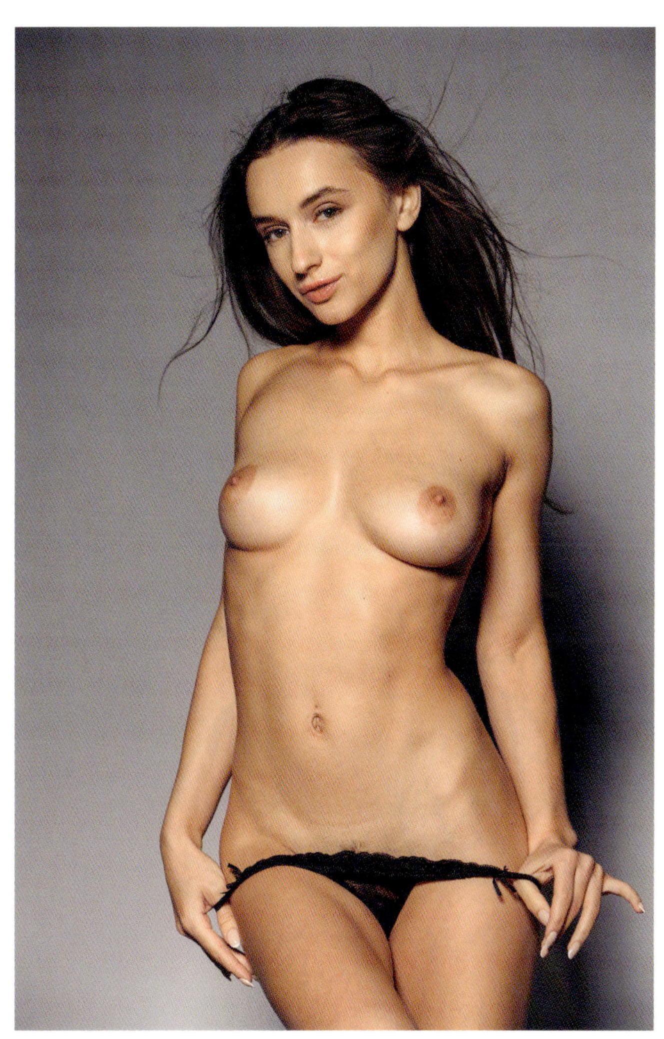

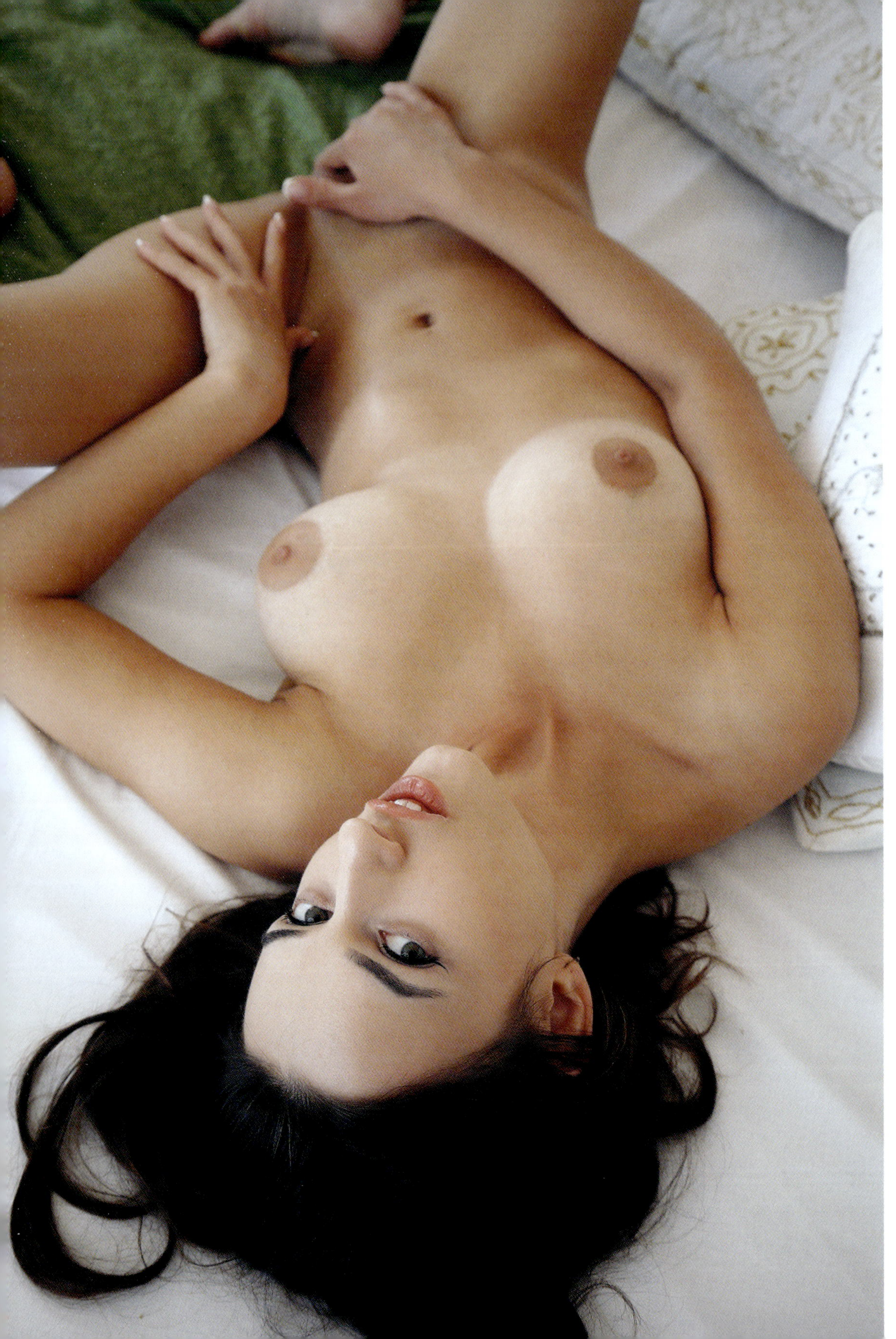

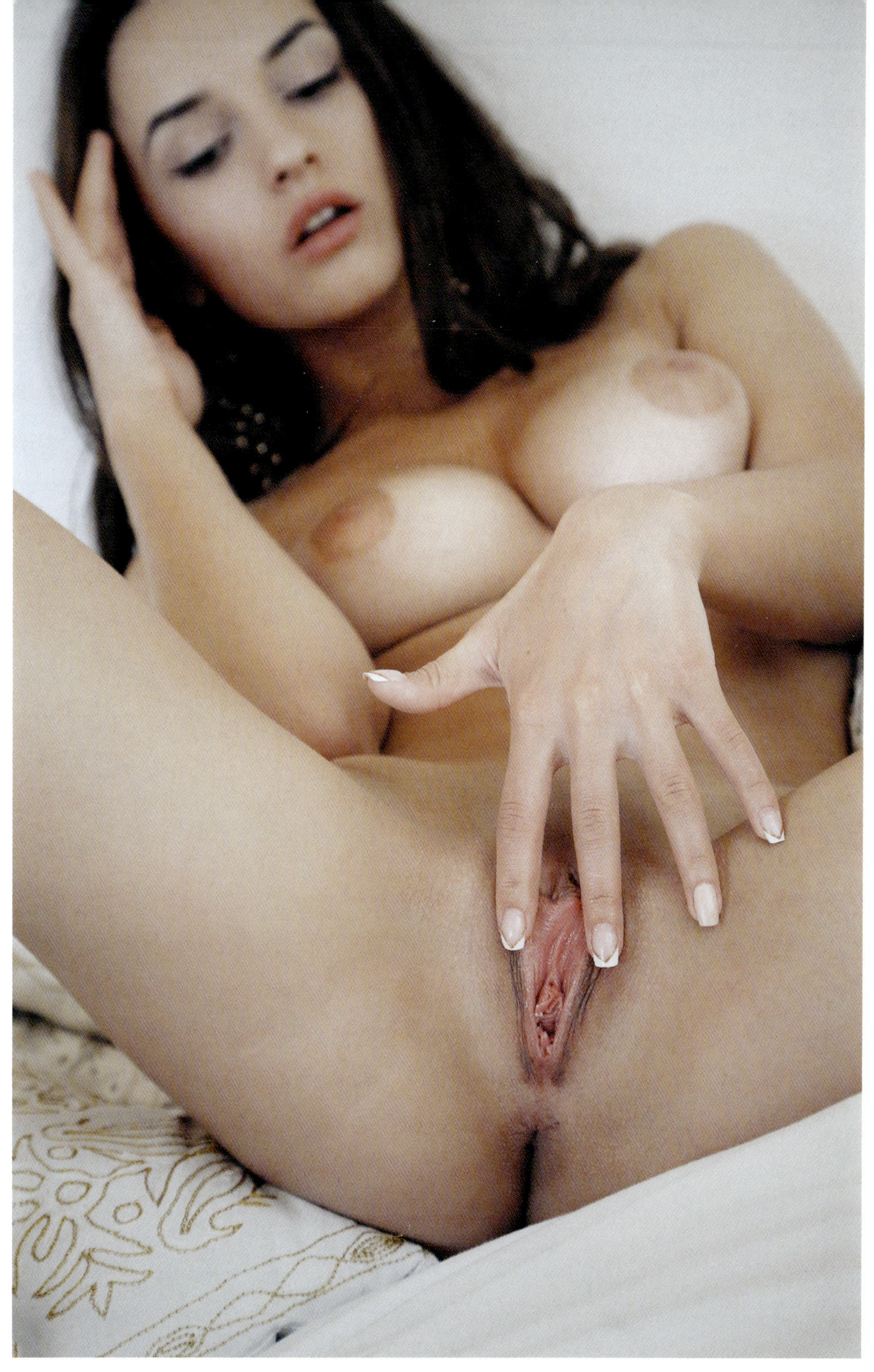

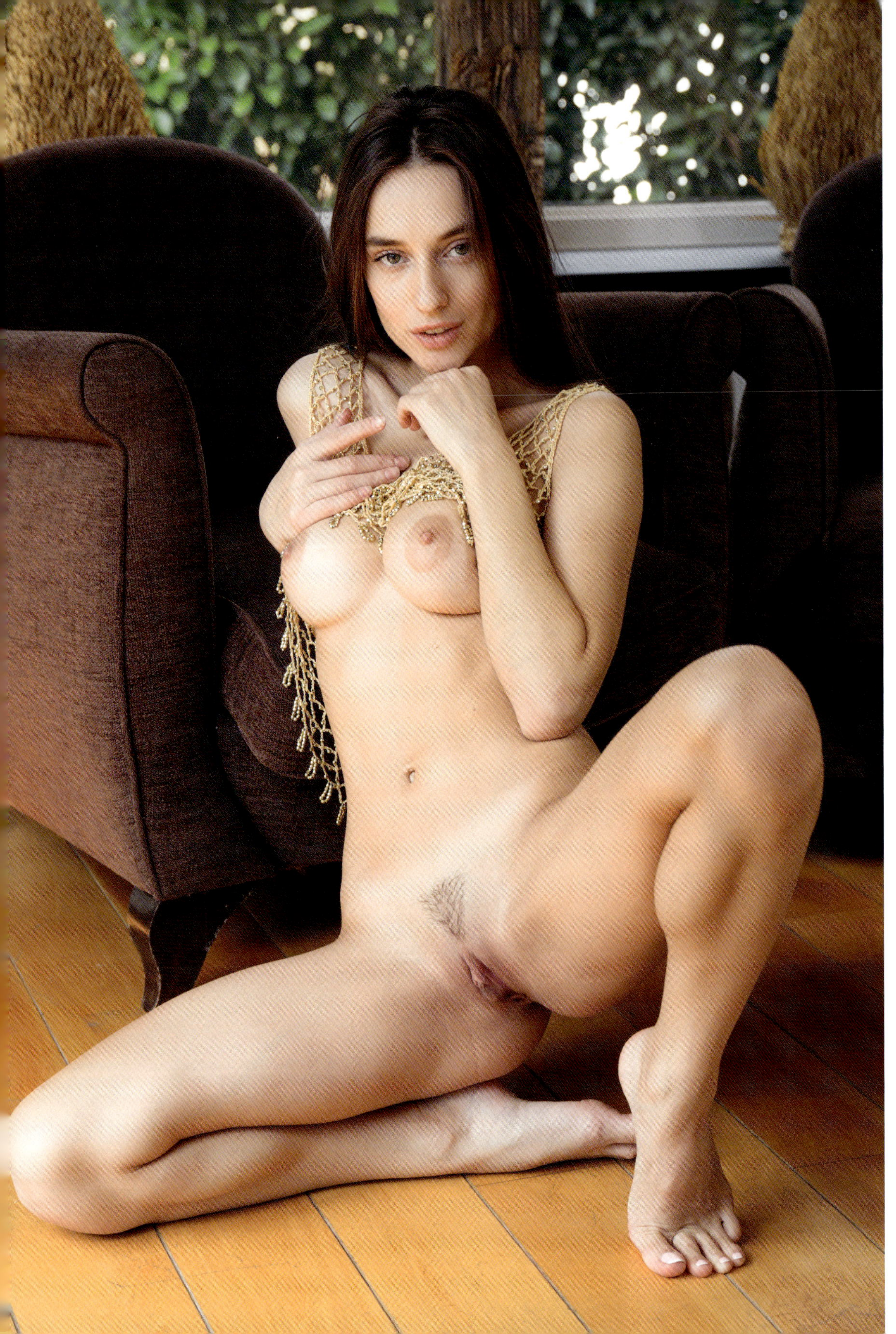

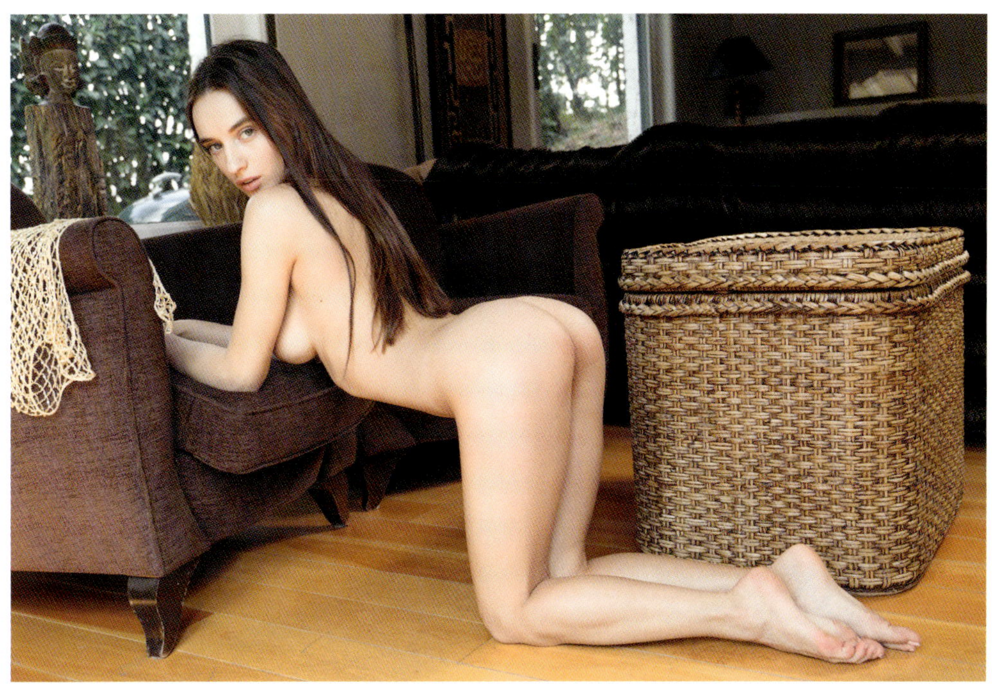

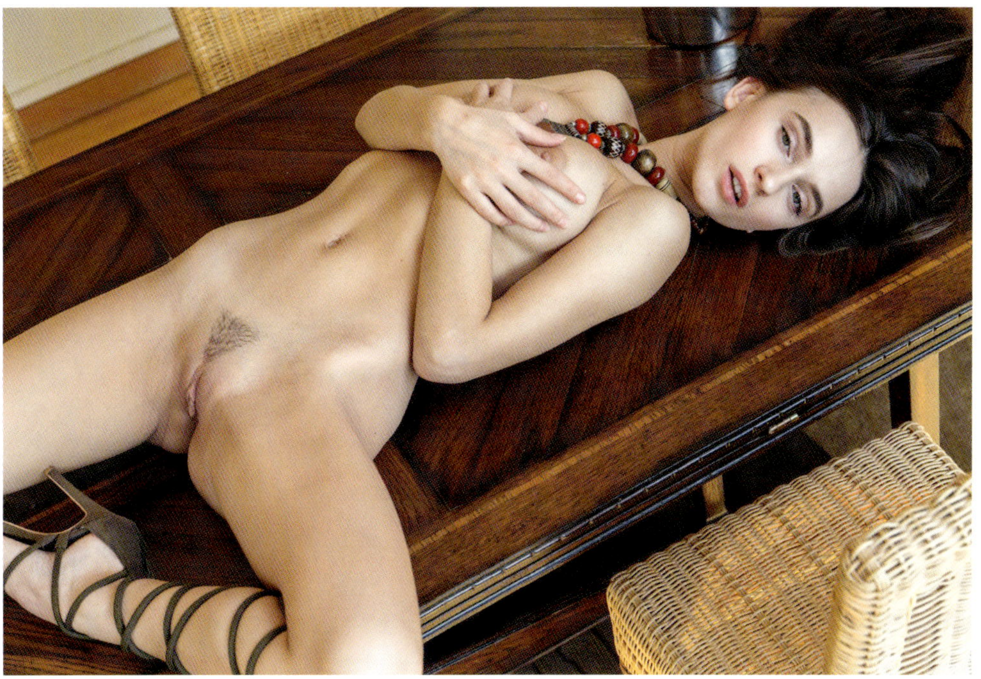

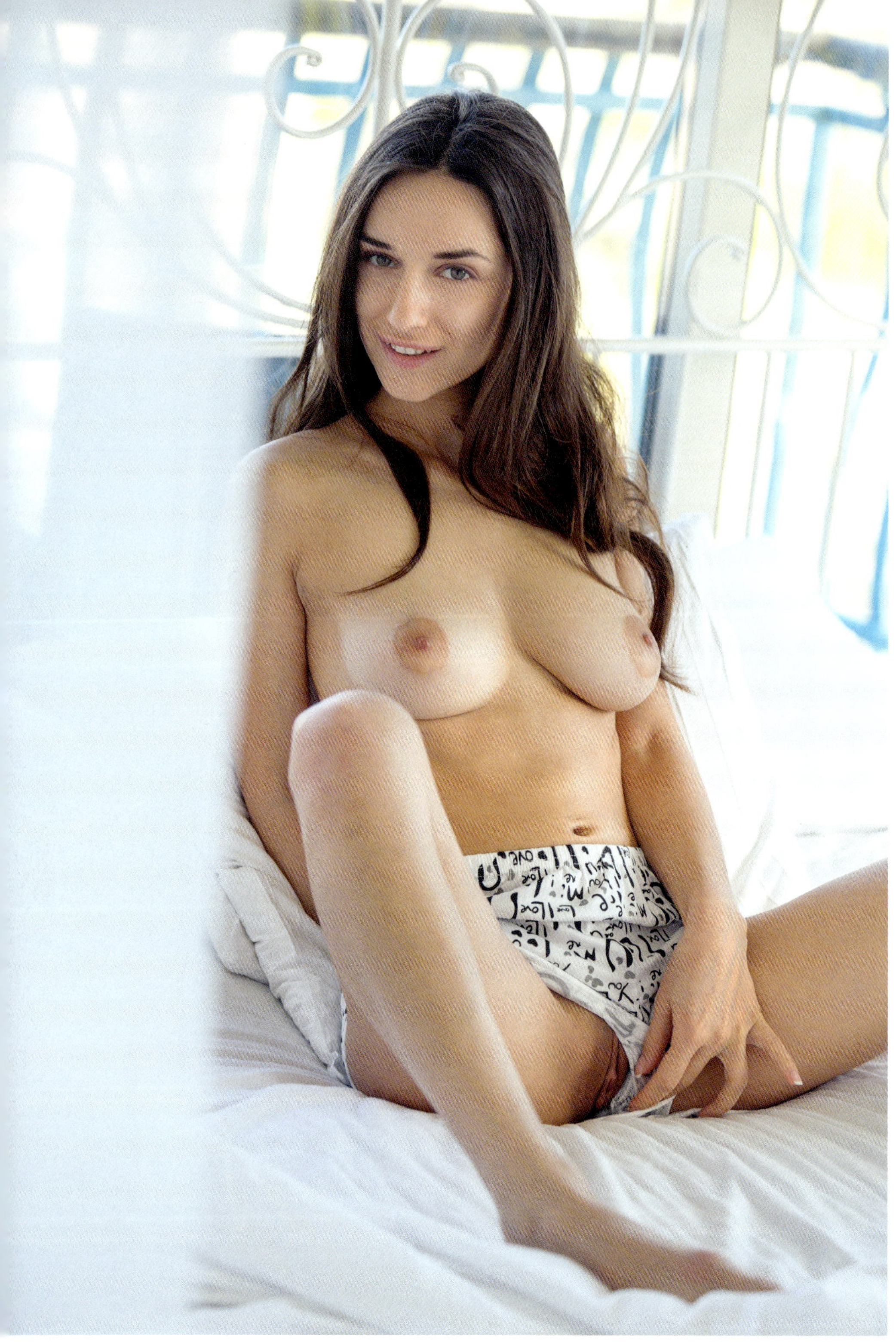

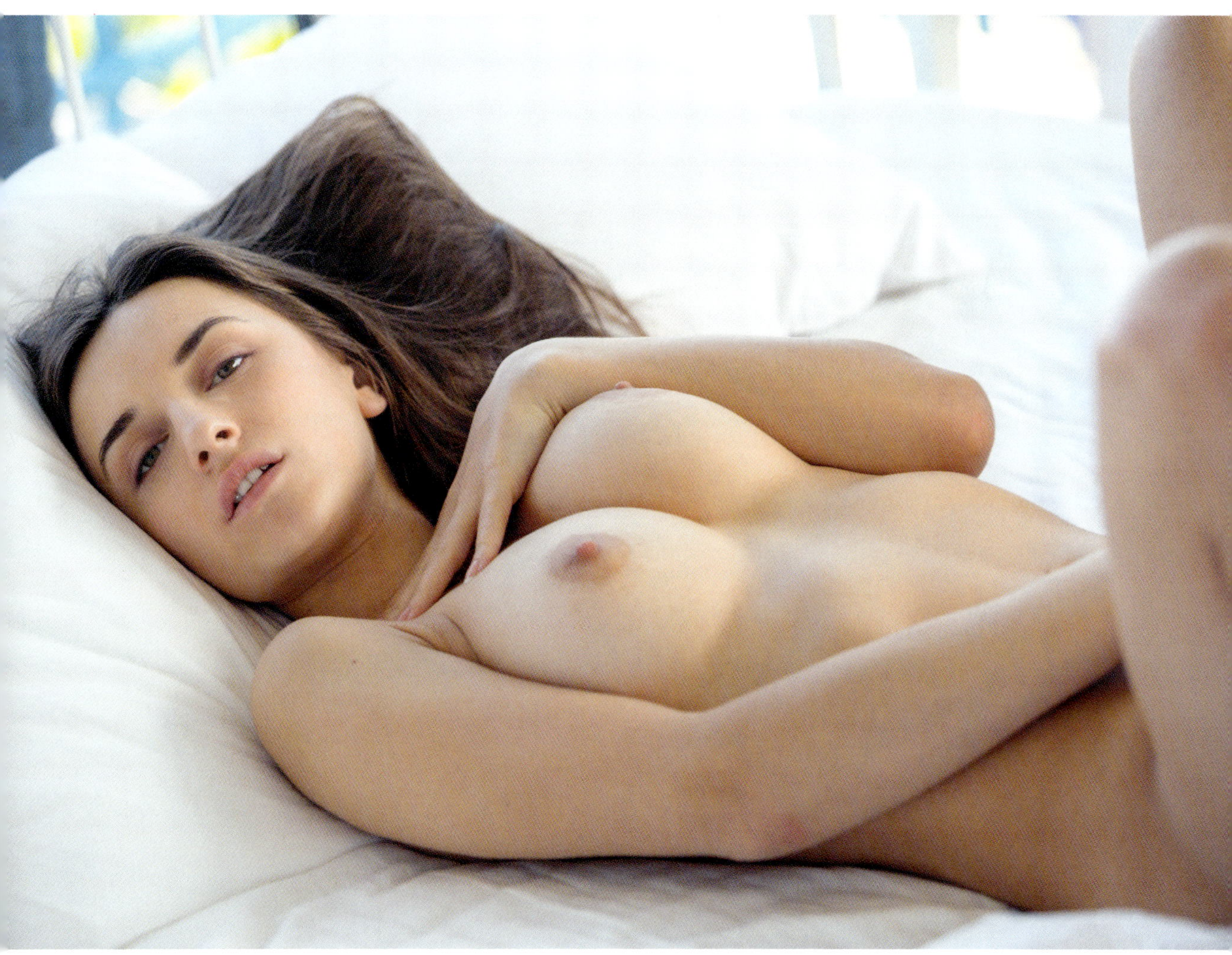

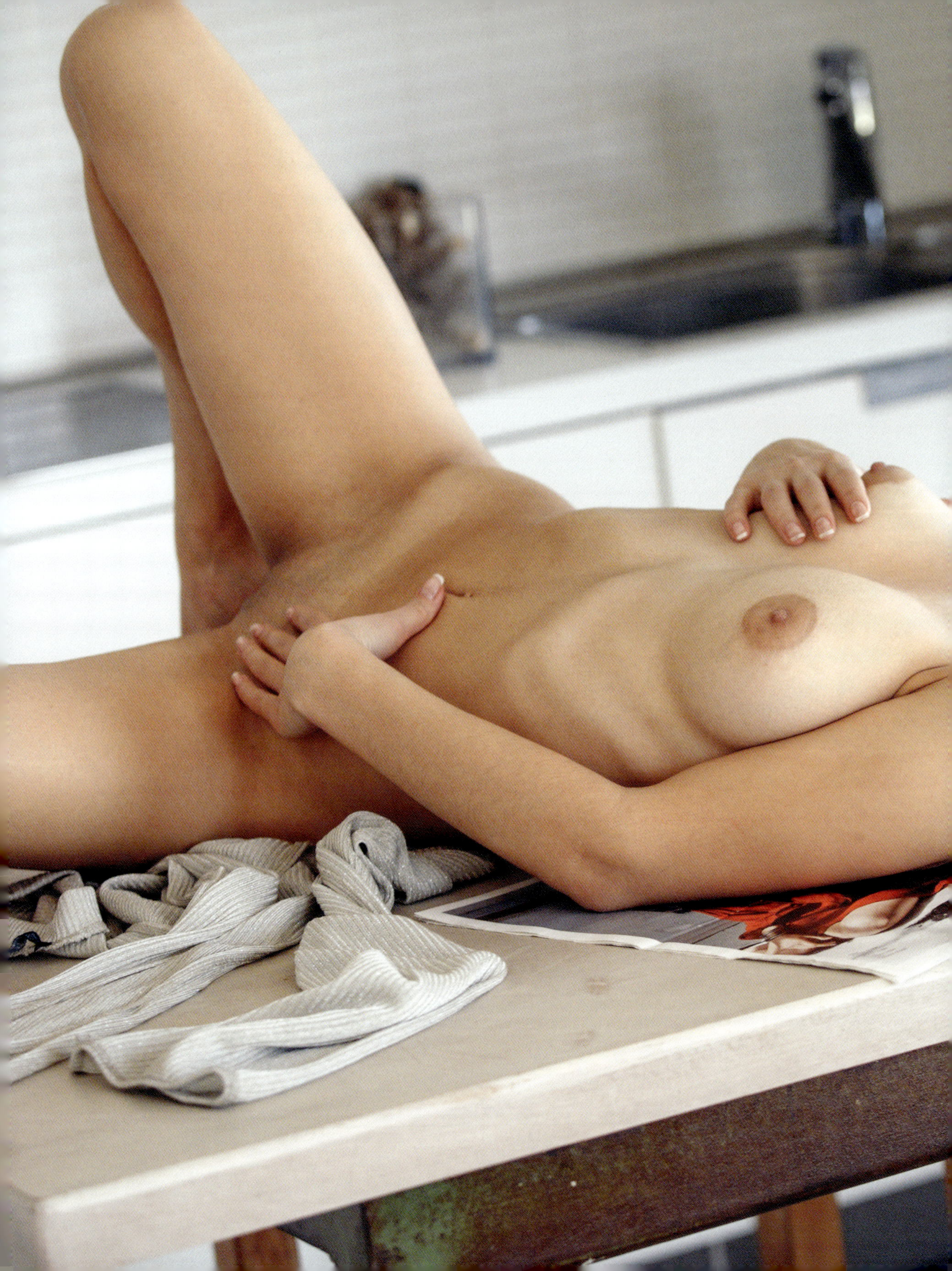

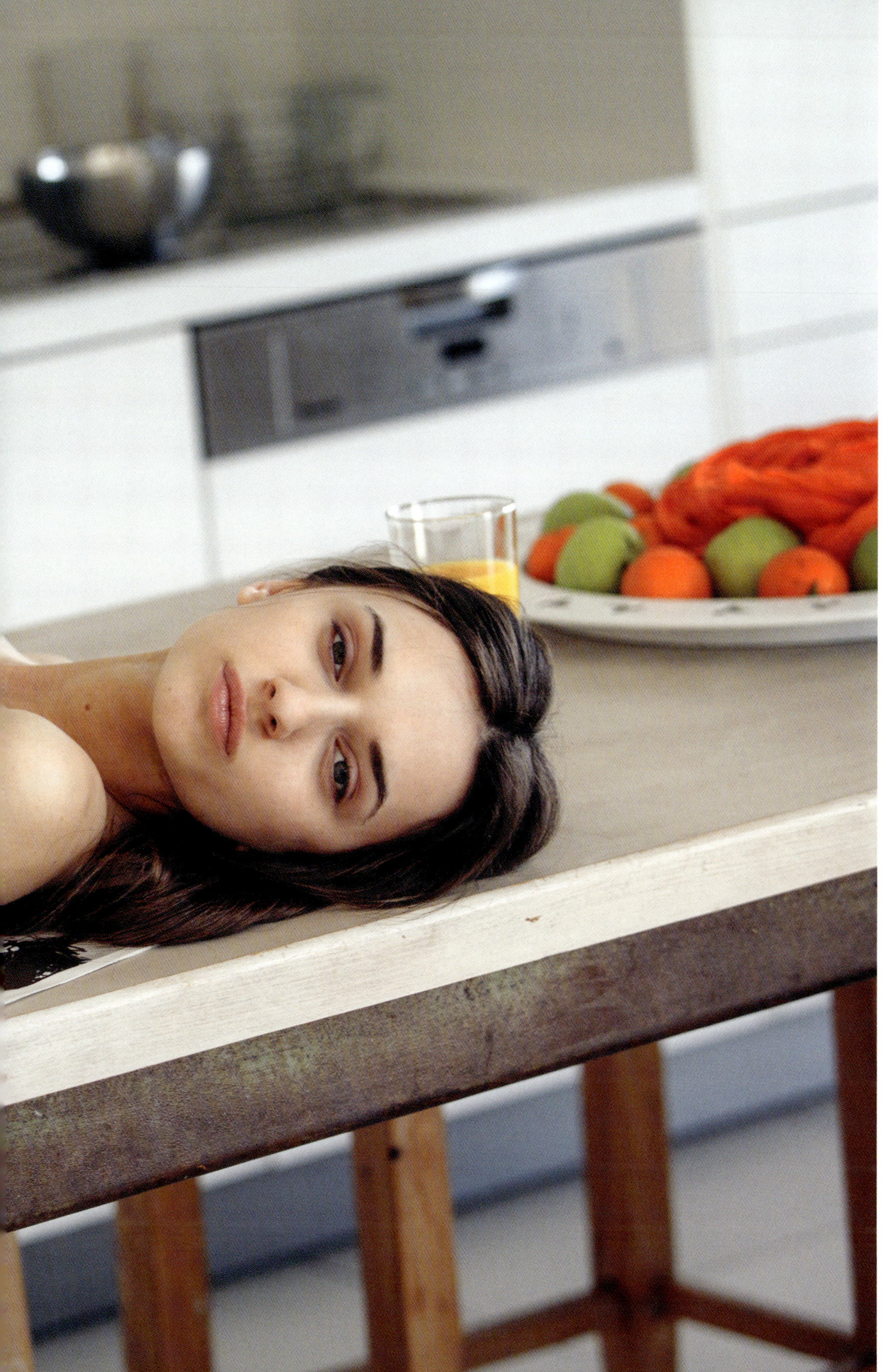

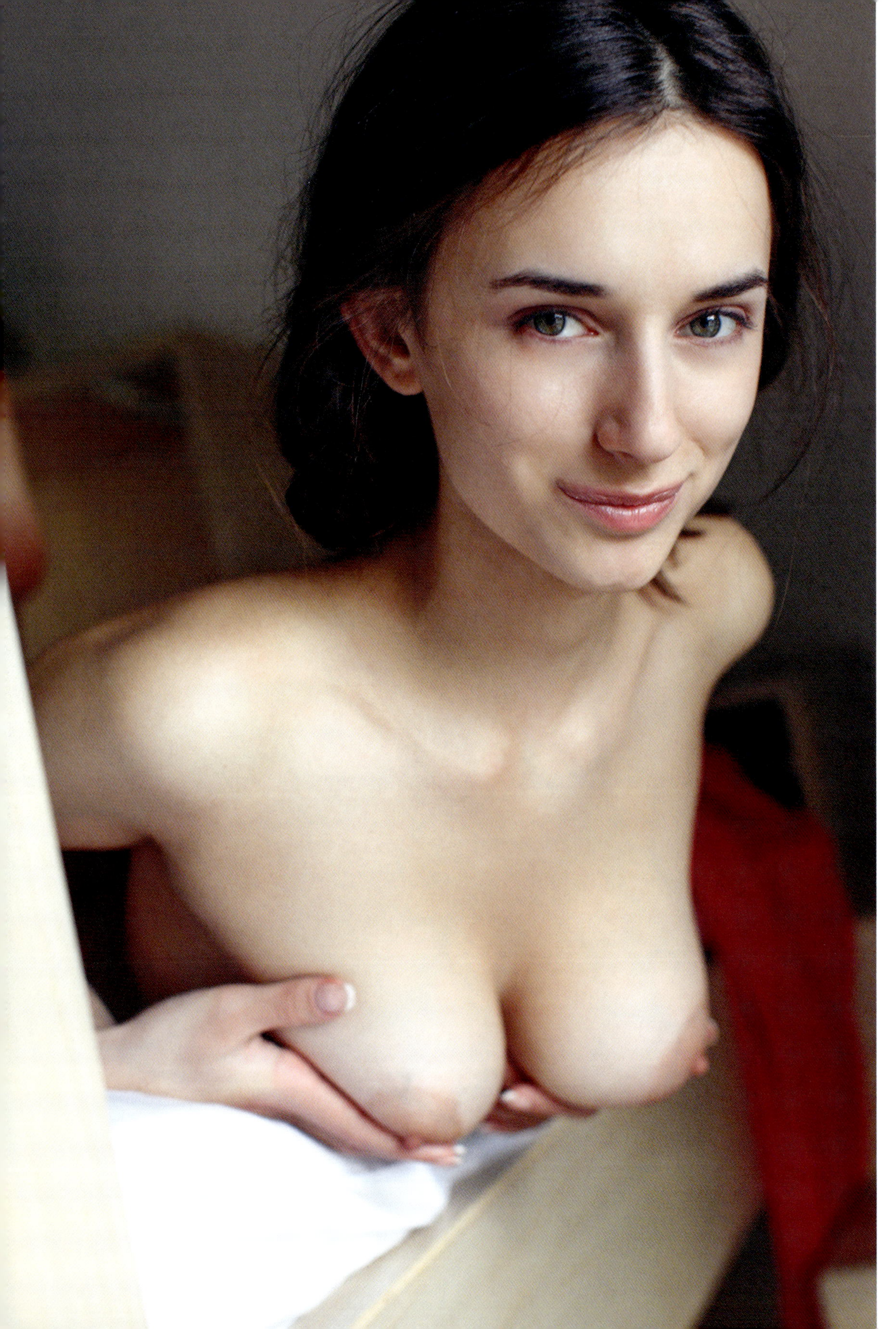

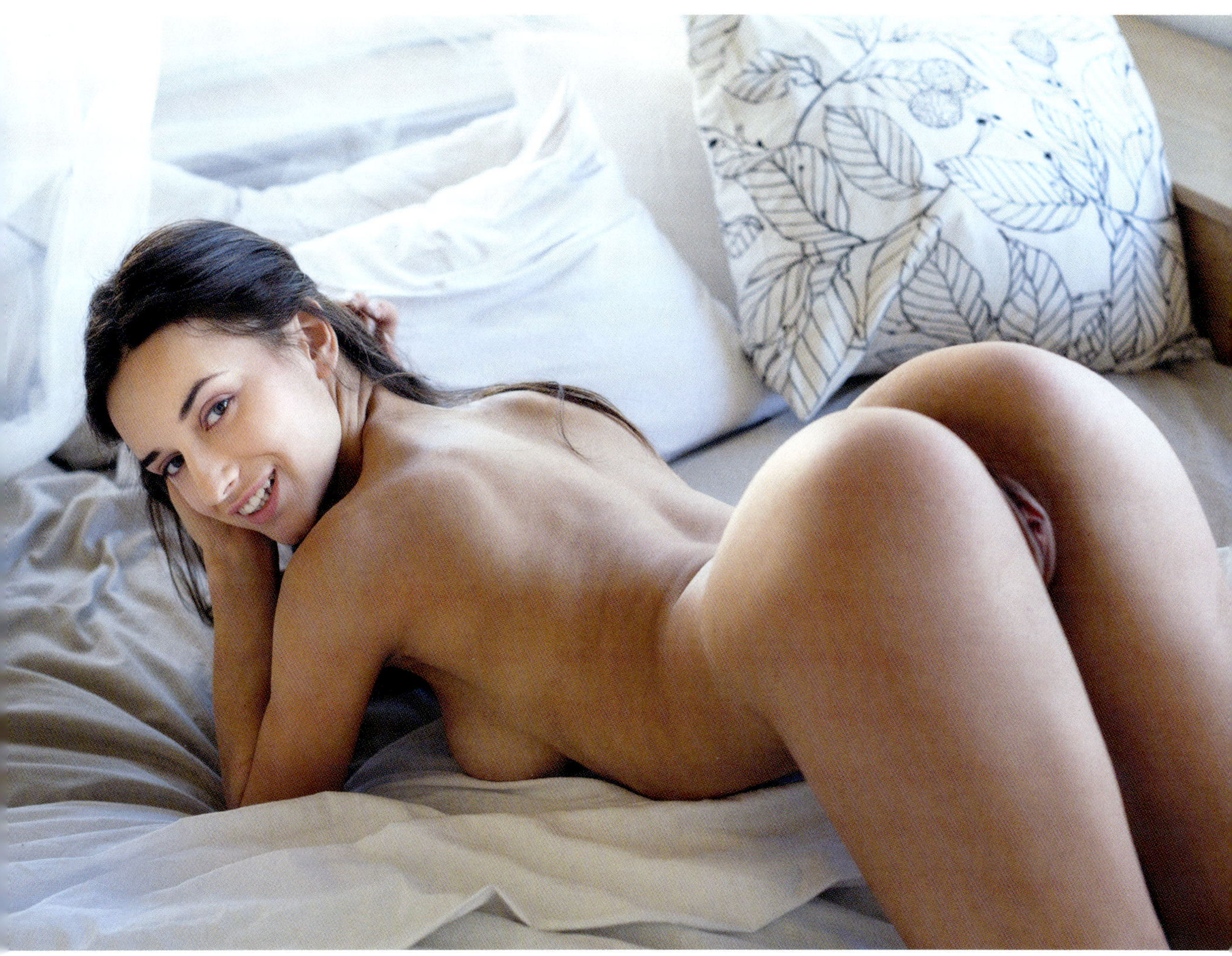

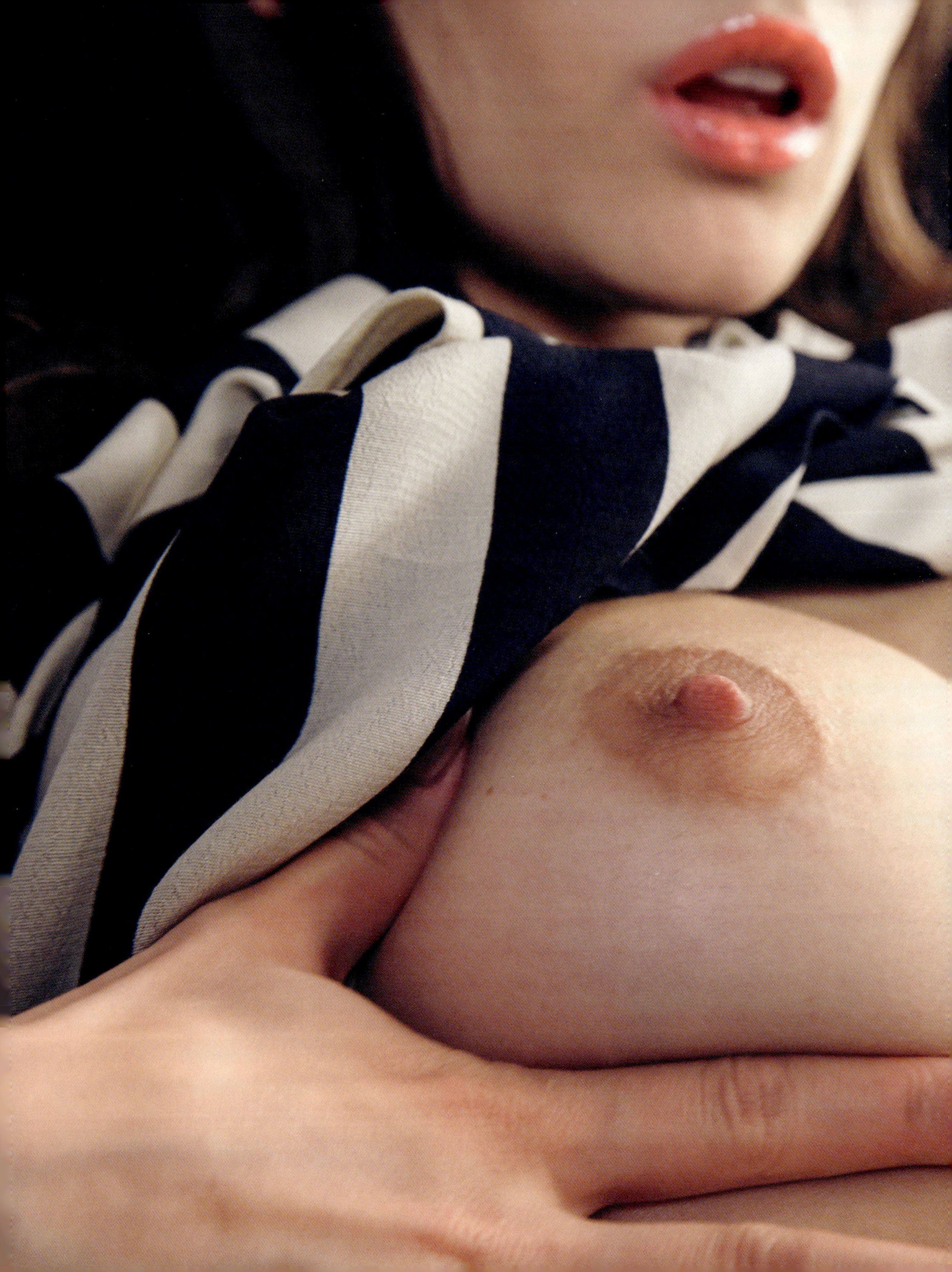

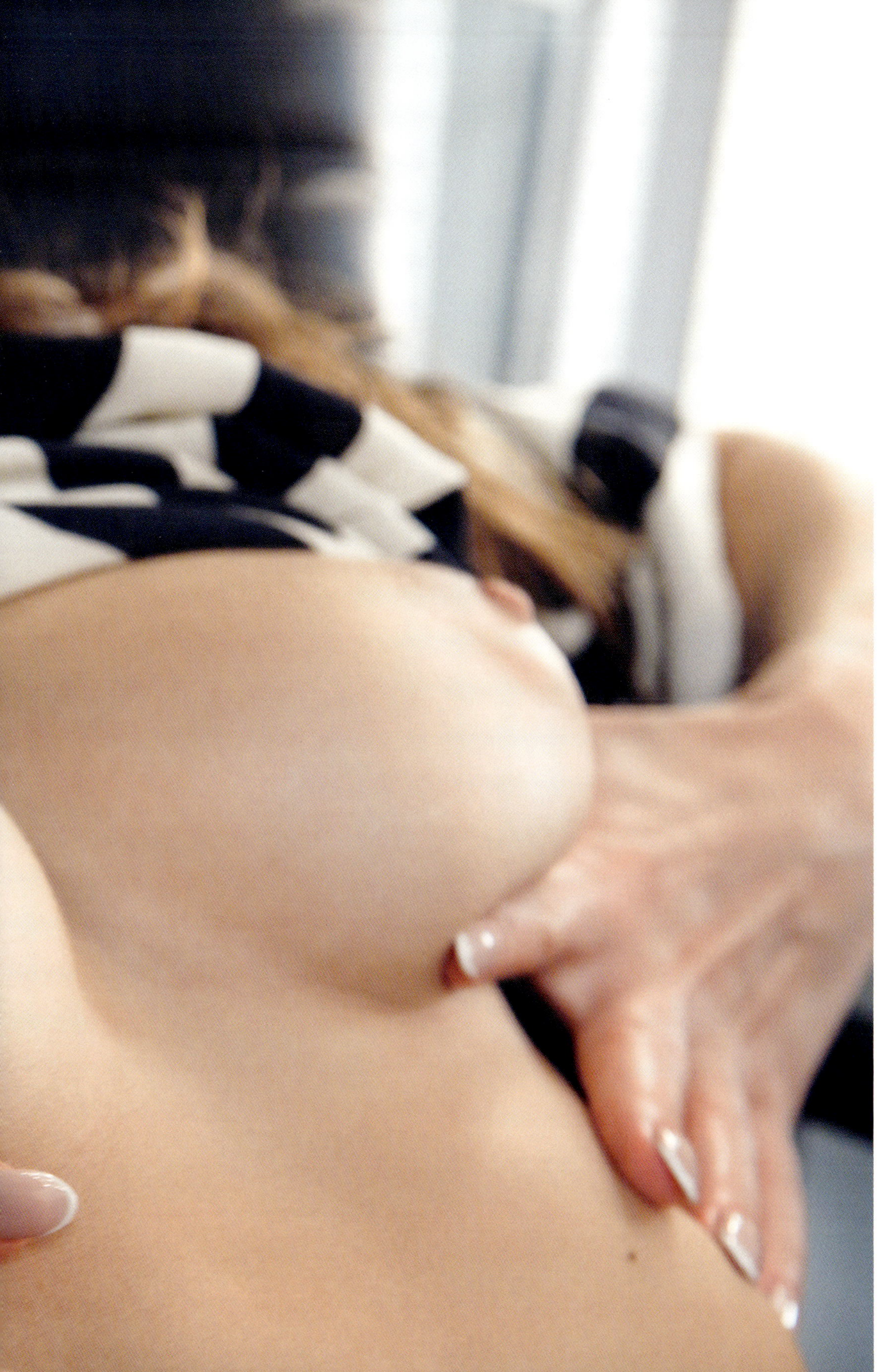

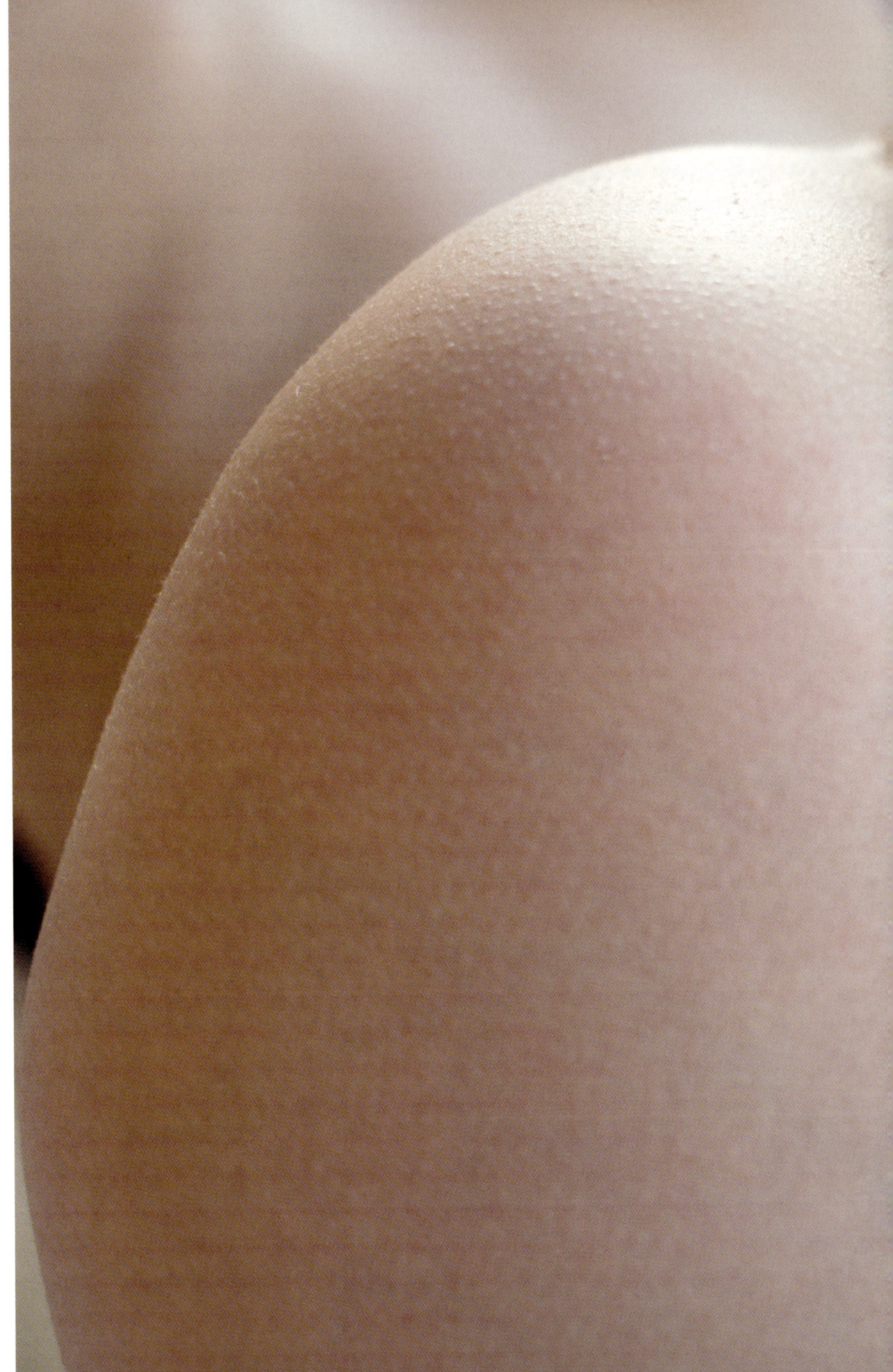

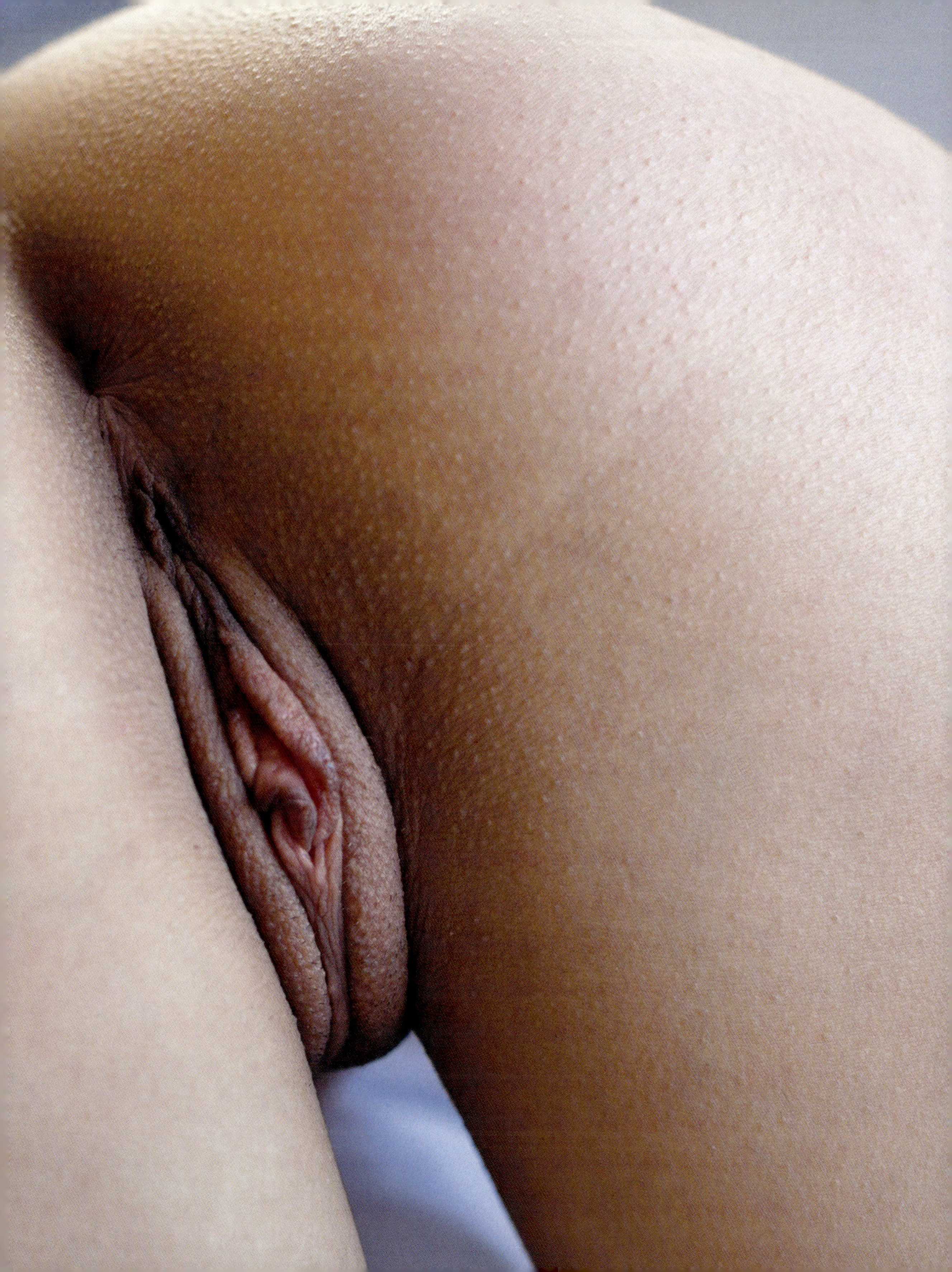

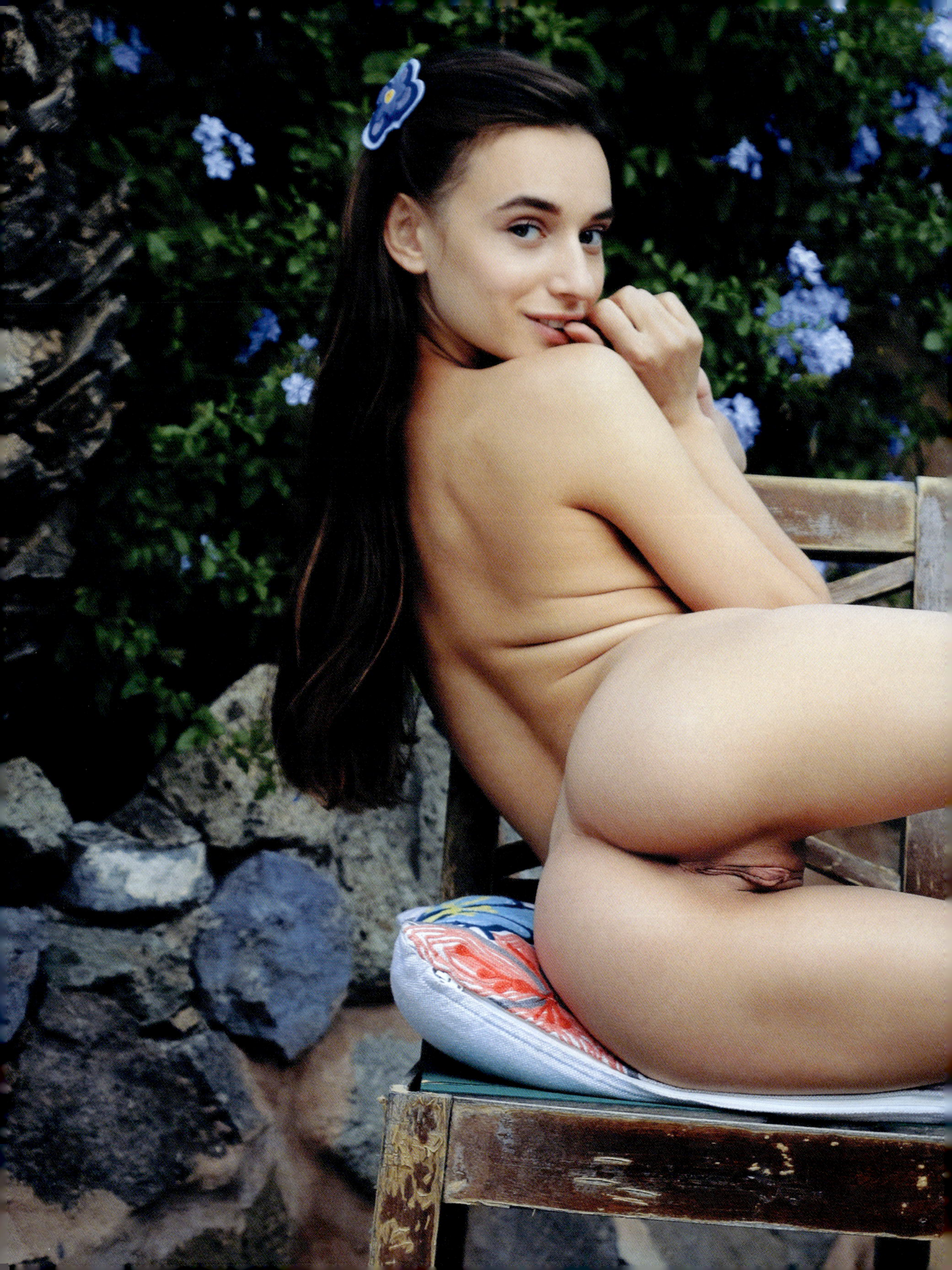

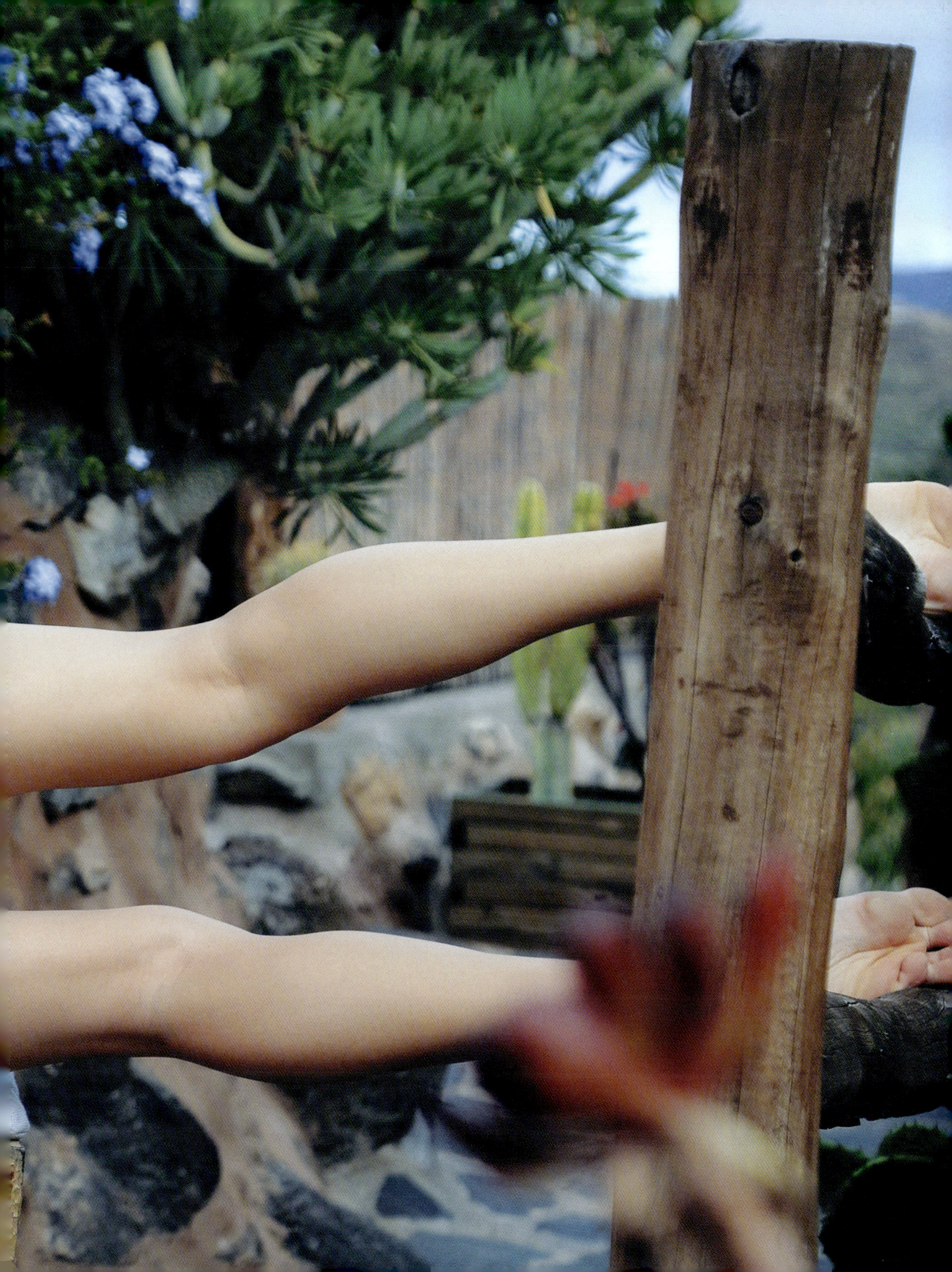

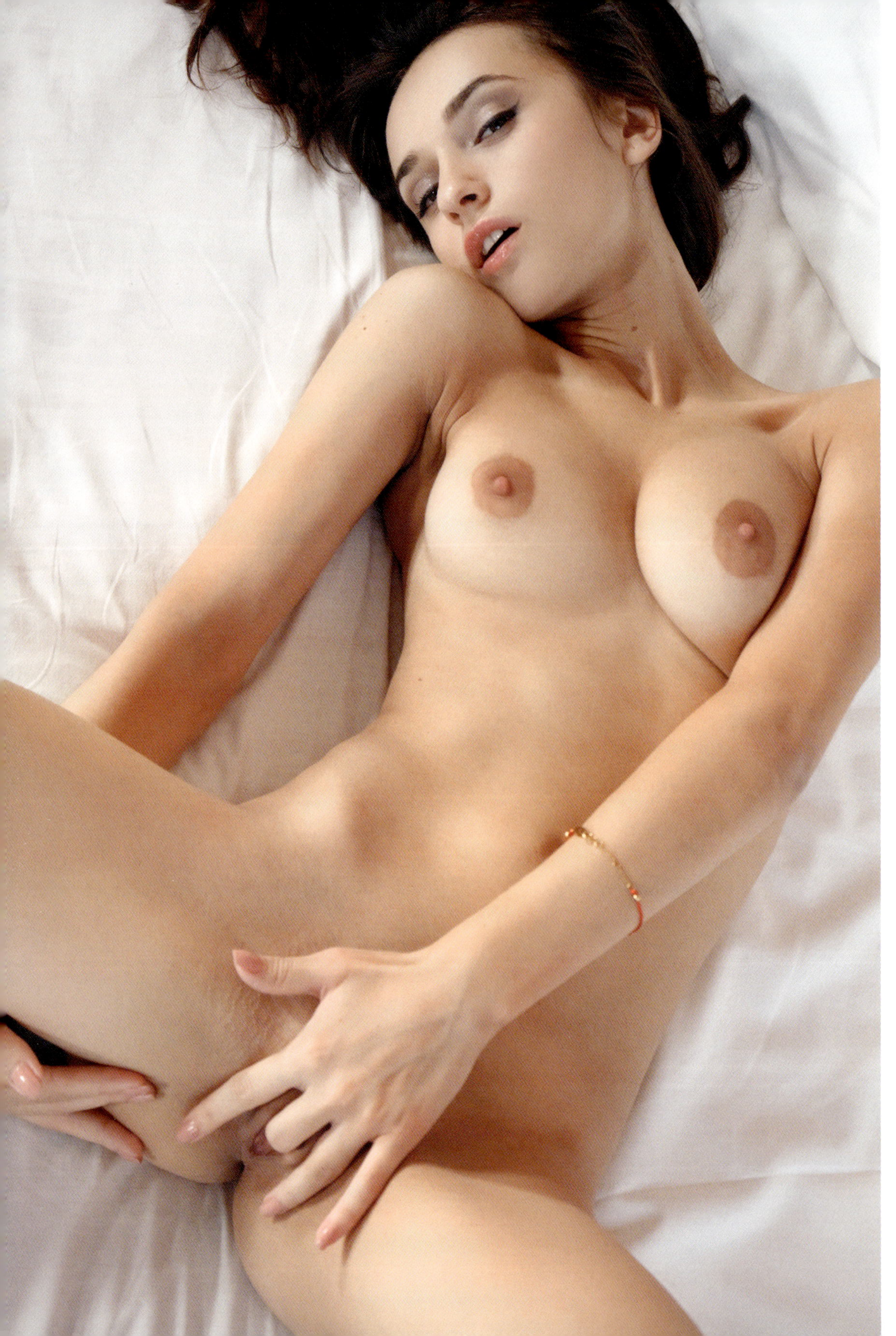

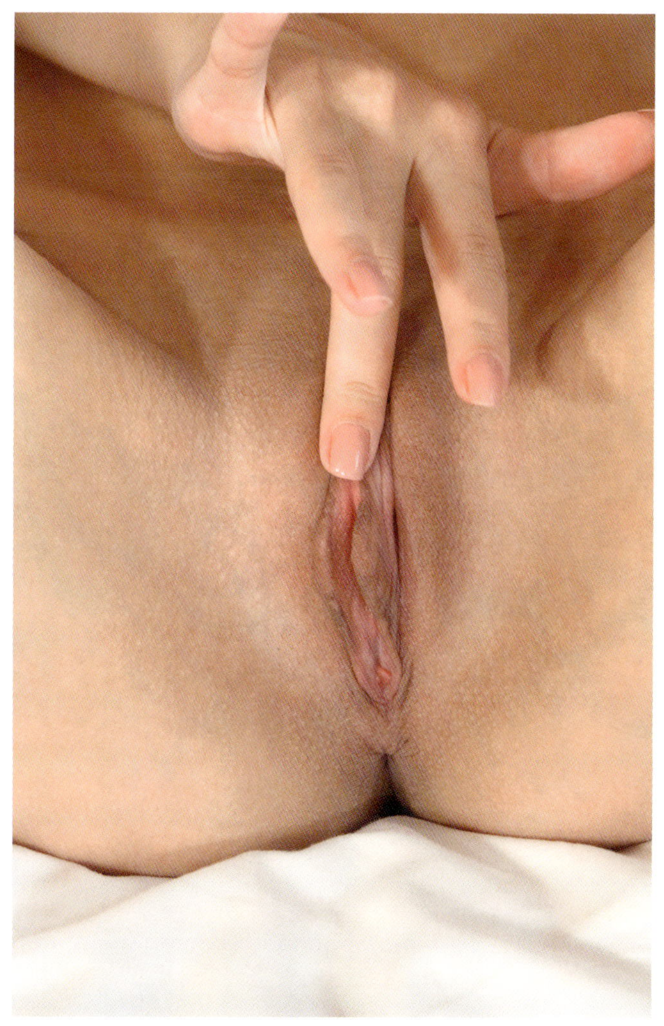

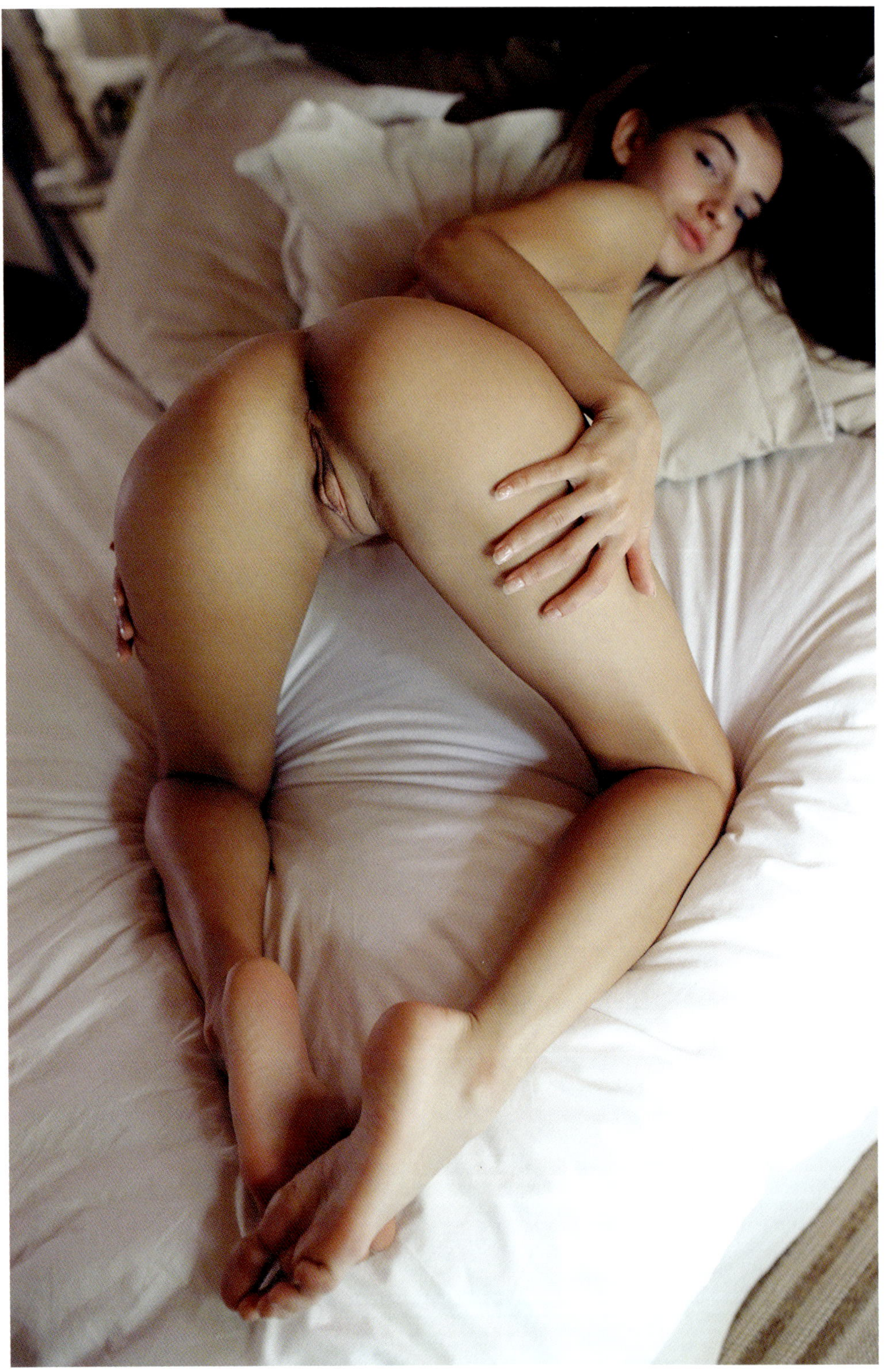

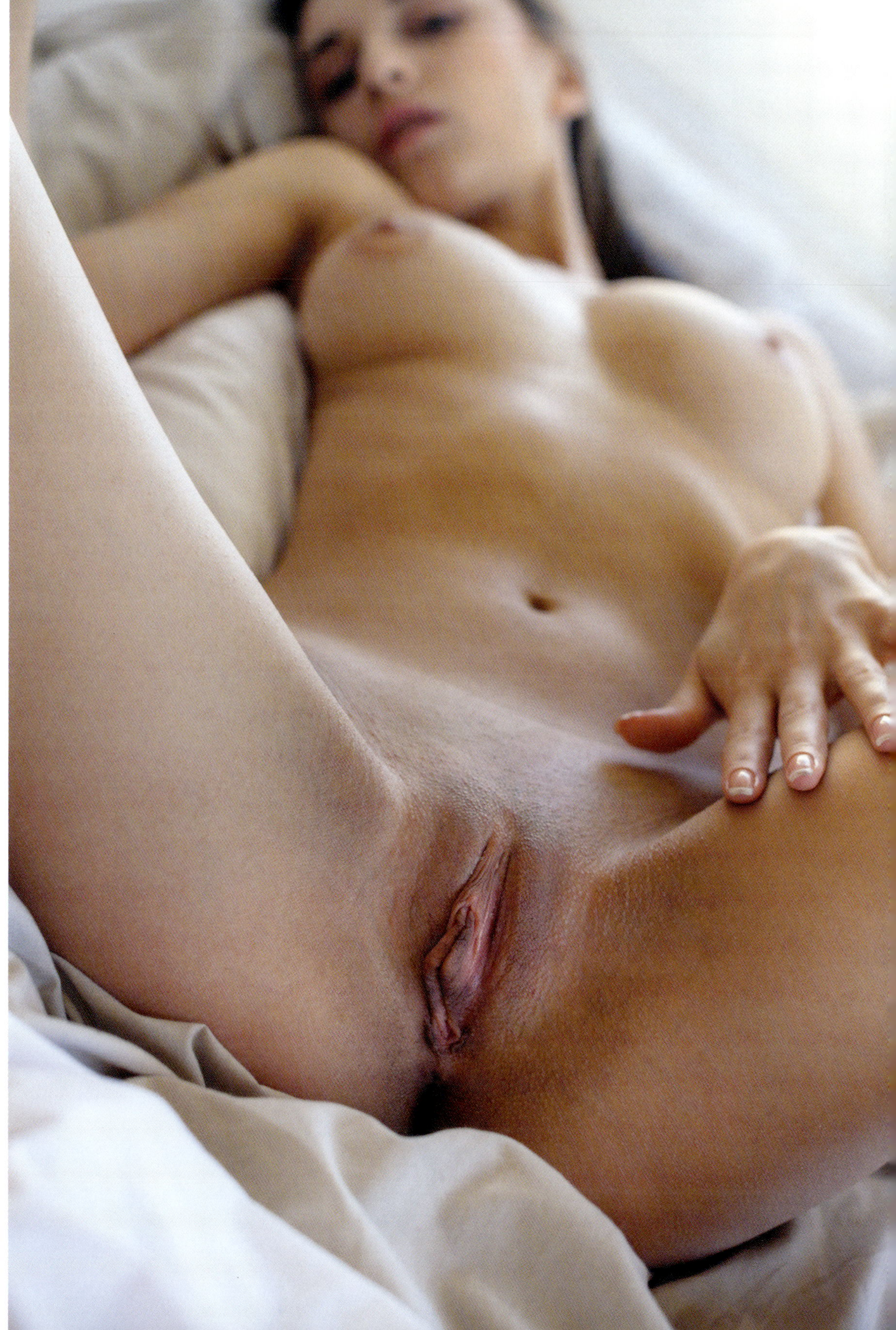

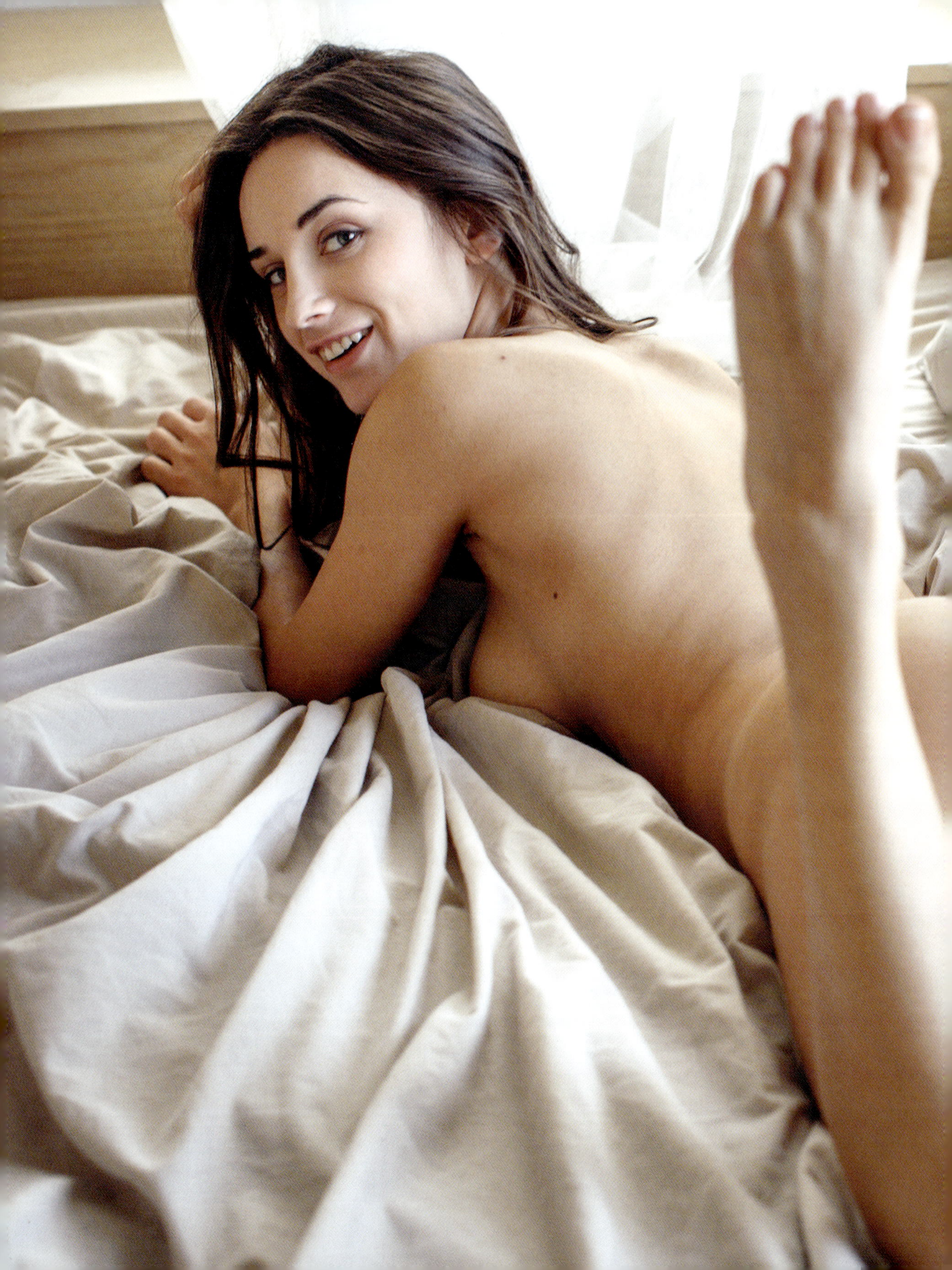

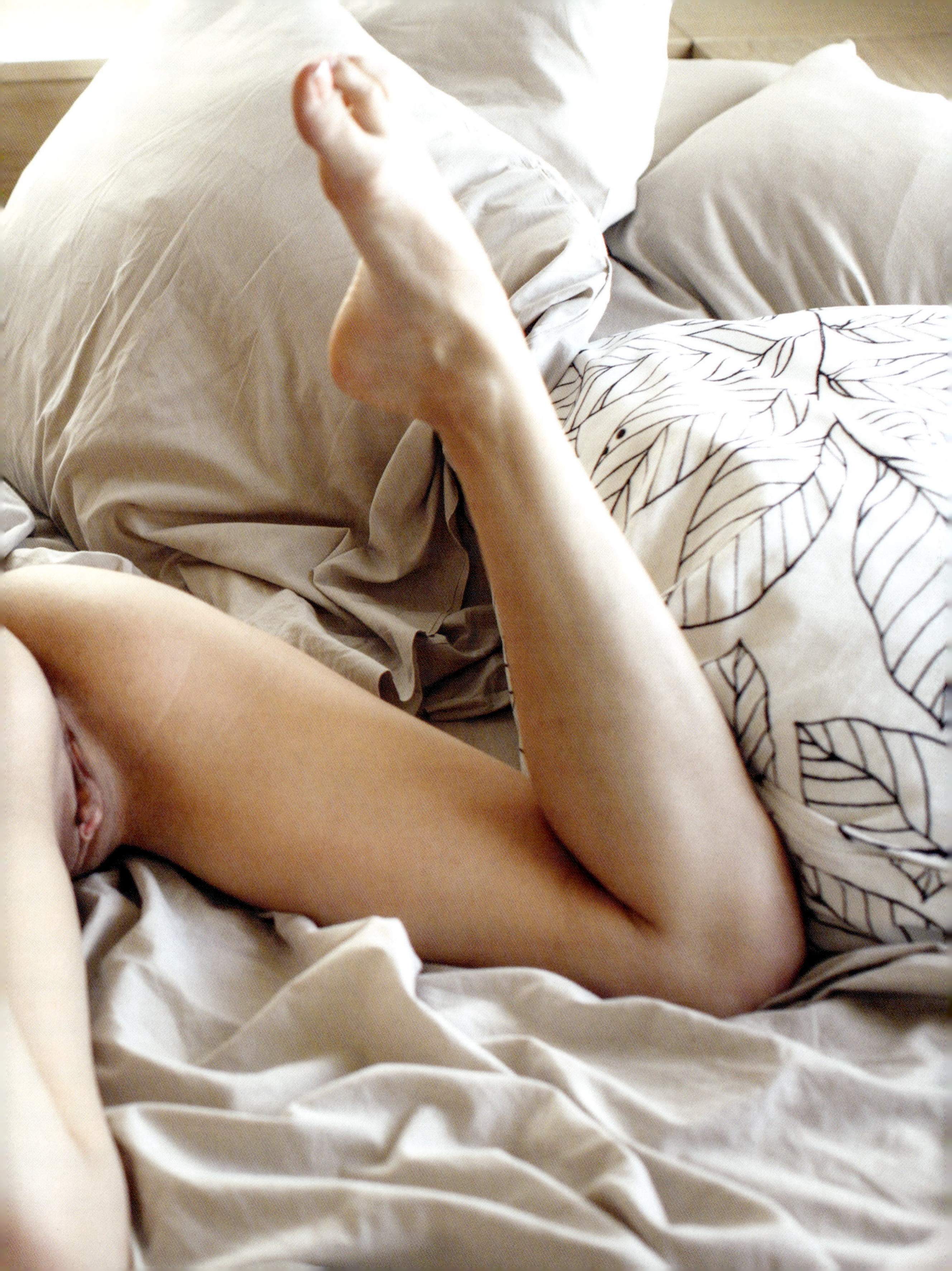

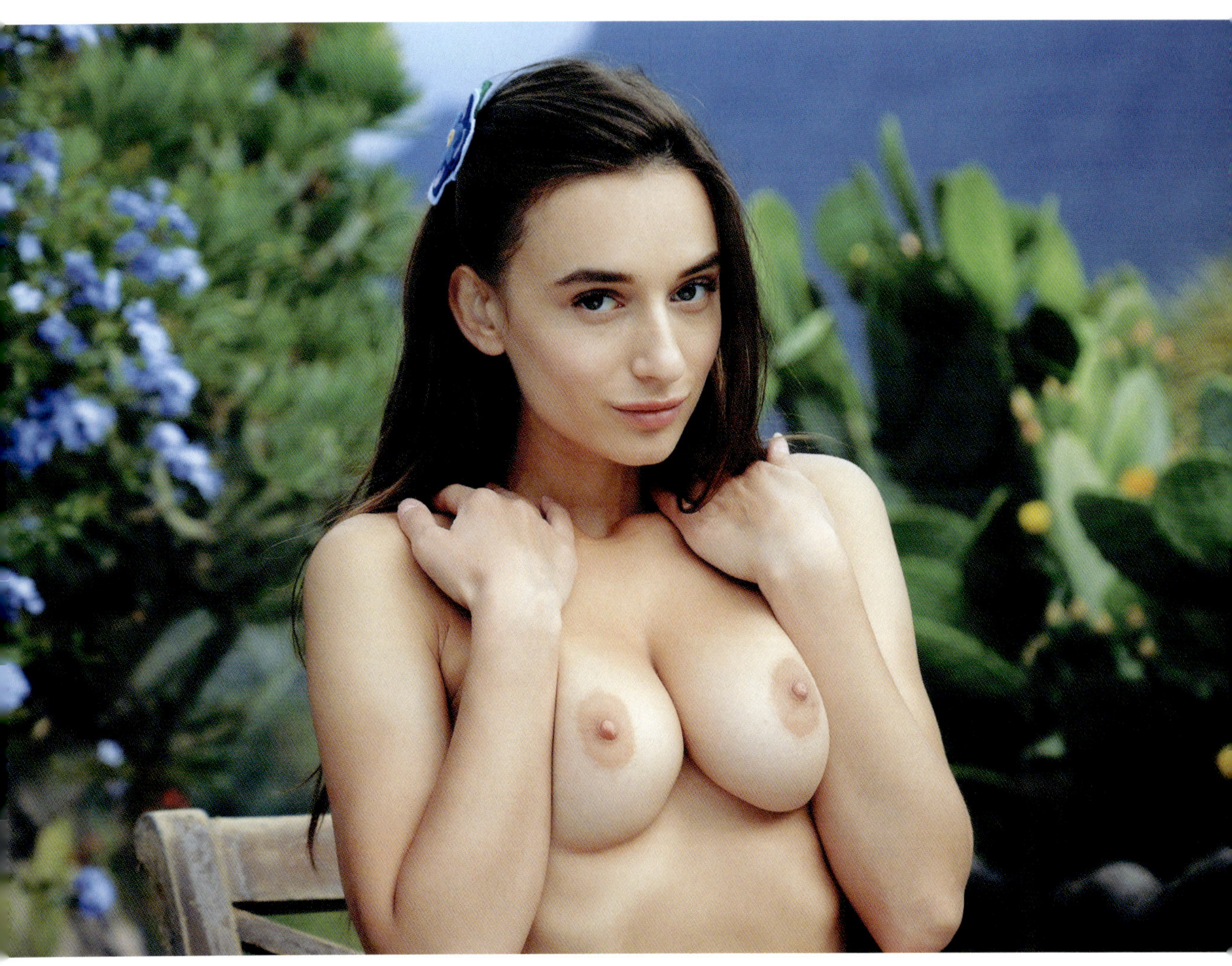

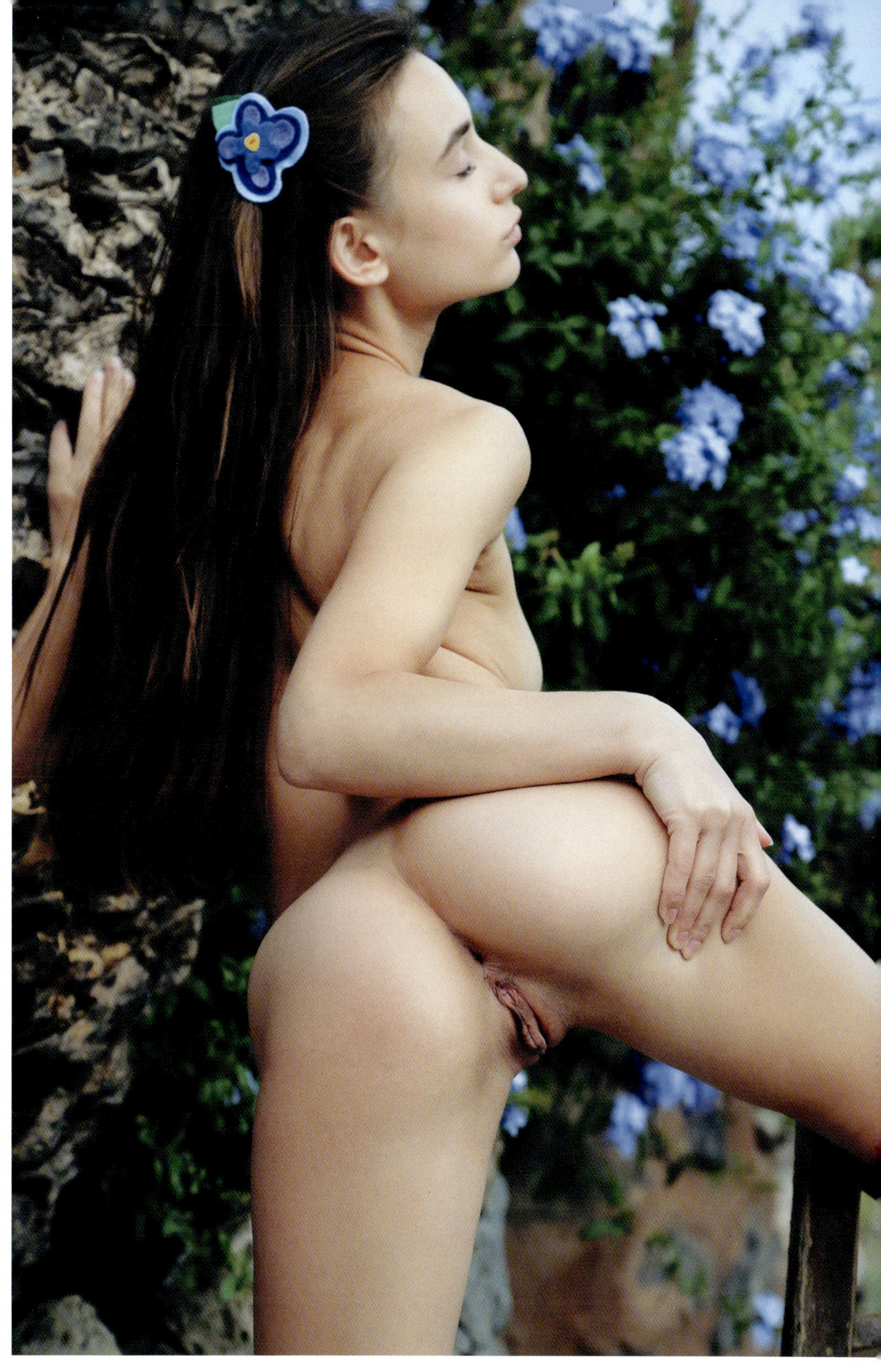

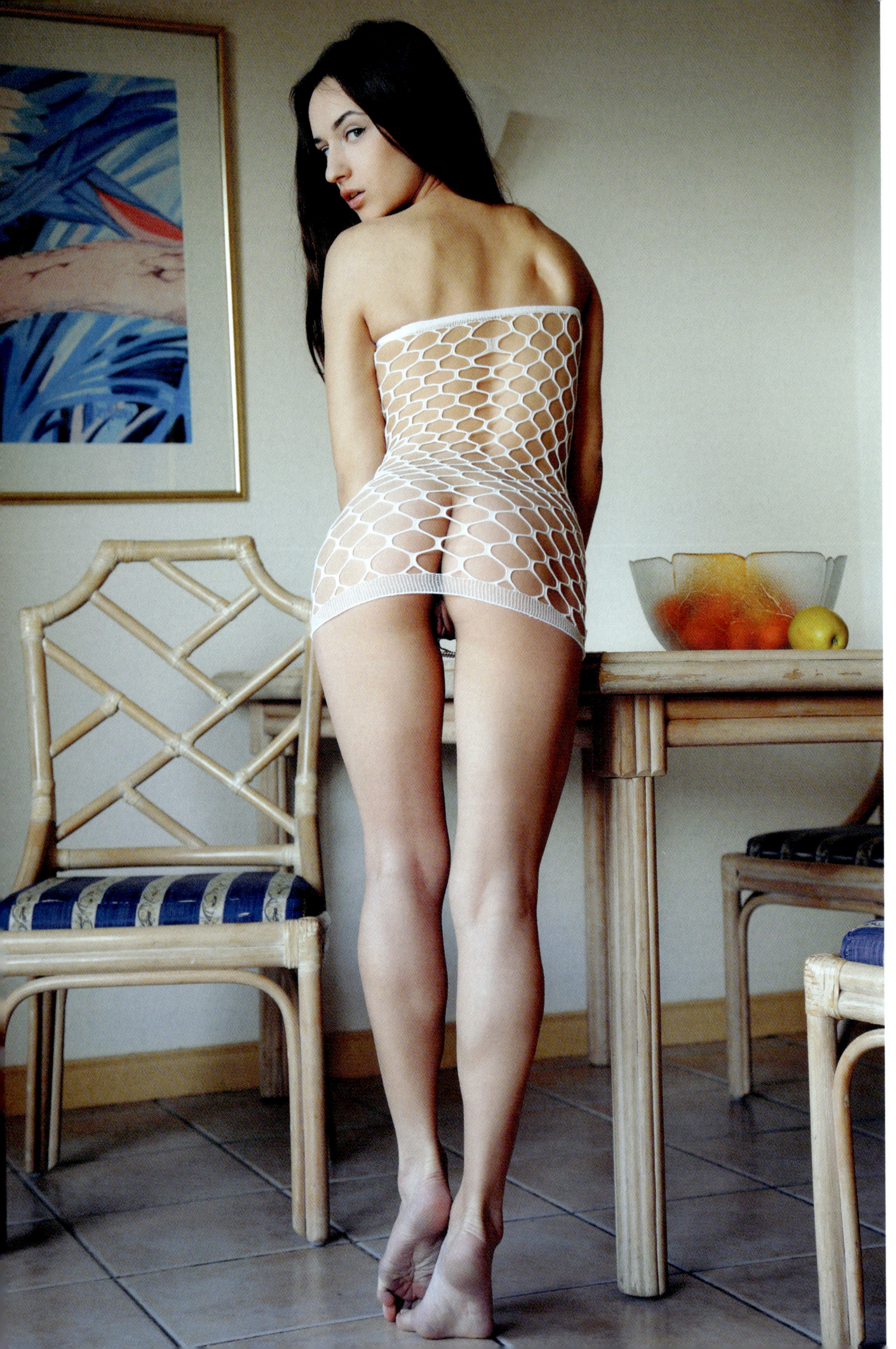

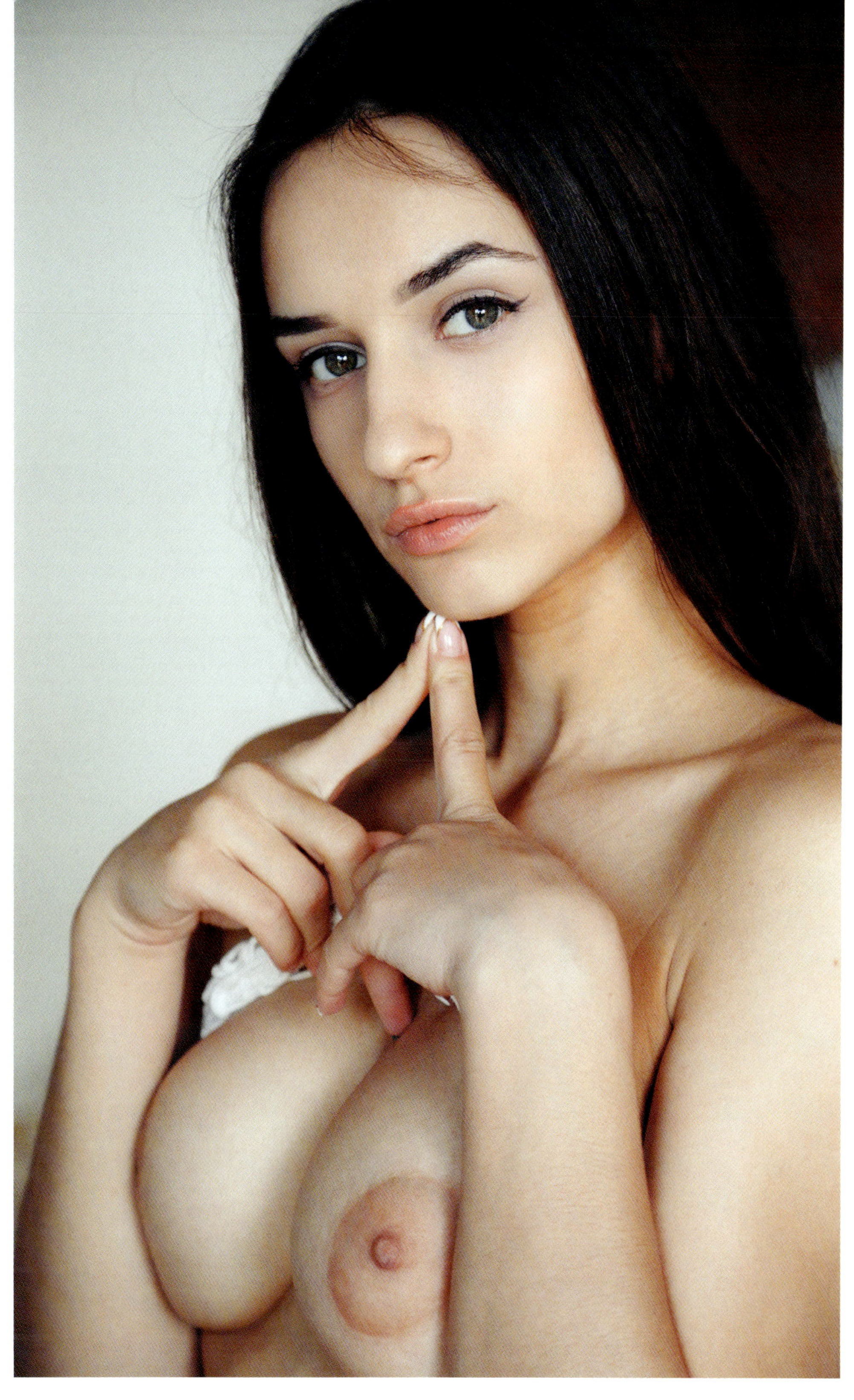

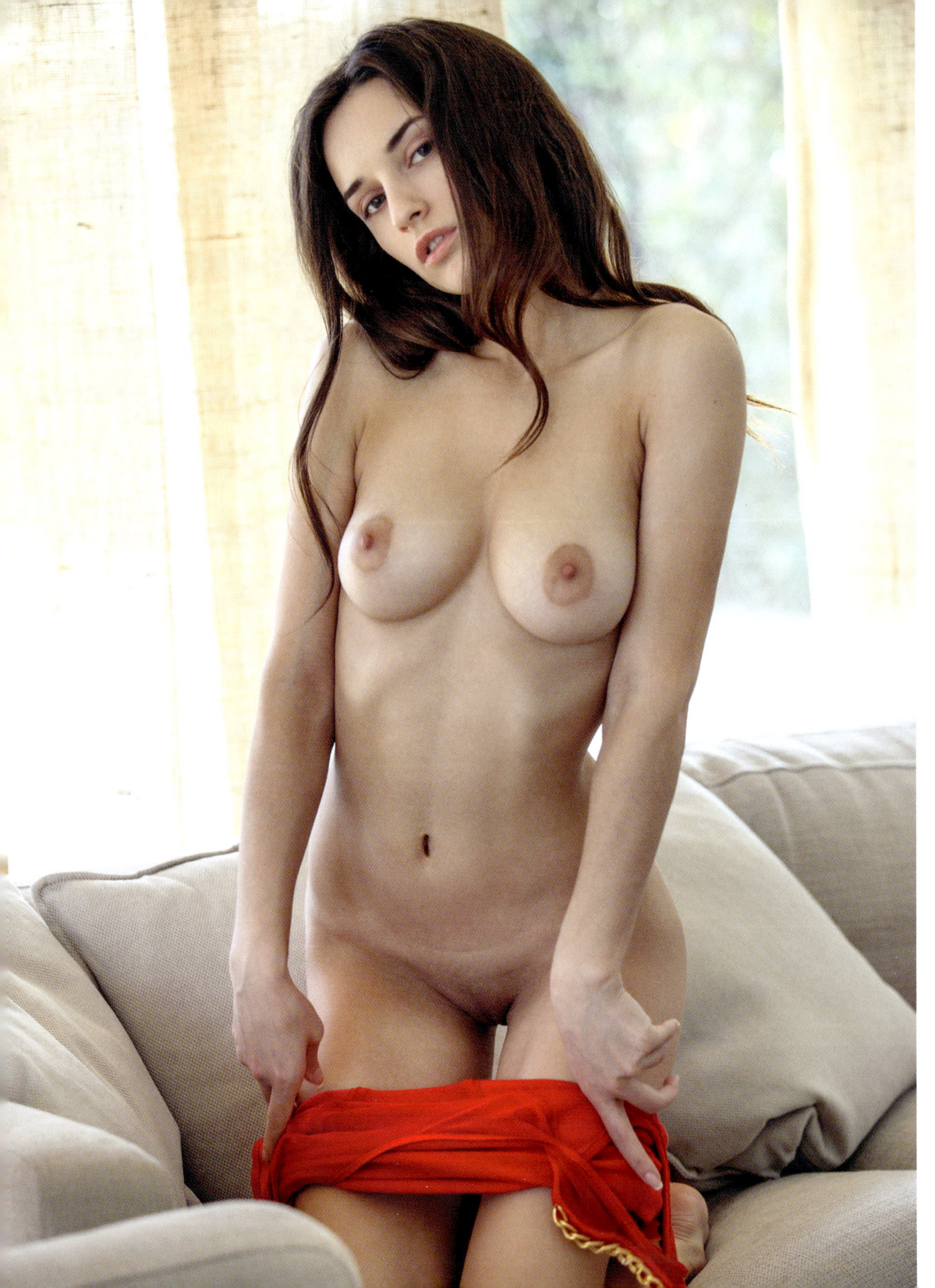

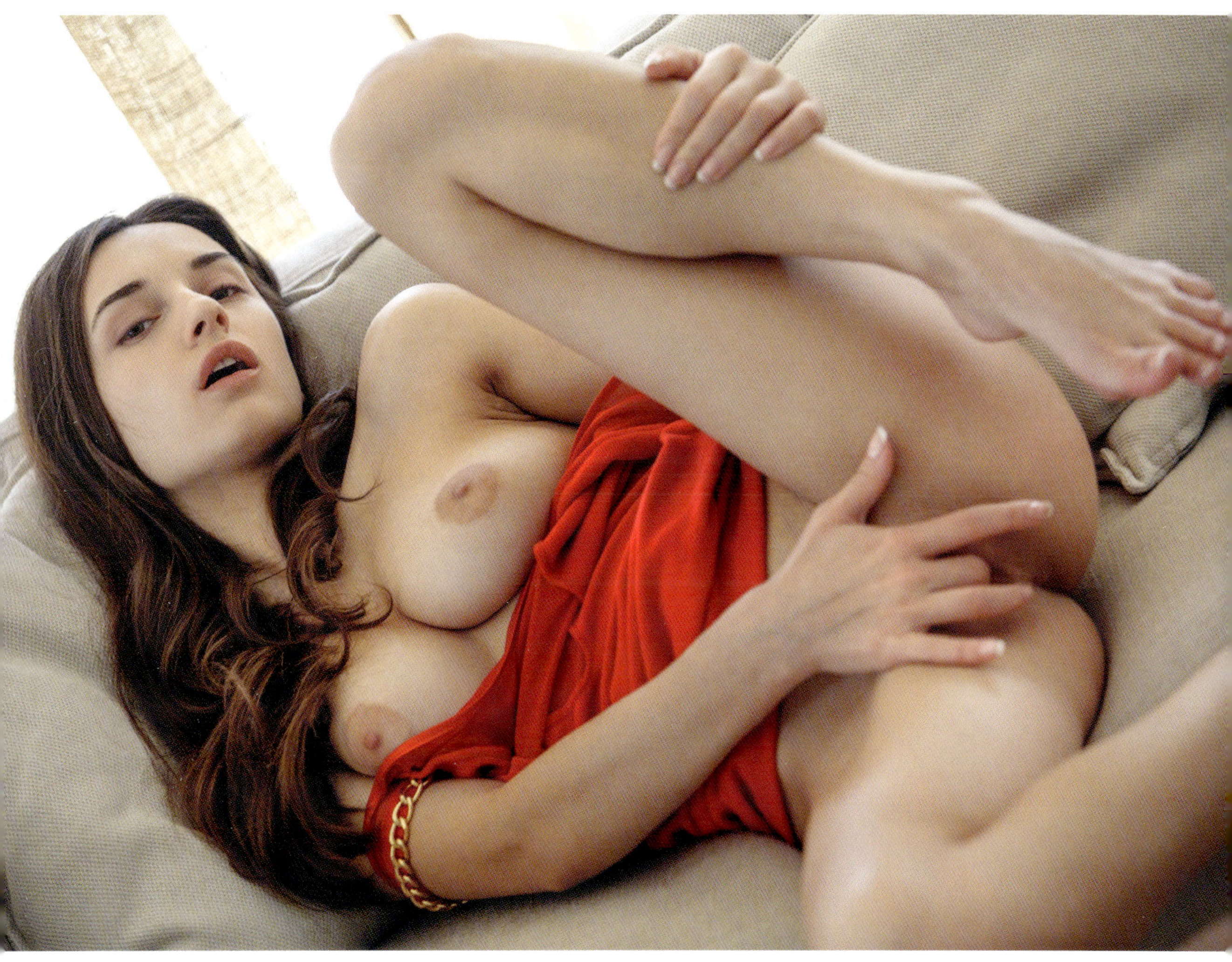

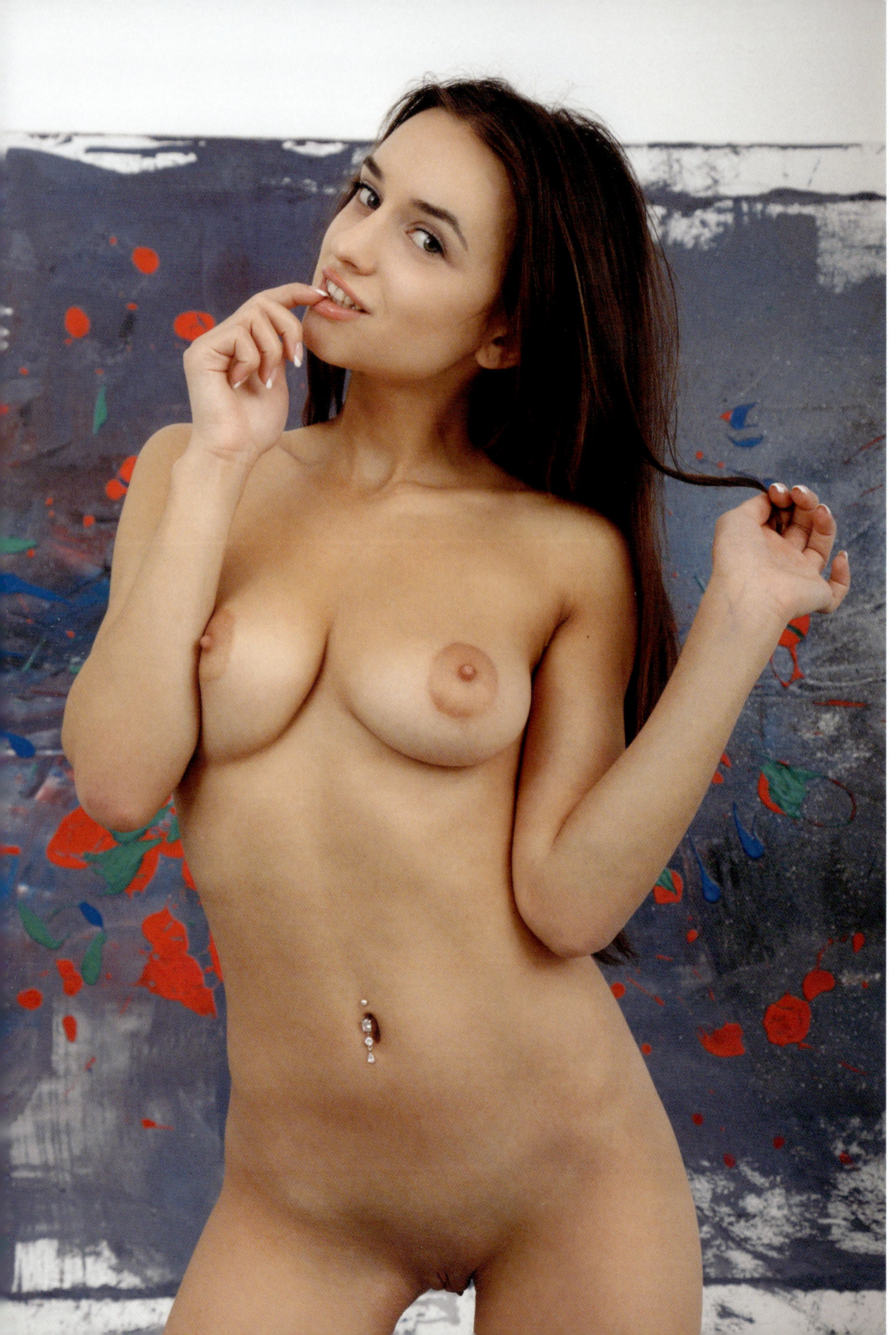

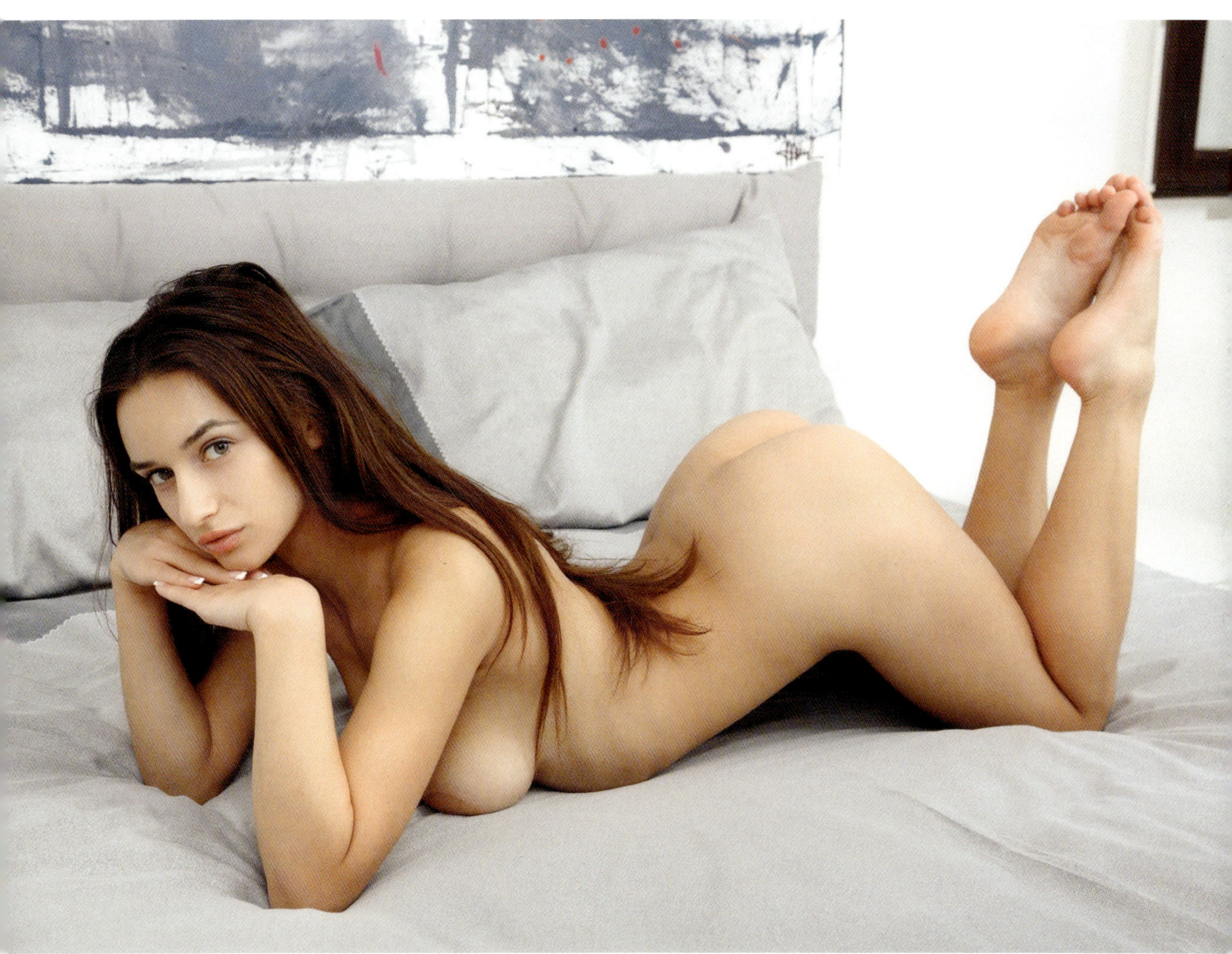

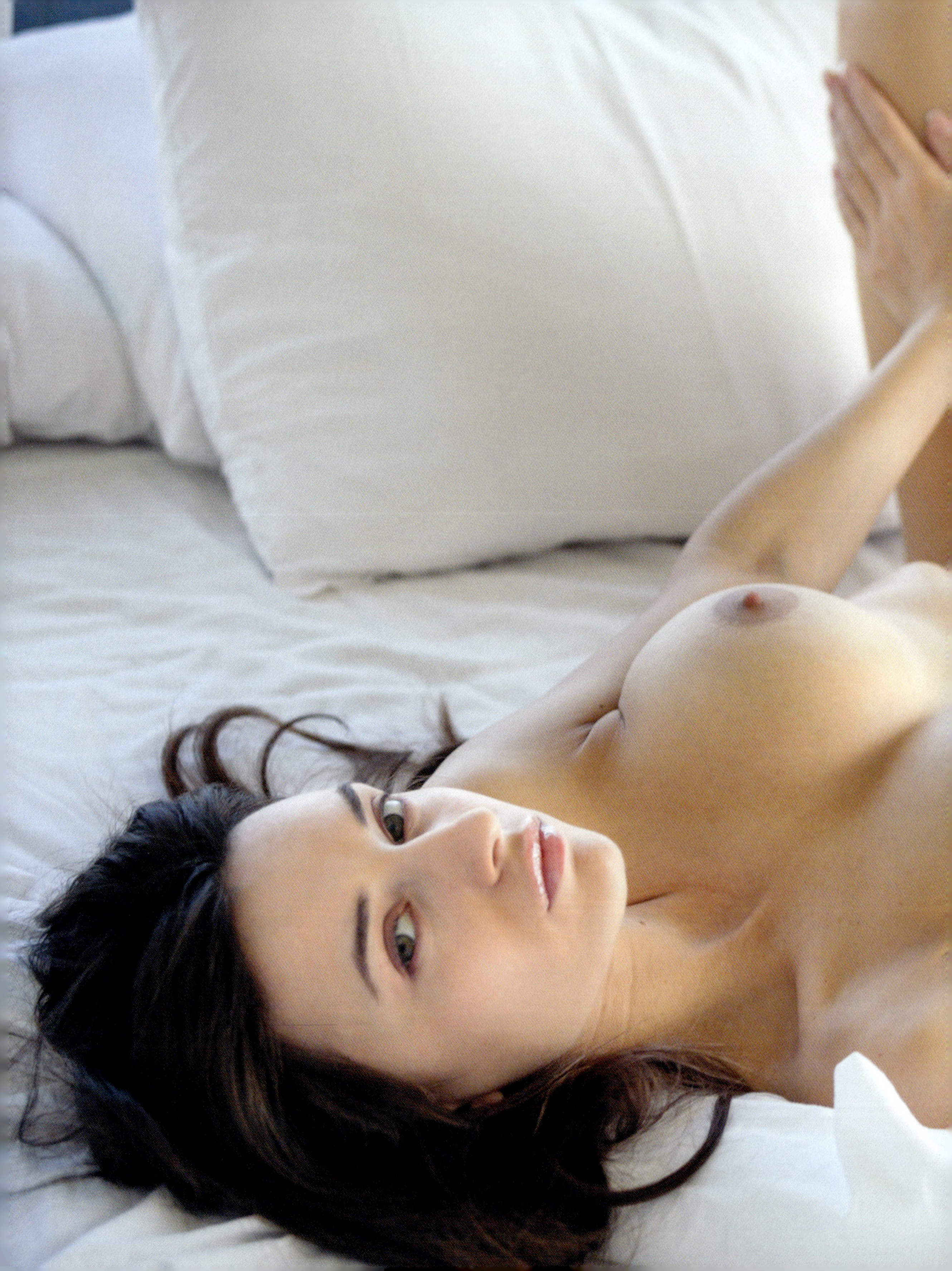

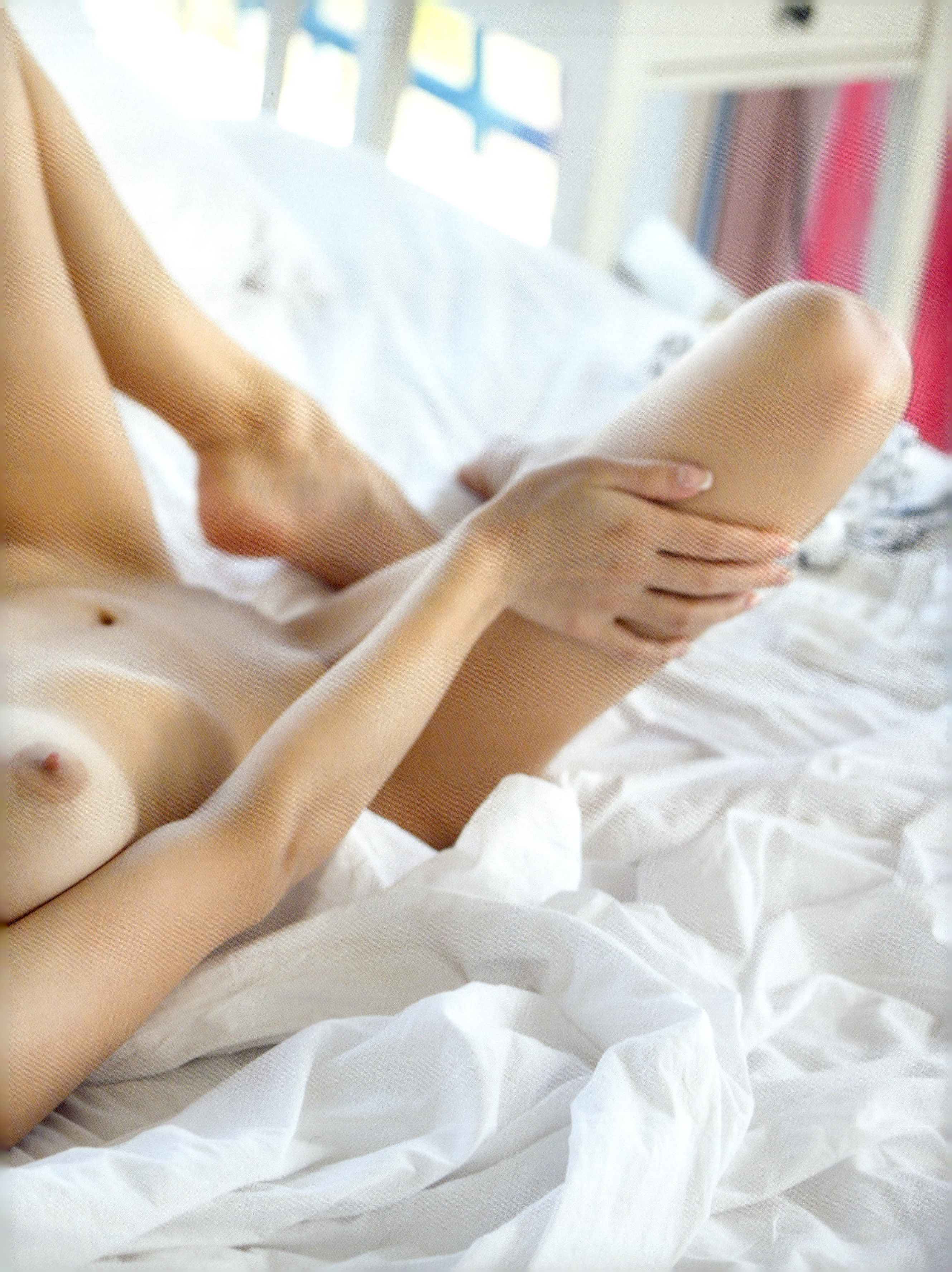

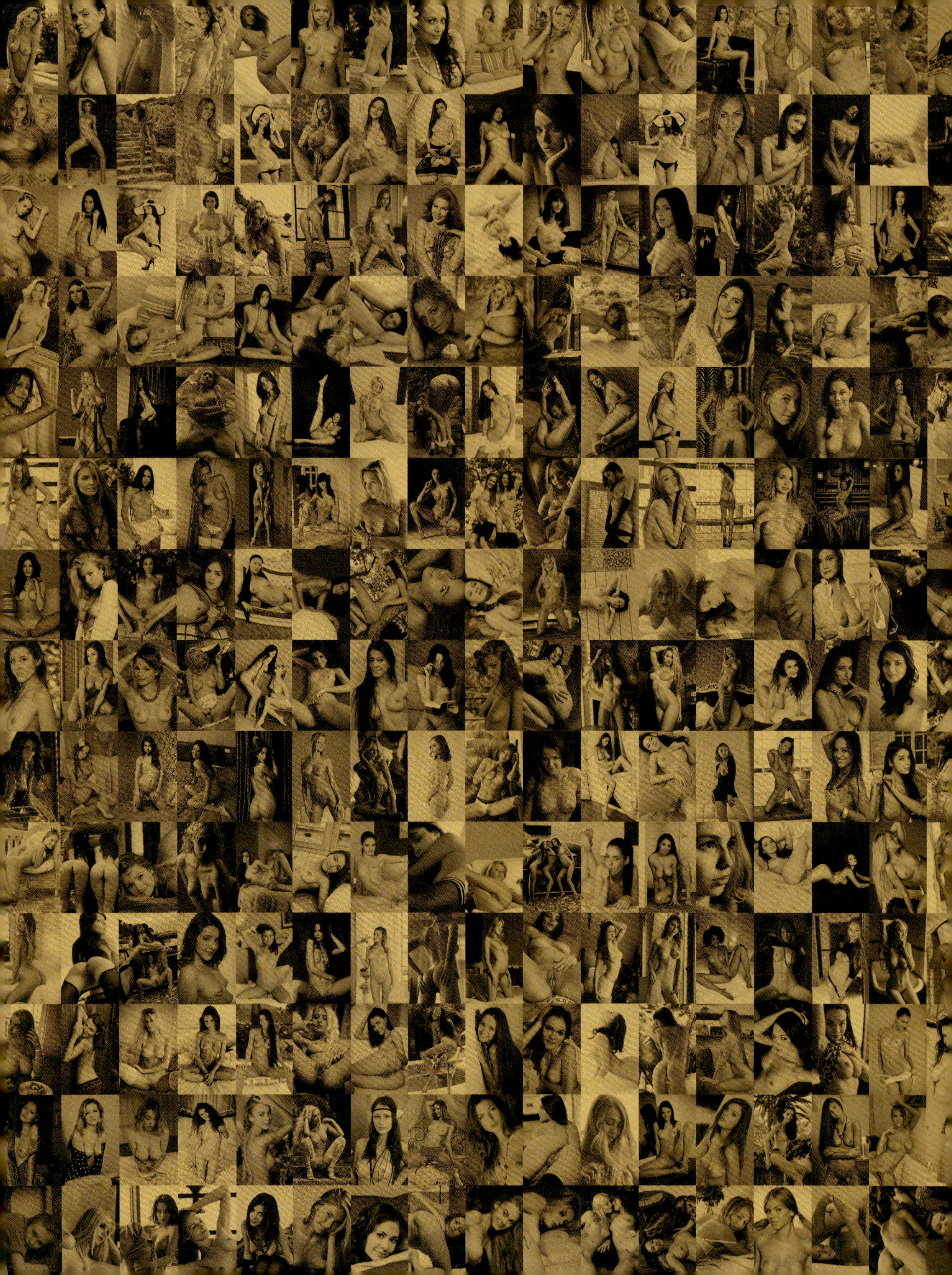